Dorset Man

Dorset Man

The Working Landscape

Interviews recorded and transcribed
by James Crowden

Photographs by George Wright

AGRE

This book is dedicated to the memory of John Fowles, 1926-2005, who lived in Lyme Regis for many years and was fascinated by Dorset's history and landscape.

First published in 2006
by Agre Books,
Groom's Cottage, Nettlecombe,
Bridport, Dorset, DT6 3SS.

Designed and produced by Watershed PR & Marketing Ltd, www.watershedpr.co.uk

ISBN: 0 9538000 9 1

CONTENTS

Introduction

Dorset is an extraordinarily beautiful and rural part of South West England with some stunning coastline. This rural, some might say idyllic, landscape has evolved through generations of men and women who have, often on very low wages, shaped the farms, woodlands and downland. It is a landscape we take for granted and the very people who have worked in it all their lives are often forgotten. Their stories are left unwritten because theirs is still an oral tradition. Many people think of Thomas Hardy when they think of Dorset, but in fact the greatest character in his books was Dorset itself – the land and the people from whom he derived his inspiration. Rural Dorset is still alive, as this book proves, but it is changing fast. The county needs a new generation of younger people who are prepared to experiment and make their living here. Local food and woodland crafts are obvious choices. Farming is in flux but the way the environmental pendulum is swinging, there is far greater public awareness of wildlife and ecology, which is good. But what concerns me most of all is that the role of the agricultural and woodland worker is still undervalued and often misunderstood. Sustainable small-scale farming is as important as sustainable small-scale fishing. For many men spending all their working lives in the open air is important, they would have it no other way, and are often fitter for it.

In the last 25 years I have seen at first-hand enormous changes in farming and many of the people I worked with are no longer with us. I learnt my farming and rural skills by working alongside this older generation, who taught me valuable lessons. When I first moved to Dorset in 1980, I kept sheep on Fontmell Down for a number of years and ran a flying flock. I lived in Melbury Abbas, Compton Abbas and Shaftesbury and was taken in hand by an old shepherdess, Ann Hodgson, who had many tales to tell. Her mother had been born at sea round Cape Horn in a windjammer as her father had a small guano business. With her introduction I very quickly became absorbed into an extraordinary way of life. This involved not only shepherding, but also sheep shearing, night lambing, forestry, turkey plucking and cider making – even building birch jumps on Badbury Rings point-to-point course with the famous hurdlemaker, Cecil Coombes. He was a great character and lived in Ashmore high up on the chalk, on the very boundaries of the Chalk and Cheese area, which stretches from there through central Dorset right down into West Dorset and the Marshwood Vale. Sadly Cecil had a stroke one day coming back from the coppice. His tools which were hidden in the wood were never found. Ashmore has since lost its village shop and post office, but still has a village pond.

Bread and cheese was often the staple diet of the casual farm worker, often unable to get back home for "nammet" or dinner. The downs on the edge of Cranborne Chase positively heaved with sheep in those days, as they have done for at least 1,000 years. I made many friends, some of whom are featured in this book. Working alongside such knowledgeable people who had not only been born and bred in the area but had let the landscape shape their lives, was itself a great privilege and a pleasure. I would not have had such company had I not chosen that very particular way of life, the casual agricultural worker, very seasonal and often precarious financially. True I had studied anthropology briefly in Oxford at the Pitt Rivers Museum where I spied a green lambing caravan used by the General on his excavations. A friend of mine, Marcus Colchester used it as an office to write up his research work from the rain forests of Venezuela. Over a cup of tea we discussed the relevance of anthropology to indigenous peoples and the importance of agriculture and hunting. Marcus went on to finish his doctorate in ethno-botany and now runs an organisation called Forest People's Programme which helps to safeguard the rights of indigenous people in rainforests. Little did I realise then that I would soon be working on the

Pitt Rivers estate, lambing and working in the woods. The only Museum there was a certain pub in Farnham where they had held the famous hurdlemakers' auctions. I felt very much that I was in contact with a very real and strong thread of rural culture, a thread that is now becoming perilously thin.

For five years I lived and worked in that part of North Dorset before moving to the edge of West Dorset. So in a sense this book has been at least 20 years in the making. It is the summation of many men's working lives, the deep insights and the humour that often goes with it. Above all, it is recorded in their own words.

In the country you learn by osmosis, by watching and listening. It is a totally different way of learning. Sheep shearing is a good example. You cannot teach people to shear. You can only really learn by watching and absorbing each minute detail. So it is with rural life. Dorset men provided me with a very real education. This book, which is their book, is a series of stories which convey their very particular sense of values. Often these values are understated and you have to find them in between the lines. To me these stories are just as important as the landscape itself; the two are interwoven and the stories are the contours. Seen this way, the men's stories provide a biographical landscape where the whole county is mapped out with anecdotes and memories. Many of these men knew each other or had threads in common. Farming, agriculture in its widest sense, shapes the land and nearly all of these men have worked on the land at some time. Some have never left it. They were, and still are, part of it.

I felt that it was essential to document these working lives and their idiosyncrasies before the farm buildings and the land become divorced from their original use and the men die out. With transcribed recordings it is possible to produce an important archive. Combine this with the excellent photography of George Wright and you have captured as best you can the essence of rural life. These portraits are the backbone of the book. Real casual farm workers are now a rarity. All too often it is contract gangs, or the land is left to the ravages of machinery or conservation by neglect. Half the farms sold in the South West in the last year went to people who had no intention of farming them themselves. That is frightening. Are we facing the prospect of a landscape composed of industrial prairie interspersed with neglected scrubland?

Biographical landscapes as I call them place the lives of working men at the very heart of the rural economy. Their lives link the land to the rural population and provide a true sense of rural identity. These men are the unsung heroes of the landscape and their way of life and knowledge is disappearing fast. By giving the landscape a voice and a visual face, I hope that we have gone some way to recording a vital part of Dorset's heritage which helps to define the Chalk and Cheese area, making links from one end of the county to the other. Excerpts from the recordings will be made available on Dorset farm Radio at www.farmradio.co.uk

My thanks go to the Calouste Gulbenkian Foundation and the Chalk and Cheese Leader+ Project which has provided the funding. I hope also that as well as being an important archive, this book will inspire other people to make recordings of their own locality and may well encourage the younger generation to value the rural skills and knowledge which is all around them. Maybe some will even follow in these men's footsteps. How many people these days can say that they have worked outside and are physically fit because of it? I hope that the readers of this book will enjoy the stories that I have been told and that the transcriptions convey the sense of a living and important tradition. Dorset is still a fantastic place to live and work.

James Crowden
November 2005

Jim and Jack Webber, in between jobs

1 Jim and Jack Webber: Hedgelayers, Stoke Abbot
Jim born 1902. Jack born 1910.

Secret is keeping working slowly and regularly. Good many have asked me what the secret is. But we don't go at it like a bull at a bank, we keep jogging along and if I don't feel up to scratch I do have a spot of whisky sometimes.

My name is James Noel Webber and my brother is Robert John Webber known as Jack. I was born at a little place called Netherhay near Drimpton in 1902. My Father was a farmworker at Netherhay. My Father never wanted to stay more than two years at one place; he always wanted to keep moving on "A rolling stone gathers no moss." He went to Childhay and then near Chard and back to Blackdown. Went into the army during the First World War. He saw action and was out there for two year and nine months, in France most of the time. When he came back out of the Army he went to Chedington then took over six horses. My Father had three and I had three on a big farm. The farm is right opposite the big house, used to be Sir Henry Peto then. Just still in Dorset. That is where my Mother died and my Father died, they are both buried up at Chedington. He stayed for 14 years up there.

Bowditch's at North Bowood, they were advertising for a carter so Father thought he'd like a change up there but I was courting a girl up Mosterton and I didn't want to go away. Anyway I talked Father out of it and he stayed on up there. So that is some of it. Jack went to school there. When he was working at Chard on a farm the cowman got called up in the army and if a man got called up a farmer could get a boy to take his place provided the boy was interested I suppose. I hated school all my life and when Father came on one evening he said, "do you want to leave school?" You know what, I said "yes" very quick. And 'twadn't very long before they got me out taking this cowman's job, 35 cows. I was 11 year old. Don't suppose it has done me any harm. No.

Farming was quite different then, 35 cows was quite a large herd then. Milk went into Chard. The boss did a milk round in Chard and I used to have to go on with him and help do the round till nine o'clock and then I had to hop into school. Then after I come out of school, I had to go back to the farm and take the horses and milk cart and deliver myself then to Chard Union and one or two of the other big places what wanted extra milk. Then back towards the Happy Return.

First World War? I was working on a farm and the farmer had to plough up extra land, so he put me on with a couple of horses and Mother said I must be ploughing all night. About 13. Soon got into it you know. We wore leather gaiters and cord britches. Hobnailed boots. We used to have drop of cider for haymaking. We grew wheat and oats and some barley, for corn really. Grew pretty good. Cows, mostly Shorthorn then. The lorry used to come and pick up the churns.

My Grandfather, John Webber, lived at Seaborough and he used to do gardening work, there weren't cars then so I didn't get to see him very much and hardly knew him. He was born about 1840. He was working in a biggish house out at Misterton. I never used to get about much. Never had a bike till I was 18. My Father, I said to my Father one day, "I'm going to have a bicycle." "Oh," he said, "where you got the money?" "I'm going to have a secondhand one." "You can borrow mine and keep on saving up then you can have a new one and have a bicycle." And that what I done. So I was about 18 before I had a bicycle and saved up enough money. What a difference.

My Mother came from Chillington. Her brother was a shepherd, pretty high up looking after sheep and other brother used to be for Dunell. So these two brothers were pretty high up shepherds. Dunell, Buckham. Never did sheep shearing. Well I never had much to do with sheep, because when we went over to Chedington and took over these six horses, I had a double plough and all this equipment. I weren't never allowed to do anything with the sheep, I had to keep going with the horses. 'Twas a lot of walking. Used to have to open up the stable about five or half past. I used to be happy letting them drink, feed them, getting them ready, clean them out because he had to be out at seven o'clock even if it was dark. Seven to two that was the working hours. Time we get back in and unharness, it was getting on towards three o'clock. Then we had a bit of dinner then we had to feed up the horses, clean them down, bed them up, that kind of thing. Some of them were shires, big horses, some mongrel breeds. Homebred. Some of them must have weighed nearly a ton each, big horses. Yes we used to break in young ones and get them in with the others.

We used to be ploughing quite a bit during the winter, putting in wheat during October, November time and then we was ploughing on and off and other jobs during the winter. On sowing spring corn again in March, April. We had a drill behind us. No broadcast. Drive two horses in the drill. My Father used to sow the grass seed with a fiddle bow. He was pretty good at it too. 'Twas organic farming really, I never knew anything about fertiliser not during all the time up there. He reckoned the sheep's backsides would do that.

Village dances, I got a mate up there and we used to go to Hinton St George, pretty good down there 'twas, Crewkerne and Clapton and Seavington, sometimes Saturday nights, sometimes Wednesday nights. Got the horse settled up then away I do go on my bike, corse the dancing used to go on till two o'clock in the morning in they days. Just piano mostly, the mate that went with me he had a mandolin, used to hammer that one as well. We used to dance till half past two then sometimes had to come home ten mile. All according, if we had to take a girl home. Sometimes just got home at half past four just in time to change me clothes, ruffle up the bed to make Mother think I been in there and off up to the stable.

Haymaking very often was a bit of a job if you had a wet summer. We had reaper binders. Still we used to get pretty well on with it drive three horses into the binder. The horses used to do about three hours, then in goes my team and out comes my Father's and then on again, keep the binder going.

Sir Henry Peto, he encouraged me to do night school 'cept I was off courting on Wednesday evenings so I did get an education after all. We used to take the corn down to Crewkerne Station, the horse with bells and topknots and all groomed out Pride of the West, I had a cracking team. Used to stop off at the Swan in Misterton on the way back.

When I left Chedington, I came here still driving horses for Mr Smith. One morning we had a field of barley ready to cut, nine acres of barley and he said to me, "I want you to cut that nine acres of barley tomorrow," and I said, "all right". So t'wadn't no dew that morning cos if there was heavy dew, you couldn't go on because the canvasses get wet and burst. T'wadn't no dew that morning so we was able to go ahead and so I was down there and had the horses and the binder down there and ready to start at eight o'clock.

So that morning I was ready to start work at eight o'clock because the boss used to ride a horse. He was gouty. So he used to come down, and he looked at me: "That field was cut in eight hours once." That was nine acres three good horses; three best ones I have ever drove in a binder. He said, "he was cut in eight hours," and sort of laughed because if it was done before, there's no reason why it can't be done again. So you aren't going to let no grass grow under your feet mind. Well I say, "all righty, we'll see what happens," so I said, "away me lads," and away they went and went on and everything went well, old binder used to break down but he didn't that day, he went beautiful all day nice piece of standing barley. And everything went OK a very hot thundery Saturday, no good for I to rush these horses, so I let them jog on in their own space and I went on till eleven o'clock and I looked up and he was coming through the gate and so I drove across. It frightened him to see how much I done, so he stayed there a bit. He stopped the horses and he said an hour and half for dinner. Soon as I shut them out and got out my watch and when an hour and half was up I was up in the seat again ready to go and about three o'clock I started getting worried. As there was always a lot of rabbits and he had to be there to see the sport like, so about three o'clock I went on and the rabbits started running and I looked up and he was coming in the gate and I suppose he saw somebody running out and he galloped up on the horse. "Stop!" he said and he dared I to leave the horses, when they was running after the rabbits as they do, shouting and drumming you know. Dare I leave the horses stood there? I just sat up in the seat and watched they falling over the sheaves and just laughed like hell to see them.

Any rate when they got the rabbits out he said, "you may go on." He took out his watch and so did I and I went on and as soon as I finished I knocked the binder out of gear and off out the gate. He come up behind me and took out his watch. "He's beat the record. Seven hours and ten minutes." So he was terrible pleased about that, cos last time he was cut in eight hours. But I know very well. It been done before, it can be done again. Well I was about 30 in they days and I never had to be beaten. That was nine acres of barley. I cut it in seven hours and ten minutes. They had to stitch it up. I didn't like stitching.

We used a fair bit of thatching straw, used to cut it with a binder but 'tis cut with a combine now, 'tis all beat up. Unless there is a special piece and then they send a binder round. Someone else went round with a scythe. We were the cream. Some horses carried on longer than others, but they never used to aim to keep up beyond about twelve or fourteen. Corse I was on every day. We break one in every year, keep a brood mare and she'd do have a colt every year and in three years time he'd be ready to break in. So if one was getting a bit on the other side, we'd break in a colt to take his place. Corse there was many more men working on the land then. When I came here this was more or less an agricultural village, seven o'clock you'd see men going on to work with their rush basket. Well as time went on, everything got mechanised and that done away with a lot of labour so I don't hardly know anybody now so many of them left. They had to go where there was some work and those houses got sold to holiday people therefore I don't know half the people here now. They come one day then the next day they go down the seaside and they come back pretty well at dark then are gone again. Don't know them half the time see.

I first came to Manor Farm in 1933. Well just about the end of the Second War I took it over. Well farming did change during the war; they had to plough up more. Well we had land workers about and there was more work to be done I suppose, but soon went down to grass again after the war. Corn was what people were short of. Tractors the first ones were them little grey Fergies. I bought two of the horses off her cos they didn't sell the horses right away. So I carried on with the horse for 10 years, well then you had a job to get them shod, and a job to get the harness, so I went on and on and then got rid of the horses and got a little Fergie. After I had 'im he wasn't man enough so I got a bigger Fergie. So then we had two. On steep ground horses were safer. Really I should have been better to have carried on with the horses. I think 'tis a very steep place down here, at least you can breed a horse. I fancy I only had a tractor cos everybody else had one. That's how we went on. I milked 23 cows as well and done a milk round, round the village. Kathy used to do the milk round, I got married while I was in Chedington, about 1928 so my courting paid off. I been in this house since 1933. Other farms like Chartknolle used to sell the keep. Poor Ikey came to bad end, with his mole traps and lurcher.

The village has changed quite a lot. I was silly I never used to book no dates. The water been with us for 20 years, the sewage as well. Electric came after I bought this house, before that, just oil lamps. We used to pump them and carry them around. And primus stoves. Cooking. Mother used to have a big oil stove. Well we always looked forward to the Sunday meal a good roast. Breakfast. Well, cornflakes, I could never tackle a fatty breakfast. Ten o'clock that was when we would pack in a meal, bread and cheese, while we was driving the horses. We had to work the horses to two o'clock then we had proper dinner or lunch, a good feed. Good potatoes and cabbage or fry some bacon. Main meal of the day and sandwiches in the evening.

We did make cider down at the Smith's and used to bottle it as well nice stuff. Yes I think it used to be a bit fizzy. The press was at the farm; the press was where David's garage was. There was mostly cider apples, David have planted a lot of trees his'self. Kingston Black, the best apples for making cider. We wadn't allowed cider, only for haymaking or harvesting. Charlie Smith always used to drive a motorbike and side car and he used to bring on 10 gallons for us down there for the day. Sometimes we did run short. There was two of us sweeping, two pitching up. About six or seven, over a gallon each. You needed it.

Bob Tolley he was very, very keen on horses. He liked cider. Running the farm was quite a responsibility, Mrs Smith used to keep the accounts. Advice be to modern farmers, I started with very little money because wages was only 30 bob a week and you didn't have the money to play with and I wanted to do this bit of farming on me own and I just as well be my own boss. And so I started on very little money and I did a few jobs with the horses, a few working jobs and picked up a few shillings the first winter and I took on in October and no hay here on the place, only about a couple of ton. So I thought to myself it was no good for I to buy in too many cows as I'd only have to buy in hay for them. I bought four cows to the sale, and had to buy some of the hay for they but I didn't buy in none till the grass came on and that was when I started. Saved up a bit all the winter as best I could, and then bought in these cows gradually but I had a lot of rough luck 'cos it was what we call redwater country, and buying in these cows they all get redwater. If they are born and bred to the place they get immune to it but buying them from elsewhere. By that time I had got about twenty-dree or something but a lot of them had this redwater and corse when they get that down drops the milk, but worried my wife all right. "I'll stick it," and they got over this redwater and calved again then 'twas all right. The milk dropped off, the cows got bad and didn't produce the milk. No one made cheese. All our milk which wasn't sold went on to the factory. Corse the lorry came through here picking it up the milk lorry. Into Beaminster with the churns. You had to be careful. We had a cooler, all put in the churn as it was cooled and stand them in water if it was very hot weather, cos I couldn't afford to lose many churns of milk. The water came from the spring into the horse trough. Yields not as much as today but they would go on longer. Today 'tis like working a horse to death. I started with short horns and then we took on the milk round, some of them wanted Guernsey milk so off I had to go to Yeovil market and pick up a couple of Guernsey cows. The rest of them I had then was Shorthorns and then when the inseminator come on he used to say, "I can't make you out. Everybody is going Friesian now." He thought I was getting out of date, so I said, "let's try Friesian." So went on inseminating Friesian and by the time I sold out I had all Friesians. They give more milk but they say tidn't so good. That's right. Cream, some people used to ask for cream, but not to make a big do of it. No butter.

Well a lot of them American troops was around here,

because when I took on the farm down there, I couldn't get rid of the apples, because they'd say who did your predecessor sell to. Well corse Smith's had made up their own apples, and so I had to make up a tale but they wouldn't take me apples, so I made up the cider myself and the Yanks was about here. So the landlord came out one day and said, "I'll take all the cider you do make, if you like." I said, "all right." Agreed on everything we did. This worked out all right the first year, and then he say, "carry on again," and after I made all the cider, out he comes one morning and he says, "I shan't want no more of that cider." "What's the matter with the cider?" "The troops be gone." D Day of course. But any rate Clarence Hooper at the Royal Oak Drimpton went to school with him, and knowing he, so he took most of it. Hogsheads. We'd make about 20 or 30 gallons in a barrel. What I used to do was, one or two chaps they'd come in and put up a cheese by night and perhaps I would fiddle with him and work him out during the day. If not every night every other night, cut it round with a hay knife. We had the old fashion press, feed the pomace to the cows, very good stuff too. I never give the horses a chance.

I gave up in farming in 1975. I had a farm sale of the machinery a very good sale. I had Fergies one was 135, t'other was the little grey one. But I had bit of bad luck. I had a jolly good sale they all said so and that 135, I bought him new for £800 and kept him for seven or eight years and he made £1,400. And so I thought that was marvellous, any rate it wasn't very long before the tax man was sending me for money. So I went to the accountant. I wanted to know what was happening. "Um yes," he said, "you had a jolly good sale. So does the tax man."

About six months afterwards, I was picking up jobs hedging and had to carry the chainsaw and hook and all the rest of it, Christ this ain't going to do so I bought the tractor what I got now. I bought he in about '76 second-hand. But when I bought him he was just like a new one. And we been doing hedges, ditches and lawns ever since. Corse I kept the transport box on him. And put all me tools in there and anything else and ride myself. And I had a hood put on him a proper safety hood and of it come on hard to rain I can get in the dry. So still got him now.

Jack: I left school at 14, went to work at Broadleaze, they kept me on in the dairy. Then I went to Knowle farm and then to Ammerham where I lived with my cousins and worked at Whatley Farm for Mr Hammett. After that I went to work on the railway, did that for 13 years, gang of four we had four miles of track to look out to. I was look out. Best job I ever had, double pay on Sundays, track maintenance but sometimes we did start at three in the morning. You could hear the whistle when they left Crewkerne station. Trouble was you couldn't hear the diesels. Then I worked at the sawmill at South Chard. Lived in Winsham, Western Way and then came to Stoke Abbot about 1990.

Jim: Secret is keeping working slowly and regularly. Good many have asked me what the secret is. But we don't go at it like a bull at a bank, we keep jogging along and if I don't feel up to scratch I do have a spot of whisky sometimes. Breakfast, now cereals, I don't get up before half past seven or eight o'clock. Have wash and shave and a bit of breakfast. Kick off about half past nine, ten o'clock. Days be long enough for us then.

I am now 102, 103 in December and Jack is 95.

2 Bert Vickery: Farmer, Thorncombe
Born 1922.

Farming's rather boring now. Corse it is. Everybody knew one another, everybody was more friendly.

My age? 81. Born at Edington, Burnthouse Farm near Bridgwater. Left when I was four year old. Then New House Farm, Ilton, where the fair people are. New House Farm, the buildings where we used to put the corn ricks have been taken over by the fair people. Years ago it was mostly let farms. They did not own their farms. Most villages had their Forde Abbey and Sadborow. Brother's 90 down Taunton. He got a wonderful memory.

I was born in 1922 and married from Elmore Farm, Thorncombe. Mother came from Manor Farm Seaborough. Farms used to change hands quite a lot a few years ago. Went to Ilton school first, then to Ilminster. Left school at 14. Never liked school. Uncle in Crewkerne offered to pay me to go to grammar school. Didn't want to go. Living at Blackmore Farm, Woolminstone. That's where I done my courting from there. It was mixed farming not too small. Thorncombe had its small farms. Ilton was 200 acres, Blackmore about 140 and Sadborow around 160.

We had a bit of all of it, pigs, milking, bit of sheep, everything. Mind you there was a lot of rabbits about and generally we used to have rabbit twice a week, one roast and the other one stewed. Rabbit was lovely years ago and we children always used to like the kidneys, didn't used to quarrel, wouldn't do years ago. Caught them in wires and traps, did have the ferrets just the same. Harvest, a wonderful time. People used to come out from the villages to finish up the corn. Getting smaller and smaller. You may get a fox or two run out, the rabbits didn't know where to go because they had the stubble to contend with. And all the sheaves of corn, poor things didn't know where to go. Used to have a wonderful time getting these rabbits. Dogs and sticks, harvest supper a rabbit or a badger. Used to have badger suppers years ago. I've never tasted one but they say they taste more like a pig. Used to have badger suppers out at the Rose and Crown and the little pub up at Wayford. Roast them after badger hunting. Just got married, glad enough to stay home. Badger fat wonderful for cow's teats and that. They reckon it is better than goose fat. Wonderful. The old tale was, if you put it on one side of the hand it will come through to the other. Lot about now. They are pulling down the hedges, under the hay barn. There's too many around.

Cooking? Porridge, nearly always a fried breakfast, good old fashion fat bacon, cook the potato in the fat, salting the pig on the leads. Always a fair bit of salt. I think the salt I eat in my time hadn't done me too much harm. Tidn't too good to always look to the future and Elsie right up to the time of her death, I told her never mind cooking me my breakfast, as long as I can, she did. Mind you I do a fair bit of work on the farm. Well I can do a 40-hour week without any trouble at all. Good to be active.

Rabbit, we never cooked rabbit in cider, roast rabbit with potatoes, we used to look out to the garden, turnips, swedes, cattle cabbage, butter milk, butter, cheese. Scald the milk in big pans, then heat it up and put it on the cool dairy floor and skim it off in the morning. Skimmed milk, different taste to it altogether.

Milking? All according to where we was to. Came to Sadborow in 1945, 45 cows. Blackmore 20-22 always two milking. Eight cows an hour. Pushing their cows too hard now. Those Holsteins, 'tis cruel. Four legs and an udder. Shorthorns and Devons, red and roany, Ayrshires. Used to rear our own calves that's how I went. Two milkings. Very strict on milking. All the cows tied up. Master cow tied up, come in the right order. All had names. Elsie used to get the cows in. She'd help with the milking sometimes had to wait for my breakfast.

Bert Vickery and beef cattle

We always had a nice cooked breakfast, farmer's wives always looked out to their families. Well you got to have something inside of you, porridge and fry up. Toast not very often, drank tea. Father had cider at eleven in the morning. Haymaking time used to always have them in for a little chatter before they went home.

Lunch would be sometimes out in the fields. Elsie used to push the pram up in the fields, stop for 10 minutes have lunch, then off again. Mostly liked cooked dinner. Lunch ten o'clock. Dinner was one o'clock. Tea six. Lunch, bread, cheese and cider. Bread sometimes used to make it. Bakers used to come round pretty well every day, Bryants, Caddy's down Clapton, Chapels from South Petherton, one out Marshwood. Two bakers in Thorncombe years ago, down Winsham, Pines. Butcher Warren used to come round.

Cheese made on farms? Me mother never made it. Poor things never had much time. Slavery. Start with Elmore and Hewood big dairy herds. Milk in churns and the milk lorry used to come around then down to Chard Road made into butter. Factory, Salter and Stokes when I was a real boy 75 years ago, back they days with their grey vans and lorries. No pasteurising then. When mothers used to go out milking, smallest children, milk straight from the cow in the bottle, that never hurt them.

Dinner at about one prompt. Used to think if we weren't prompt for dinner we would spoil the afternoon. That was our main meal and when they say going out to dinner. Dinner is one o'clock. Always had a nice joint of meat for Sundays. Poor old farm work. Monday washing day, used to have the old copper. That was their busy day, used to have cold meat.

Had our own lamb. Mostly pigs. Slaughter pigs not anything else, if you start with big animal you don't want too much on your hands. No refrigeration good old fashion meat safe and marble. Most of it was salted in. Salted it on leads. Used to tie it up to the beams, and smoke it that way, some people used to send it down Taunton to smoke it. Nearly always Saddleback. Kill as you went into the winter, don't want to kill a pig in the spring, let the weather help as well, keeping quality, 'tis cooler. Salt would do it. Pig killing. Fair bit of bargaining went on. Petrol… you know what I mean. I'll let you have some pheasants, if you let me have some beef. Barter they call it.

Tractors? Used to have horses, then the old Fordson tractor. Father bought a new Fordson for £140, Hawkes down Taunton. That was going back, I must have been about 10 year old, iron wheels, no rubbers, ordinary, Fordson then. Fordson Major, but when we came to Sadborow a new Fordson then, but that one was on iron wheels, come up through the fields, cleats, lugs to dig in. Some used to complain how the cleats cut the ground in the dry weather, used to put bands around to go on the roads. Tractor came in, the horse went out. Titans came in during the first war. They went on for a few years with horses. Used to call them "iron horse" with attachments for shafts.

Crops? Winter corn? Years ago mostly spring corn, barley, field of wheat for the reed. Barley and oats was grown more then. They reckon they're coming back, really good feed, ordinary feed, oats. More knew what they were doing then. Then we had the thrashing tackle, reed comber Mr Pratt from Chardstock. Three or four thrashers, steam engines. When we was boys down Ilton, used to get ever so amused to see them come, used to have a thrasher on behind, then a trusser and very often a caravan and a steam engine. All going on a steady speed, took 'em some time to line up but they used to always start thrashing eight o'clock, used to get proper excited to see the thresher come. And then they started with the big tractors. It was very dusty. That was when the cider was drunk. Well there was not much other. We made cider on the farm a long time ago. Must have been thirty year ago, right up to when a lot of people stopped. And that bring back memories. Nearly every farm had their own cider press, three or four orchards. Used to sell the apples to Mitchell and Tom's in Chard. We used to keep back apples for ourselves and then go in with a horse and cart. Tom Putt's was a good one, Blenheim Orange, Jack apples, Morgan Sweet, lovely apple to eat. Like down Ilton, they orchards are all now built on. Tarmac, concrete. No orchard out at Sadborow.

Rationing? Wartime not like other people. We done very well. Good substantial food, flour by the sack. Used to take the grain down Lockyer's mill and I remember they used to have a siding, near Woolminstone. Old Mr Lockyer, his carter, three times up and back in a day. Made the horse go fast. Old man used to work them hard. We used to go to Sadborow mill have it ground up for the pigs, eventually went into cattle feed.

Potatoes? Half acre or an acre always used to grow enough and the workmen always had a couple of rows. Milk, potatoes, eggs. Farmer's wife always used to look out to the workmen better than the farmer. Sharp's Express, Banner, Arran Pilot. Not really early potatoes. Wheat and barley varieties. Phil Morgan, nice straw to make reed, Redstart, binder twine, Red Star. Ricks was quite a skill, not everybody can build a rick with sheaves, liable to slip out in sunny weather. Always start to the middle and work on to the outside. It was skilled, they used to put them up well, thatch them at the top.

Stitching up, can tell a tale. Used to work hard, used to put in some hours, big 15 acre ground up Sadborow, stitching corn, oldest boy in a carry cot. Put the boy down somewhere in the fields. Darkness gradually came, couldn't find the boy for quite a bit of time. Elsie putting in the hours. Stitching up. Six for oats, four then tie the tops. Wheat, eight. Barley not very many, put a pick in, pick them all up at once. They reckon oats supposed to stay out two Sundays.

Horse and cart, all according. Used to go on steady. Horse used to know all according, brought back to the farm where a thresher could get in mostly on hard ground. Very often round ricks, nearly always round. Those reddy hay barns came out about 1945. Threshing tackle. Had to wait till they was in the district, from farm to farm. Not easy work. Used to wait a little while. Rats a problem during the war. We had to put wire around by law when you started thrashing, so you could kill them. Always had to put it round before they started, those rats also went in the corn ricks and you could see the holes in the hedge.

Farming's rather boring now. Corse it is. Everybody knew one another, everybody was more friendly. Farmers not got the time, none of us as sociable as we used to be, had to make our own pleasure years ago.

Me wife started off a concert, trying to raise money for troops and then charity. £28,000 for cancer research she was always one for trying to get a shilling. We always enjoyed village life. Tea: cake, bread, butter and jam. Generally cake in the home. Rock cakes, boiled egg, good currant cake. A lot of bread and butter was eat a long time ago. Bread, cheese. Elsie often cooking a meal at midnight when I come in. Wonderful really.

Sheep? Dorset Downs lambs sold at Crewkerne Market. Chickens: Rhode Island Red, white Sussex. Fruit: apples, pear, plum, cider orchards, cider clubs. Never hardly drunk any. Me Father did. They used to drink too much, especially farmers. Horse and cart. Horse knew its way home. Farmers used to go to market that was their little treat hard life… Cider presses, one in Thorncombe, one at Sadborow.

Pheasants make a wonderful meal. Shotguns, nearly all farmers had them. Vans came out. Two different bakers, plenty of callers, Mother's Pride. First car 1939. Courting, got a car just as we started courting, Ford 8 for £70 sold him for £100, had a running board. In demand for them, petrol rationing. Got married 1945. Bicycles; 'tis only occasionally you had the car.

Jams and pickles, bacon fat saved in earthenware jars. Always a stone floor, meat safe and marble, gauze lids on top to keep the flies out. Cheese dish. Blue one generally, cheddar and blue vinny, "West Bay mackerel," I can hear 'em shouting it out now.

Dick Measures with a duckling in transit

3 Dick Measures: Organic farmer, Toller Whelme Born 1923.

Oh God, the funniest years of my life. Swill was a story in itself. Kept about 100 fattening pigs. West Dorset. King of Swill… Swill went on beautifully for a long time.

My Mother? The impression you get, it bugged me all my life. If you weren't actually suffering from some ghastly disease like flu you ate your breakfast. There was always a bottle of aspirin on the table, you were expected to get out and hoe the turnips or get on and make the hay so you could never rest. You just didn't rest. If the sun was up you had to be up there. It still goes on. Yes. I was born in Charmouth we had a riding stable. Going way back 60, 70, 80 years, now. Used to live in that house opposite the church, a row of three Georgian houses, well we sort of ruled the roost before the war. Life was chaotic. My father was a solicitor in Axminster, Measures, Chapple and Rowe. Well my mother, mainly in horses. All her family were out in Burma, import, export. There were six or seven in her family. I think her mother died of drink. Gin. Having too many children in the Far East. I was born in January 1923.

School? It is a long story. I started off in the village school in Charmouth. Dame school, blue-eyed boy. Could draw beautifully, intelligent, all the rest of it, then I blotted my copybook. My little girlfriend about six years old, crying in the passage way so I went up to her and put my arm around her and said: "Why are you crying Jean?" "I wet my knickers," she said. I said, "Don't cry, take them off and as we go into the classroom put then in the wastepaper basket and no one will be any the wiser." And of course when the headmistress came in she looked in the waste paper basket and said, "Whose are these?" "Oh they are mine." said Jean. "Dick told me to take them off." I was no longer the blue-eyed boy, dead loss that was the end of me. And my school career has been like that ever since.

I then went to St Albans in Lyme Regis. Well that sorted ended up in disaster because the Headmaster ran off with the Matron. The school disintegrated from that stage onwards. Well then I went to Chaffyn Grove in Salisbury. All right for a bit. I bred tame mice back here at home, put them in my grub box and took them back to school. I sold these mice to all these kids and the whole place stank of mice. Sold them for sixpence a time and they would breed like flies until the whole place stank of mice. Headmaster searched everybody's tuck box by which time I had got rid of all my mice…

When we left Charmouth my mother took a farm in Loders. Perwen used to be Callington in those days, a small farm and there we used to make cider, the far end right at the far end, we had quite big orchard with lovely trees. Tom Putts, Morgan Sweets. About three trees left. Now Perwen is a thatched house lying back 20 yards from road, stream running under foundations. That was my introduction to farming. We had about 25 acres and we used to milk cows by hand. Well a mixed lot, Devons amongst them. The bigger the teats the better. No we didn't make cream, used to make a hell of a lot of cider with the intention of selling it. But it didn't work because the war broke out. I was 16 when war broke out. The army was entrenched on Eggardon Hill and my sister was quite pretty and they used to come down in their droves and they used to drink the cider. So you could say the cider went into the guts of the army. She married one in the end. Searchlight party got two of the local women into trouble. Yes. The Spyway, and then the roadhouse on top of the hill, used to have dances every Saturday night. We had the lot, the mill, the press. We employed a farm worker who knew how to work it; we lived in a rose-coloured world. We were drunk. Used to have cider for breakfast, cider for lunch, cider for tea, nothing mattered. Never learnt a bloody thing at school.

I then went on to Reading. War was on you know. No. The Army didn't get hold of me. I got into trouble. They said you have got to go on a 30-mile route march. It was 30 miles. They gave me an anti-tank gun to carry. Well you stagger on and stagger on. Well I threw it away; as far as I know that anti-tank gun is still at the bottom of that ditch. Yes. War was well and truly on then. Went farming during the holidays, 25 acres, milking cows and all the rest of it. The Ministry of Agriculture bloke perked up and said "This is the sort of bloke we want," and the Navy bloke said "No. I think he should be well and truly situated on a destroyer, which would probably suit him even better." So I said, "No. I am in a reserved occupation. I have a farm and I shall be running it". And they could not say "No." It was a reserved occupation, farming.

So the Ministry of Agriculture got me and they sent me up to Manchester of all places. Well Manchester in those days was a dead loss, just a mass of smoke and soot. Attached to the University. So I went round soil sampling trying to make farmers plough up everything. Reading taught me a hell of a lot. I got a prize for being the best student of the year. Fifty quid's worth of books. Terrified of the country starving to bits, so it was potatoes, potatoes, potatoes. I don't think it was all that bad but they had to take steps. If the Germans kept sinking ships at this rate there would be nothing left to eat, so we went round these farms, round the back of these factories making them plough up this five-acre patch to grow potatoes, they'd say this, "We'll plough up the patch and plant potatoes but you won't get any." "Why's that?" "Can't you see?" and you'd look up and see a smog coming down. And in a lot of cases this is exactly what happened. The spuds would come up, look nice and green and the smoke would blow in the wrong direction and chlorine gas would descend on the spuds and the whole lot would go yellow or white. The whole damn lot would die. So you can say my time in Lancashire was a bit of a dead loss.

"Do you mind going up to the River Irwell and taking some samples because the cattle down the river are dying?" Well you'd go down to where they were dying and the water wasn't just water, it was flowing, blue or green from the dye works and they were pumping it out into the troughs and the cattle were dying of fluoride poisoning. And they would abort and go thin, go lame and their teeth drop out. Just told the people to mend their ways a bit but nothing much happened. With the war on, everyone belching out more smoke and chemicals, the farmers didn't really stand a chance.

Well then I baled out of that job as I said I wanted to go back to my farm and do that. My mother happened to take the Western Gazette and happened upon a small advert, "Tenant wanted for Pipsford Farm." So I took French leave, came down and went over the farm. Was like a desert. Last bloke in there was just interested in horses. All he did was just breed horses. Goes right over the hill to the Hooke-Beaminster Road, couple of hundred acres. I came down and thought this might have possibilities, because it was so derelict. All they had done was plough it up to get the subsidy £2 a acre for ploughing bloody grass. Well they had done all that and grown nothing. So I put in an estimated rent of 30/- an acre. Happened to know a farmer in Beaminster and he said "bloody fool you should have offered them nothing for the first five years." Place was derelict. Well I said everybody else will be doing the same thing, I'll offer 30/- an acre and being Duponts they took it, and I was then the proud tenant of Pipsford Farm.

We didn't have much money. Once you were a tenant, you were there. An archaic tenancy agreement. Chronic. I had to make 25 chains of hedges a year, but if the hedges are 50 years old then it's forestry. Chainsaws were just coming into their own. So it was quite an effort, although no sooner had we got in there than they wanted it back. Because their sons had decided they wanted to farm and so from the word go I was on a slippery slope to nothing. But they didn't increase the rent and provided I went on abiding by the agreement they couldn't chuck me out. I made sure I made 25 chains of hedges a year, not an inch more or less. And they'd come and measure it too.

Well I realised the skids were on. We were there for nearly 30 years. Milked cows, dairy. Churns went to the factory in Beaminster. You had churn sniffers. Yeah pretty hard life really, because besides milking the cows, you had to make the hedges. And the war was on and so you had to keep ploughing. We had tractors, one Fordson, one carthorse. If you made any money it went into machinery.

Shortly after getting there we had a plague of abortion just like that and you were hand milking cows and a lot of cows hadn't cleansed and you'd be sitting there with the afterbirth wrapped around your neck and sweat pouring off your body, but provided you filled the churns it didn't matter. Price for milk wasn't bad so long as you kept going. We used to employ prisoners of war to give us a hand haymaking. Italians and Germans. Italians weren't so good, bit too neat but if you treated them well they worked moderately. But when the Germans came, that was a different story, provided you gave them a packet of fags every day, give them a good midday meal they would work wonders. Parnham was a prisoner of war camp. No escorts. In the end we would go down and pick them up. They loved it. A lot of them were peasants. In actual fact they were doing what they knew best. You'd sit back, smoke cigarettes and they'd do the work for you. They had their sort of know how equally as good as ours. They knew all about making hay, we had about four or five.

We used to put up rick after rick of hay. Used to go down to the Chesil Bank to cut rush to thatch them. Labour in Vain, near Bexington. Got into terrible trouble one time. Sent a young tractor driver down to pick up a load of these rushes. On the way back through the narrow lanes he passed a bicycle and the boy jumped on to the bank and let his bicycle slide under the trailer, bashed it up a bit, didn't think much more about it but a week later the cops came out and said you were in an accident the other day, and then they started. I had squashed the wheel of a bicycle and terrified a boy. "Where was the tractor licence? Where was the insurance?" And it went on and on. "Where is your gun licence, where is you wireless licence, dog licence?" The whole bloody lot. Of course I had none of it, so I was hauled up before the beak.

Between times I was driving down to Charmouth and a pheasant flew out of the hedge. I ran over it, stopped the car opened the boot and there behind me came Colfox JP, MP, Lord of the Manor in a beautiful Daimler car "HEY BOY! That pheasant belongs to me." "Indeed it does not." I said. "It was on the road. I killed it on the road." I opened the door. Threw it in, slammed it shut. "I'll get you!" he shouted and he bloody well did, because when I went to court he was on the Bench. Didn't declare an interest. Well I had already taken the pheasant back to his place. Waited till it was crawling then dropped it on his doorstep and ran away. "Yes Measures... Right. Right."

Cost me £200 then. I reckon the fields belonged to him, either side of the road. Bridport on the way to Charmouth so that was him. So I wasn't very pleased with Colfox.

DDT that's another story. When I was at Pipsford I was also looking after sheep we had about 200 mixed. Welsh in matter of fact. Let them out of the back of a lorry you'd see sheep scattered over Dorset. In the end I cornered the lot, shut them up in a barn and there they stayed. I brought down a load of grass on a buckrake and they loved it they did well. They had lambs no trouble but even then you had to dip your sheep in organo-chlorine. Arsenic had gone out in spite of the fact it was fairly good. Arsenic for everything worked pretty well. Blokes making the stuff probably died in their hundreds. I was the strong man that pushed them in and pulled them out, getting soaked in this stuff. Couple of hundred sheep and lambs push them in, pull them out, so I thought the usual dip was not on. Took too much time and was dangerous so I made my own dip which was a long passage way, so I made it watertight all the way down, drive the sheep into this passage way all you had to do was go down turn them up roll them in it and that was that. I was always a bit cagey about putting heads under. That was all right, organo-chlorine because you had to use it, you got completely soaked, the smell was ghastly. Dieldrin was magnificent stuff, let them out and that was that.

It was then that I must have picked up sheep dip poisoning in a big way. Because after a while I went bloody ill. Dieldrin was so good, you put the powder on don't you, also DDT dust, we also had a field of barley. Wireworm and leather jacket were eating it fast and furiously, did the same thing there. In this case I got O&J House, used to be the local contractors. They sprayed the barley with DDT. They sprayed the field and within three days the place was littered with leather jackets, dead ones, and the rooks wouldn't go near them. They must have known not to touch those leatherjackets any more. I started feeding cattle, feeding my own hay, my own silage, the cattle got thinner and thinner. Some of them aborted and I wondered why. I started feeding corn to my lambs and sheep up on the hill and one or two would die, nothing thrived. You'd send your dying ewe up to Bristol and the answer would come back "neurosis of the brain." That's no answer to anything.

Then one of the agents came round trying to sell me sprays and foodstuffs. Still alive today. I said "Yes I could do with some more of that." He said you can't have it, I said "Why's that?" They found tomato growers growing tomatoes on straw bales up in the east of the country and the straw has been sprayed with DDT and they are finding that their tomatoes are dying, so you won't be able to get that anymore. Then it suddenly dawned on me that the holdover of Dieldrin in the straw and grain, in your farm as a whole was something colossal, and the more you fed, the worse the cattle got. It was banned soon afterwards. You've heard of Silent Spring and all the rest of it?

It was then that I started seeing double, wake up in the middle of the night with nightmares, panic, absolute panic. Sort of seeing double. We weren't actually eating the stuff. Well from my point of view things went from bad to worse because you found that if you did any work, you broke down more organo-chlorine in your liver and got an attack like. Well you know what a fly is like when it goes round in circles when it's been sprayed. Well I was virtually going round in circles, and also my sheep were going round in circles, so well I decided this is it, it is Dieldrin.

Then I started writing to the Farmer's Weekly, even The Stockbroker which was on its last legs, but nobody would publish any of my letters. No. No. No. "Would affect sales." I gave them all the details of what happened to cattle, sheep, left myself out, didn't mention myself, but they wouldn't publish a damn thing. Well after all that I started getting very ill, hot flushes, teeth fell out, you name it, I had it. Amazing toothache. I suppose it affected the nerves. I was getting nerve poisoning. Absolutely. Gulf War Syndrome. Fantastic toothache. I felt perfectly mental. Giddy. Nausea. Heard of Lake and Green? the doctors in Beaminster? Well I went down to Green. He said, "you have got brucellosis," and he had my blood tested. But it wasn't brucellosis. Said, "You must have been fiddling around with some sort of poison." So they sent me up to the Middlesex Hospital in London and it was there that I met the boffins. And it was there they said, "This is Dieldrin, DDT". One of the boffins said, "The last case we had in here with these symptoms, had been spraying mosquitoes in Sudan. Swamps. He went yellow dropped back to seven stone and died". So I said, "This is rather hopeful". He said, "You only have one chance, go back and never touch any more sprays for the rest of you life otherwise you'll go round the bend". Diagnosis. You tremble very slightly. Trembling the whole time, going round in circles.

But since then, after that, talking to several farmers round here, they had to chuck up farming because of it. One lady milking a herd of Jersey cows, every time she went into the cow stall sprayed the cows with DDT to keep the flies off. She ended up on sticks, she got paralysed and that was the end of her.

Nobody thought about suing the company. You didn't have a chance. They told me in hospital in London, "You might get better, but from time to time you may have another attack but you'll get better". So after a while, the best part of two years, I appeared to get over it, but a lot of them didn't. They went slightly mental, never got better. A shattering thing because you couldn't pin point it. Well that was Dieldrin out of the way. It was this that encouraged me to go organic.

To make more money we kept the beagles for George Pinney. Twenty couples, about 40, put up new pens and new gates, OK. Right went on for quite a while, we didn't hunt them, we just fed them, they were bringing out dead sheep, dead calves. Doing the countryside a service. Not my job to collect them, someone else did that. Just dumped them in the yard, skinned or maybe not skinned. Then after a while, things got a bit hard. Picked up sheep as well, we kept the beagles for 10 or 15 years I think. We were out of Pipsford by then. So from 200 acres we went down to 25. We had to use all sorts of devious means to make money.

The beagles helped one hell of a lot. In the latter stages, sheep were being brought in. A lot of them skinned, a lot of them weren't. Yeah. I had to chop them up and put them in a boiler and cook them. Smelt wonderful. God. Yes. I'd feed them raw quite happily, but then farmers would start phoning me up. "I've got a dead sheep. Can you come and pick it up?" So you might, but then they would say, "there is no reason for this sheep to die, do tell us what's wrong with it." And so after a while you got so wise to it. You didn't bother to cut it up, "Why did it die?" You ask them one question: "When did you last dip your sheep?" and more often than not, they would say, "About six weeks ago or a month ago." So I said: "Right, well your sheep has died of dip poisoning." And you were that slow, that you didn't realise that you didn't have to put their nose under the drink. You dip their head under the water then they are going to breathe in stuff, and time and time again if you cut them up and looked, they had abscesses on their lungs. Lung cancer, as simple as that. And they would die anything as much as three or four months after dipping. And you got wise to this. I'd feed it to the beagles, not much is going to kill a beagle, believe you me.

Yes, well, another story is the swill. Oh God, the funniest years of my life. Kept about 100 fattening pigs, swill was a story in itself. West Dorset, King of Swill. Everybody else had chucked it in years ago because of swine vesicular, terrified of getting it. Keep on feeding swill, we'll get foot and mouth. Well when I came down here, one of the jobs I took, was at Chantmarle looking after the cops, looking after the swimming pool, as I can swim like a fish. Police training centre, I looked after their swimming pool, a brand new swimming pool, 100,000-quid job, sole charge of water. Up to 80 degrees C to suit myself, couldn't care less, burning 200 gallons of oil a day. They realised I kept a few pigs back here, and said: "We have a problem, we have to bury our swill, which comes from the kitchen, would you like to pick that up?" which I did every night, and brought it back here and fed it. Pigs and ducks, raised on police pig swill. But little by little, they go and put a telephone in the boiler house, well

I looked after the boiler house. I thought I might as well pick up more of this swill, and bit by bit I phoned up one or two people and before long I had the lot, didn't I. West Bay, Bridport, Chideock. A wide radius of swill, I never paid anything for it. You were given it for free, you ran virtually a bus service, picking it up, about 10 years in a big way and it could have got bigger and bigger, but being me I would never employ anybody, I had to do it all myself.

Damned all restrictions but you got the inspectors. Yes. You had to boil it of course. Went through with my usual experimentation. Started off with pressure jet burners, oil, this sort of business. You have to boil it for one hour, twenty minutes and its got to be seen to be boiling. Well pressure jets were all right except it was running away with oil, and so I thought I will do one better than this. So I went in for blast furnacing, in other words you get sawdust, cow dung, paper anything you like and put it under the boilers which were baths, long baths because you had to put the swill in one side and take it out on the other side of the wall. Whole lot of ghastly rules, fantastic rules. Fair enough. I went into this. Bones, everything and you would skim the fat off the top and sell the fat and get paid a pound a gallon for fat, good money, went into lipstick and soap. Had a couple of tanks out the back and used to put all the fat in there, used to come down and collect it, one hot day a couple of heifers came down and started drinking it and they got a taste for fat you see. One drank about three gallons and another one drank about four gallons. They died within about 24 hours. Excess of fat.

I went back to solid fuel blast furnace. Now the blast furnace was so simple, you get a Hoover, turn it round the other way and blast air into it. I used to pick up sawdust on my rounds, hospital waste in plastic bags. Christ you never open one of those bags. Believe you me. Push the whole damn lot in and set fire to this side, and now the whole thing was a bubbling mass, and the inspector used to come down, and say "Well yes," put the long thermometer in. They'd come roughly once a month, poke his thermometer into the cooking swill, leave it there for about 10 minutes, and I said "You had better take it out, pretty soon." "Oh no. I have got to have it in here for 10 minutes." Well on one occasion, he took it out and the whole thing was melted all down the sides. "Do you realise this thing cost £200?" I said: "I didn't put it in." It was so efficient this blast furnace, they sent a posse down from Bristol to examine it. What's the point in examining a Hoover turned round the wrong way under a lot of hospital waste? Well they came, made notes and sniffed the air and said, "Yes, this is very efficient." Because the blokes that were using pressurised steam were using a vast amount of money, raising steam, apart from that you get cold spots in it. And if you had a vast amount of steam, you could understand but if you a clobbery load of swill, you can't get the steam through that lot. My system was so fantastic that as you went round collecting swill, you'd collect cardboard, hospital waste, school books and Christ knows what. The fuel was free, the food was free, I'd burn the bloody lot. Virtually burn mud, so that went on very well.

Never did more than about 100 pigs, used to buy them off Herbie Snell. He's dead now. Time and time again he would bring in pigs for me and I would fatten them up. If he wanted any he would buy them back. I loved Herbie because you'd have some cattle for sale and I'd ring up and the majority of dealers would say, "You got a plain lot here Dick, I don't think I can move these for you." Herbie would say, "These are lovely, just what I want. I must have some of these," and he'd praise your stock up no end so that of course you would sell them. It's like that. So unusual to have somebody praise your stock.

Swill went on beautifully for a long time, then we had a bloody snowstorm, do you remember? Way back, 10, 15 years. You couldn't see any trees hardly, just the tops of the trees. I was running entirely on swill, no meal whatsoever, it looked a total disaster, I couldn't get out. I couldn't collect and after about four days I had finished all the swill. So I took a .22 down and went up the track because I was going to shoot the first pig, a sow, cook it up and feed it to the rest of the pigs, obviously the only thing I could do. But I got about 100 yards up there and a voice came from the other side of the hedge, "Hey Dick come and give me hand," this was Rob Dupont. All his sheep had got snow drifted all the way up. And as we pulled them out, a lot of them dropped dead. Just like that. Shock. So I used to drag them down on galvanised sheet and I had a stack of dead sheep under the hedge about 10 foot high. And I started cooking sheep to feed pigs. They scoured so terribly, ran out of them too much fat, so I thought I am going to lose this lot, about 100 pigs. All sorts. Phoned up the helicopter, £200 a drop. You got to buy the food. So I thought better to kill the lot. So I thought I will have one last chance chuck in the sheep without cooking them not even skinning them. I chucked them into the sty and one sheep per stall, all the way up through. Those pigs knew exactly what to do, they knew exactly, start at the tail end and worked straight through the sheep. And you'd come in the morning and all you would find would be the fleece, hooves, a bit of horn, a bit of head. They stopped scouring, cooking it a waste of time. So I said well, if the inspectors happened to come up here, they couldn't come in and if they did they wouldn't get away again. Well these aren't sheep, these are turnips. But it saved the day beautifully.

Kept pigs, sheep, ducks. Still doing ducks, that's the trouble you can't retire. Virtually free range, you have to bottle them up otherwise the foxes will eat them. Free range bantams and ducks, running around.

The cops are always stopping you, they want to know what you are doing, Right, well one day, one day I was driving to Bridport the siren behind me. "Do realise you are causing an obstruction?" I said, "why ?" They said "the cars behind you are slowing down and hooting," and I realised why, I was so fed up with being visited by the cops, that when I was visiting Bridport one day I bought some legs, silk stockinged legs in the window, you know the sort of things, I put them in the back of the van, stuck them in one of the bins upside down. so anyone coming up behind would see a beautiful stockinged leg sticking out of a bin. Well when the cops stopped me on this occasion, they said: "Do you realise you are causing an obstruction." "Why's that?" "Well," they said, "people coming up behind slow down and hoot." So I said, "that's nothing to do with me." And they said, "what is the meaning of this?" So I said, "you do realise that I collect from the hospitals don't you?" And they said, "yes, yes." Didn't smile. They didn't like it. "Take these legs down. You can't do this sort of thing." So I took the legs down and hung them up in the swill shed for many, many years till the silk stockings rotted off. But swill was always a joke.

I always remember one time I broke my leg, and sent my daughter off to Bridport to collect the swill and up by the traffic lights coming up from Charmouth way. She started off with a jerk by the Town Hall and half a dozen bins fell out of the back and floated down the road. She said, "I tried to borrow some dustbins and get it back in." Well a bloke gave her a bit of a hand. Well she came back in tears. "That's the last bloody time I am going to collect your bloody swill!" she said. Well I can understand it. It would have ended in disaster.

"Dick Measures, licensed swill collector no 12684."

4 John Symonds: Gravedigger, rat catcher, cidermaker Born 1944, Whitechurch Canonicorum

Rat catching. I had it with flying colours… A massive area it was and all farms. It suited me down to the ground. After rat catching, that was when I went on seriously grave digging.

I was born in Hincombes, Whitechurch Canonicorum, 1944. We did get a bit closer to the sea afterwards. I was a wartime baby. There were four boys and four girls. One boy died, one's farming, other one's grave digging. Howard he lives in Bridport now. He must be over 70. How long he can go on I don't know. Unbelievable. Robin's the one that got the farm at Twyford. But I think he's soon going to retire in a couple of years, He have done well, he bought a little place.

Father was a farmer and his father was a farmer. Father had a smallholding, used to do odd jobs around the farms and then during the war he was on the fire engine in the village. Pull one's I suppose. I got a feeling he wasn't Home Guard then. I must have been about four. Father took a farm at Butt, Ryall, about 90 acres, and he used to rent a bit more land and that was where we were all brought up. Looking out down North Chideock side. Down there, so we got closer and closer to the sea. Ninety acres, we used to milk about 20 cows. Twenty to 25 cows by hand. There was eight of us, three cows each.

We all went to school from there, in Whitechurch. A good mile and in all winds and weathers, no transport, never thought nothing of it. Had to be there by nine o'clock. I always went to school when I was in Whitechurch School. It was Lyme Regis I got caught. The big woman, corse they wanted me home haymaking didn't they? I left school when I was 15 but I never went very much the last 12 months. I never went Fridays at all, that was games, I hated that. And swimming, I hated water. I used to hide in the lane and watch the bus go on. My parents never said nothing. I used to get into a bit of trouble but I missed the bus didn't I? Even then I had to walk half a mile to catch the bus to get to Lyme Regis and that was a long way. You had to be up early.

My Father was Whitechurch family. And when Mother met Father her was in service up Pitt farm for Barnes's and Father used to go up there haymaking and Mother always said Father used to chase her round rick. And they wore long dresses in they days… She must have tripped up.

She didn't do bad. She had eight of us see. No cooker nothing. Not down Butt. When they moved to Butt we used to have the butcher call. I can remember the baker coming with a horse and cart. Out there so many times a week. The butcher did come Saturdays. The Co-op grocery van come later years. We had no electric, not until we had a generator and that was 1963 the hard winter, '62-'63 and then we had a milking machine the following year.

We used to milk by hand. Father's brother, he was out contracting. We had two little Fergies, but they come there when I was 11 and I used to stay home sweeping in the hay. I was 11, '55, I got a photo, we used to help make the hay round other farms as well. But a lot of the time, they used to come back and help us. But we did do contract work, when time went on a little bit, we had two grey Fergies. TVO 1962-63 Father bought a 35, three-cylinder but he wouldn't buy one with diff lock, cos there was more to go wrong. Just the plainest. Diff lock was useful, Oh God yeah. Now there's four-wheel drive.

On Grandfather's side he had a farm in Whitechurch. He had a little farm down there, but Mother's Father he lived at West Chinnock when Mother and they was born. And then he moved down to Pilsdon with Mother and Mother lost a sister down there, and they had two boys and then must have moved to Eype Down where there's a bungalow to. He built a wooden bungalow up there Charlie Wills did. He was a keeper. Gamekeeper most of his life apart from a poacher and one or two other odds and ends. He was a lovely man.

Horses? Oh bugger yeah. Before tractors come, brother was ploughing, Howard was ploughing and done all the mowing with them and then the tractors come in. An old Ford but he didn't last long, Father went out and bought the Fergie, but we still used the horse for turning hay and small jobs hauling the milk out every day. And picking up everybody else's milk, the milk, we used to haul it out to Ryall. Christ yeah in they days about six different farms, but there isn't one farm left now. That was all churns 'twas hauled on to Beaminster milk factory. All went there in all winds and weathers. We used to have about five churns a day, they weren't all filled up as you didn't mix the night's milk with the morning's milk. We used to carry the milk out of the cow stall as we never had a dairy then. We'd carry it out, tipped into the churns behind the cows with the calves going up and down like buggery and carry it across the yard. Mud and shit, never seen anything like it and put it in an old big bath where the cows do drink out of and tie it back be night. And that's the only way we could cooled it for years and years. Until they got modern and then they come round and inspected the buildings and then the cows had a pipe in front of them. I can remember the changes all right. I was lucky to be doing the old things which we had to do, all the copsing done be hand, up on the hills the thistles, wouldn't cut it with anything else cos you didn't cut the grass off did 'ee.

I remember once we got the tractor stuck, the Fergie stuck and when I was down there copsing, got stuck in a gateway and Father went down with a horse and put the horse on her and pulled him out. Pulled the tractor out, pulled the bloody Fergie out he did. Father never drove a tractor and when something like that happened and brother got stuck he was in his element wasn't he. Chuffed to bloody beans. Horses. We kept ours on there for just hauling the milk and doing odd jobs but then I started riding the bugger. Father didn't like that, cos you got to keep the last horse when you keep him for a bit and I was riding him round instead of doing work, and I was only about 12 or 14. He didn't like that. He thought I might get horsified. He was rubbing a bit, his legs on the implements and the gates and that was the excuse.

We only had they drop of milk. I know Howard left, he went driving the lime lorries. He stayed there all the time, then I stayed there till I was 22 or 23. Then I left and Robin was left, he was doing contracting, digging graves and that. Bugger we used to do the milking and Mother come and help milk, get it done then go back to working, haymaking or dung hauling or whatever. Sisters? They seemed to get a bit townified I think. They disappeared into Bridport. One went, buggered off. She used to do some nannying at the end of the lane where we lived by night and then she went off with these doctors up London and then the next thing she wanted was Father to sign to say she could go to Australia with them. And Father wouldn't sign but Mother, somebody must have done, her went and she been back two or three times, cost her nothing. She worked for doctors. She went out there got married to a Dutchman got four boys and that was it. T'wouldn't have hurt if a few more had gone out there I should think.

One of them married a postman and one of them worked at the knob biscuit factory. She worked there for years and I went up there driving for a few months, bloke up there lost his licence and I used to go round delivering these ruddy knob biscuits. Driving bit was all right but I didn't like being away from the farm. But you had to do anything to make a bob. That's how we got through I suppose. My Mother never had washing machines never had nothing did 'er.

I started digging graves. I used to help Father filling in cos he always did it down Whitechurch. He always done odd jobs, I suppose I went on doing it seriously 20 odd year ago, I suppose. Got to be. Doing logs and digging graves. When I left the farm I got a bit uneasy, I missed out in life, I was always working, you never thought of going anywhere, I didn't want to go off to shows, I didn't want to go anywhere. I was always

John Symonds, telling a story

home working, tractor and odd motorbike drive round the hills. Things like that. When I left I done four years on the building in Bridport, that was an eye opener. Bugger. I was earning 20 odd pound a week for five and a half days or something. Never seen money like it, then I done that for four years. Then I was on hedging and all sorts as well. And then I had the super job when I was doing hedging one day and the man said he was giving up rat catching for North Dorset District Council. But I liked the job and I had it. I had it with flying colours. I went for the interview and that was it. It opened my eyes up and I done four years at that, based at Sherborne area and Beaminster RDC which went all round Winsham, big area that was. I went all through Evershot and right the way up on to Milborne Port. A massive area. It was and all farms. It suited me down to the ground. I had some experience, rats, mice, fleas, cockroaches everything you can bloody think of. Done the lot. Done the lot. Hornets, not DDT we was using zinc, Warfarin was the main one, zinc strychnine, we had access to it in the early days but when they got a bit modern they pulled it back. But for mice and that we were using something which used to knock them out quick. Once they eat it, it caused a heat between the skin and the body and they blow up and we had some wonderful things happen with them. They just curl up, you might see one up there and all of a sudden he fall off onto the ground, wobble. And then he is gone, he didn't die that quick, if they was kept ever so warm they'd come round. And waddle on again.

I done the grave digging after that. Altogether I done eight years at rat catching. We got a salary. We was working more or less from home, so many hours but it was all flexi. Everything was flexi. Nobody could tell you how to do it because they didn't bloody well know how 'twas done. That was the snag. Especially with hornets. In Netherbury once, they had a hornets' nest up in the roof in the Old Rectory. I shall never forget it, I went to the top of the stairs and there was a door in front of I that went into the attic, and of course I opened the door a little bit, and you could just see one hole that they was going in and out of and it was black. And the woman said I'll put the light on. I said, "Don't bloody do that." I already had the torch on and the hornets started coming through the door. She said, "What are you going to do?" I said: "You gas them." I could have gone and got a pipe but 'twas difficult. Because there was light in the passage. So I said: "You hang on I am going in there." I had a spoon, this is true, a plastic bag, an artificial bag and I went in there and I had a torch and I put the torch on quick to see where the buggers were, cos I could see them hung up on a gert dark beam like that. And I held the bag underneath, I had a spoon and hooked the bugger off in there and they was everywhere they was. And I did it so quick I tied the top and Oh My God! her was panicking and I thought what am I going to do with the buggers now? So I chucked them into the mini van – I had a grey mini van – drove up to Beaminster tip, still open on the top, cor before I got up there they had gnawed through, and they was crawling about in the van, they was everywhere. And I chucked the buggers down over side as quickly as I could. But I still found them in they van for a long time afterwards. Well they was mesmerised or something. But they see the light and try to fly out.

Cider in Netherbury? Warren's cider, Jack Scott he was another one used to make it there. 'Twas a lot of cider apples down there, Warrens still make it don't they? We went up to Powerstock one night. Good little do that was, a good night. There's a lot of small lots being made. We have been making it up Chillington for years. And now I have been off with Tim Chichester this year and off at Kingston Maurward with the horse driving the apple mill on their Apple Day. And I made mine down Chillington with a horse. Round and round with a mill, there's a lot of people interested, saying they will do it next year but whether they do or not…

After rat catching, that was when I went on seriously grave digging. That and logs, I been doing that every since. I kept the pigs and I worked the horses in the woods. At Chillington, I worked them a lot there, specially when I went there first, pulled three acres of larch out. Big stuff too, and with a horse. Then send the timber on. I did keep pigs there, I kept 40 sows. There and Cricket St Thomas. We had a lot of pigs on contract selling them at eight weeks. Eight to 12 weeks, 27 acres of woodland. And that's where I still mess about and make the cider. Ah you got it…

Bob Tolley? That was very sad. We be relations somewhere through Mother, and Mother's family was Podgers of Mosterton and the last of her relations lived at Buckham Mill up the lane. But Mother always kept in touch with them and when I was growing up 17 or 18 Mother used to say to me, "I've seen Mrs Tolley, who was a Weatherell, and whatever you do, don't have nothing to do with that Bob Tolley. He is mad as a hatter," and she didn't know half what I was up to, so I had to keep bloody quiet. But I never met him, he lived in Thorncombe they days and went Chard that way and I went the other way. But 30 years ago, a good 30 years ago, I was living in Stoke Abbot, and old Reg Hunt, the farmer up the road said one day, cos I was still catching rats around like at Honeycombe Farm. Ikey Chubb sad end wasn't it. So Reg Hunt said, "bugger I had a dozen bloody calves come in here last night, sucked all the cows out." And he said they belong to a madman moved up to Honeycombe Farm, just moved up there. He said, "he isn't going to have the buggers back for a day or two," so he didn't know who it 'twas, so I ended up going there, telling him for Reg, only to find out that Bob had been to market, bought these bloody boss calves, took them home, instead of shutting them in for a week or two, let the buggers out. They went to Harry Studley's, sucked his cows out, then to Reg Hunt's, that was my first meeting. Hang on a bit, better take another drop of that old cider…

My cider went green, don't know if the green goddess got in there overnight but 'twas all right. Somebody gave me some tablets to chuck in it. Improved it no end, never mucked about with cider like that. Cider on the farm, oh bugger yeah, down Butt. 'Twas Kingston Black. Everything in the orchard went in there, Father used to make it fairly early, because of the early ones, Morgan Sweets come early and we used to make the cider fairly early. Picked up the Tom Putts that we needed and then the rest would go on for cider. What the other varieties was I wasn't sure but it was a biggish orchard. The old orchard is still there but a lot of the trees have tumbled over, and haven't been replaced. Back in they days, 'twas always drunk, 'twas always used. Nobody asked where the apples come from or what they was. We only just made cider, nobody doctored it like they do today. We was brought up to it, how you can make one lot of cider and get ten different ciders out of it? I can't cope with that. Everybody used to come haymaking, loose hay, everybody used to come out from around. There was a bloke used to come out from the garage, the postman, all sorts of people come out, but in return they did plant some potatoes, couple of lines of tiddies in the fields, so they come haymaking and put the tiddies in and keep them hoed. But they always had cider, and Grandfather was the best one at it, he used to drink about eight pints a day at least and take another four to bed in a bag every night in bottles. He'd get up at ten o'clock in the morning and he'd drunk all that lot, and then he would have another lot. He always went to pub during the day, but then he'd bring back that brewery cider. Bloody hell, he changed over to that. I don't know whose cider it 'twas. We used to get it up at the Sun Inn, Morcombelake. That was it. We never drunk it, it was chemicals. Father always said, "the old bugger's gone over to chemicals."

I always remember old Charlie he was a marvellous man with a gun and a catapult. He could put a candle out at a distance with a bloody catapult. And he'd knock a fag out of somebody's mouth and he taught me to shoot as well Charlie did. I don't know when he was born, he was 90 something when he died, Charlie was. He used to sing in the '50s and they took all these old songs, Peter Kennedy, he used to go up and sing on the telly. Then they made a record, the Yetties, and all that. They still ask for him now, but he had a lot of songs. When did he pass away? Buggered if I can mind now. He been dead a few years, I got a record of what he made 'twas all in there where he moved from. Funny thing was he landed up with we down at Butt, after coming two or three stops from West Chinnock. I come other way haven't I. Crept over the border again. Everybody was related to one another, they never went far, tidn't like today,

There was dozens of little farms right through the Marshwood Vale; Whitechurch, Ryall, some might have only had a dozen cows and a few heifers. But they still made a living, and 'twas real old fashion, the odd pig, but now 'tis, in a few years time there won't be anybody left like the Barnes and the Creeds. They stopped delivering milk in the villages, hygiene put paid to a lot of it. Very few delivering today. A few year ago somebody in Stoke Abbot still doing it. If you take milk now, when we was youngsters and we used to go out and have a few pints, and headache, the first thing you'd do was take the cream off the top of the milk and 'twas cream, 'twas like that, put a cup in and Mother would know you'd been there because you couldn't get all the cream off, it was so thick. She used to moan and groan sending it on with no cream on. Now if you buy a bottle of milk now they have taken all the cream out and put water in. When we was young we had all that didn't us. Old Charlie he used have a pint of milk, a pint of tea, three knob biscuits in there with sugar on top and then he'd put two eggs in and stir it all up, every day he'd eat it like porridge, I can see him now drinking it. Raw eggs, he used to have a spoon and stir it up. They knob biscuits, Mother used to bring us a pint cup up to the stall in the morning when we were milking the cows and dree knob biscuits in there and sugar on top. Well time her got up there with it, they had expanded, can you imagine that, with sugar on top. And when you just finished milking the cows, you might have gone under the cow and started milking and hear Mother coming, and there was another 20 minutes before you got out to eat the bugger. You know we'd always look forward to it mind you, 'twas breakfast all in one, we'd go down at nine o'clock but we was eating that at seven o'clock in the morning.

We always had a cooked meal dinnertime, and breakfast but we never stopped between nine o'clock for nothing till one o'clock and then five o'clock we had tea. Grandfather always had his knob biscuits, and some of them used to be burnt because sister used to bring them back broken and burnt ones, bag fulls so we never really bought too many.

Mother cooked everything on the fire you see, except for Sundays and then we had oil, paraffin oil cookers with the round burners and oven on top. Well that was all we had and the girls used to help cook Sunday dinner, but the rest of the time we had stew. There was always stew on the fire and 'twas either rabbit or a bit of lamb. Don't know where half of it come from. Used to get chucked in the bloody pot. Always stew and then her always made the jam and her cooking wasn't very good, the cakes were terrible… but her done it. Mother never made bread. Her had enough to do without that. I can see her now, see the old bugger there now, everything was black, her hands on the old fire with all they saucepans and that, and her would get it all over her face, and she'd have a black nose and Father would say something…

Funny thing we never went fishing but we always went down to get mackerel. When there was mackerel. Never done any fishing, we always waited for somebody else to catch them. They were always down there, giving a few away, they was lovely. I ain't too good on the water that was why I didn't go to school on a Friday.

Burton Bradstock was always the best place for fishing, you come down through Seatown, but that was a fishing place

Cogden, more serious up there. Mackerel, you could see them specially if you get thundery weather and they'd come in.

How many graves have I dug? I hate to think. I've travelled all the way up to Mere and all round here, at one time I used to do a lot, but I have cut back now. I'll cut back a bit more shortly. I tell you what. They got bigger over the years because what has happened these undertakers, they buy so many coffins in a standard size. Very few undertakers tailor the coffin. I get no more for digging a bigger hole. If you get a re-opening now, when there is already somebody in there, it is usually easy digging, as it has been dug out once but when the coffins used to be 18 inches, about average. Well now the buggers are now up to 26 inches, so you got to take more out. Chip more off on the sides. Well you got to be careful, because somebody next door, you can often tap and you can hear it is hollow next door. You got to be very careful, you see years ago they'd put them pretty tight, wadn't a lot of room between them, cut two or three inches that side and then you got to allow for the handles and then you get a bit tight to they next door. I seen them come in before now. Many times. Most of them is machine. I done two the other day be hand, a bit in amongst it. You don't get paid extra for doing it by hand, you don't get much out of the undertakers.

They phone us up and mark the grave. You get him ready the day before depending on the soil. Otherwise they soon fall in if the water come along. The sides come in and you got to be there. I been there, dipping and dipping and dipping and digging out and you know, they are soon coming out of church and you jump out, and then all of a sudden you be hid behind a bush and you hear flop… and the whole bloody side go in. I've only had one where we have had to leave him on top, but usually we can get him in and level them up.

An expert on soils? That's right. That's right. West Dorset. South Somerset. You'd be surprised, I know where 'tis gravely, where 'tis clay, where 'tis sand and you go up to Podimore and it is all pebbles, gravel and all fall in. Christ you get a lot of greensand. Chalk, you can get run in chalk up Dorchester way. You dig a hole up there and it just come in like that. Unbelievable. The worst place for water is Martock because the graveyard is lower than the river and nothing soaks away, and that is terrible out there, But the oldest one I do is out Stoke sub Hamdon, used to be a wall out the back of the church and I think he is 1300. And years ago there was a wall there and everybody was buried lower side and we have had them fall in time and time again as you dig down. And you got to dig it all out, you just find piles of bones. We was out there one day, my boy come on he was 11 to give I a hand, and I was there with a digger and had to pack the dirt downhill. And I was there digging away and the bones was coming out and I said to him cover them up if somebody come, cos you got to be a bit careful, because you always say you put them in a bag, and collect them and then you put them back in again. But all these heads was coming out dree or four heads come out, and anyway one bugger rolled on across the churchyard from the top of the heap and the vicar come round lower side and I thought we be for it, so I stopped the digger quick. But you couldn't help it. An old part of the church like that. Nothing you can do, so my boy run down with a shovel to pick him up and vicar said, "I want to see, I want to see." And I didn't know what to do, so I went off and buried some more bones round the side and he was looking at me, and the boy brought him up on a shovel and put him up on top and the old vicar, was looking at me and he said, "any more bones?" I said, "not a lot." "Interested in that skull," he said. Never seen one before. But they be very naive vicars, unless it be somebody else's wife. Anyway he said, he was looking at it. And he said, "I wonder if it is a man's or a woman's skull?" Cos we was talking about it I said, "'tis a woman's." He said, "how do you know that?" I said, "it has got its mouth open…" He went "WWWUUuuu". *Much laughter…*

I worked for five undertakers. Used to work for quite a

few up round Sherborne and that, but I cut back now and go no further than Yeovil. You can dig them, you can try to pick the weather to dig them. But on the day that is it. And you can always bet too, that if you get a wet day there is water in the grave and they all disappear quick, but if it is a fine day they all stay yapping and laughing. You have to hang around. Terrible, terrible. And then you got to fill it in and sometimes the funeral isn't till three o'clock winter time. And then you don't get much light, you got to rush on to get him filled in. We be usually back in the churchyard to top him up, we get called back occasionally. Always put the turves back on the mound, you know which churchyard is going to sink, but down your way Winsham the bloody stuff just go down like that. High as you like, and it go down, terrible digging down there, gravely. We know a bit about that. Cremations are easier but I don't get the work. Don't want too many. I think we get out share. I like it enough.

Horses, I've got the two. Then I got another two, a pair of driving horses, which I use for the do's, shows, odd weddings and funerals. All sorts. Then I got another driving one and a donkey. Which he do a few odd jobs. Carol singing tomorrow night. No, Wednesday night. I had horses, I've always worked with horses. First one, the farm horse down Butt, then we used to go out with the milk, then come back we always used to drive him as kids then walk up the shafts and get on his back and things like that. But when I got married I bought a horse, and that was the end of my first marriage. The horse I think, the horse finished my first marriage and I had horses ever since. I think I got up to a bit of mischief. I think.

But I started Bob Tolley off with horses. That's why Bob bought a horse because I was going by his place one day and when I see his missus sometime afterwards. I said Bob's going to get a horse and he bought one off Jack Ware, Fifi, and he only had that horse put down two year ago, and that horse must have been 30 all right. And the one we did Bob's funeral with, the horse that's the first foal he had, that was. Was a lot of people there, lot of people knew him. Biggest crowd since the last public hanging. There was a lot of people who would have gone if they knew on time. I'll never forget that day. We walked from the farm with the horse and the coffin on board and we got down and David Wakely said "Park across the road in front." And the church was packed then but I never seen so many people milling around in Broadwindsor in my life. They just like a swarm of bees coming down the road, it was unbelievable. 'Twas hardly room to get the coffin in the church. Bob and I was always friends all the time. My birthday is the 21st of January and Bob's the 25th the same day as my Father's birthday and we always celebrated mine first then his. We always used to go out on mine, only Bob and I never took our wives or nothing, and there was usually a bit of snow about or sommat or another.

The story about the tree in Beaminster? *Much laughter.* Yeah I've heard about that as well. Funnily enough. They love to see I come round at Christmas time. Hoping something's going to happen, the buggers, the real story? Well I don't know really. I suppose I was around there in they days in Stoke Abbot. Down there with horses and drinking and I don't know what was going on and then they asked us. The butcher ask I to supply a tree and put him in, in the hole which I done. And one day I went and had a pint afterwards and he said "I'll come over and pay you. Somebody donated the money to 'ee." Well I said, "That's all right." But he didn't come in the pub and pay. He then got in the pub the next day or the next night. Kept saying he was coming he was coming. "I'll bring the money tomorrow". "Well," I said, "I'll chop him down if I don't get paid." That was a joke that was. Well the landlord said bring him in here and I'll give you the money for charity when you cut 'im down. Come to bloody Boxing Day and us all had a drink didn't us. He had lights on all right. He had a fairy up the top too. Yeah we went in the pub and had a few pints and went up Hooke and had lunch and Julian said, "we'll cut the Christmas tree down this afternoon." Well bloody hell. We come on back didn't us. It was a bit of a muggy afternoon. And the bloody chainsaw, lopped the branches off and the whole lot went down across the road. Nearly went through the butcher's shop. It was the biggest one they ever had. Had to be a big tree, good 30 foot high and a good bushy one too. And that helped him a bit, slowed him up as he came down, stopped him doing too much damage, I think. There he was. Anyway we took some in the pub burnt it in there and then we scarpered. This was Boxing Day, I think it 'twas. Yeah, 'twas. We scampered, so I was in Beaminster staying for a day or two, I was living at Broadwindsor then, but I was in Beaminster staying for some unknown reason and a policeman was going out to Broadwindsor and putting a note on my door. "Would I come into the police station. Pop in." It was Godfrey. And he put three different notices on there. I was working for the council at the time in Bridport catching rats and he phoned here two or three times, but poor Julian up Hooke, he got locked up. He was off to the Hunt Ball and they locked the bugger up. Vandals and all in the papers it was. "Vandals cut 'im down." So I never done nothing and it was New Year's and Julian rang I, as well and said, "do you go on and see them, you're in bloody trouble for this, the electricity board you could have electrocuted people." So 'twas just before New Year's Eve and the police rung up in Bridport Council Offices for I to go in, when I found a police woman I knew and her said "They are gunning for you all right. But don't you tell them I give you a lift down there from Hooke to Beaminster. They will keep you in overnight. Take everything out of you pockets but don't mention my name."

Her drove I in there in an old Ford Anglia estate but the bloody thing broke down didn't her. Half way up through the bloody wall, the car broke down, anyway she let him run out in the road and I went in, and said who I was. They was highly delighted wasn't they. So I had the interview with the young copper. He couldn't spell, he couldn't understand what I was saying. And went all through this, about three times, and then I said I hadn't been paid for the tree so it was still mine. It was mine. But her told I it was, "Your tree but what's in the ground isn't yours." So I made a statement and the other copper came in and read it. Asked me a few more questions and let I go see.

So then the councillors at Beaminster wanted to make sure we was done. But in the end we had a warning, a severe warning and a telling off. Naughty boys. Won't do it again. But it didn't stop at that. Word got around. Shouldn't have done. I always regretted it… Did get paid in the end and I gave it to the landlord to give it to charity. I never saw the fairy. I expect the chap that ordered the Christmas tree, he took the fairy. He was that type of bloke. The fairy was perfectly all right. Let's stop for a drop more cider now… Very nice bit of mulled cider. Come back in an hour's time and I'll tell 'ee a bit more.

5 Norman Strawbridge: Gamekeeper, Forde Abbey Born 1925

When I was 17 I took over the horses, and done all the ploughing. We had 40 acres of ploughing. I loved it. An acre a day. I loved ploughing with horses, peewits sweeping down...

My Great-grandfather was done for smuggling and was a model prisoner in Dorchester Gaol. Out of six brothers, five emigrated to New Zealand, one stayed. My Great-grandfather is buried in Stockland. My Grandfather was buried in Thorncombe and my Father in Marshwood. I am famous now. Mark Roper had my portrait painted. My portrait is now hanging in Forde Abbey.

I was born in 1925. 31st July, Thorncombe. Down by the river, Synderford, that's where I was born. I tell who has got the house now, a Member of Parliament, Oliver Letwin. My Father was a farmer, had a smallholding and as he had such a big family it wasn't enough, so we took a big farm, 60 acres, at Marshwood. That's why he shifted because all of we youngsters were coming on. I am the second from the youngest. I've got five brothers and one sister. My Father came from All Saints, Stockland, Smallridge. So I was brought up really at Marshwood. I went there aged five. Colmer Farm part of Sadborow estate. About 160 acres. Dairy, a few sheep, mixed, mostly dairy. Milk then went to Cow & Gate, Beaminster. We used to have to take it up in the morning on the stand in churns, no tractors, all horses.

Six boys and my great Grandmother emigrated to New Zealand in 1852. 1,500 of them now out there and that was six years ago. Some of them are policemen, all sorts. One relation was the mayor of Nelson. One of them, he volunteered in the First World War and was sent to Gallipoli with the Anzacs. He got wounded and was sent to Malta where he died of his wounds. There must a headstone out there somewhere. My grandfather he was a bit of a bare-knuckle fighter and somebody knifed him as he was getting on a horse. A four-inch knife. He survived but it got in the papers. My Mother came from Chardstock and her Father had a smallholding, he was really a carpenter.

My Father rented off Sadborow estate. Farms then were used as an investment and let out. I went to Marshwood school and when you were 11 you went to Thorncombe by bus. I left school at 14 and worked at home on my Father's farm. I left school the day the war broke out. I stayed on the farm, my brother volunteered for the army. And when I was 17 I took over the horses and done all the ploughing. We had 40 acres of ploughing. I loved it. Loved ploughing with horses. An acre a day. And when you were mowing you could get up at five o'clock in the morning 'cause it was cool for the horses and go out the morning till nine o'clock, to take the milk up and you had three or four acres by then. Lovely really put the horses in for feed, and then ready to put the wagon on to get some hay in, which weren't too hard for horses. They had to hang about while you pitched it up. Small carthorses. Not the big ones. He bought them off my uncle, he used to break horses in and sell them. And wages. When I first got married… £4 10/- a week.

Farming during the war. I belonged to the Home Guard and we used to go out all night down West Bay guarding the coast. Bit of fun really. So long as the Germans didn't come. Yes there was a false alarm one night. I was in the Home Guard and I wasn't old enough to be called out but I got a message one night that the Germans were landing. They done it on purpose. And I had to whip around some farms and tell them to get ready and come. I think they done it on purpose to see that they were ready. I can remember it happened twice. I remember it happened once in church in the middle of a service, they said this country has been invaded and two or three of them got up who was in the

Norman Strawbridge at Forde Abbey, lunchtime

Home Guard and went out. So they done that twice. Must have been after Dunkirk. I lost several cousins in the war. One was killed in India flying. We had searchlights everywhere. You would be out on your pushbike and there was searchlights everywhere. There was searchlight that got a German plane one night and he dropped his bombs and they landed up on Pilsdon there, there was this great big ruts, they never went off. I went down to Bettiscombe and there was a bomb hole you could look down. Didn't explode. I reckon he's still there. And one night they dropped hundreds of incendiaries. We used to go out and find them and the fin would be left there. I had one for years, the rest burnt round, all over the fields down the Vale there. Exeter had a bashing one day. I was down in hospital couple of days afterwards. I had something done to me arm, that was smashed about, you could proper smell it, terrible smell up through them ruins.

On the farm we would eat rabbit stew and kill a couple of pigs a year. Don't do to tell the government as you were not supposed to. You didn't do bad really. My Mother used to make a bit of butter in a pot get the cream and shake it. Sometimes half an hour sometimes a bit longer. Then you just washed it and you had lovely home made butter. Jam, she would make a bit of jam, you couldn't get a lot of sugar. Honey. I cut out a lot of bees. We had some bees, been there for years in a an ash tree. I had a ladder there and I got up the ladder and Father had some sulphur he had melted on some paper and I pushed it in a hole, stopped it up and went down the next day on a Sunday and we had two four-gallon buckets of honey, comb and all, not solid honey. Pity really cos it killed all the bees.

My Father paid me very little, not a lot. I was always happy, I can never remember being bored. You always had something to do really. Your horses and one thing and another. In the war you had to grow an acre of potatoes and we used to grow a field of turnips that had to be all hoed. Swedes, mangolds, that's all you done during the summer, hoeing weeds out. Bit boring but it's not all day. You had the cows to do and it was ten o'clock by the time you had washed out the cow stalls. So you only had from half past ten till one o'clock. And then from two till three or four and then the cows again, so it wasn't like you had a full day at it. We had mostly Devons. Don't give much milk. Not a big milking cow. All dairy about 30 or about that.

My Father used to go to Martinstown once a year. They have a sheep farm there and in the autumn he would buy about 25 sheep and winter them and then sell them in the spring. Colmer that goes back hundreds of years. A family called Colmer in Henry VIII's time. They lived in the farm for generations. Then a man called Ayres bought the whole estate back in 1938 I reckon and he done all sorts. Put up new cow stalls and houses where they were needed. Spent a fortune on it. Rent about a pound an acre. It all works out to what a wage is. I don't expect it's much more than that now, getting on for a week's work before the war. So you could reckon on £200 an acre now. So it hasn't altered.

Worked there till I was 21, 22. About eight years I think. They always used to do that. I'll tell you what farmers used to do years ago. They used to have son work on a farm and let them rear a cow a year till they got married and then they could take on a smallholding with about 10 cows. To start off, then get a bigger farm All that's finished now. No farming left now

Cider? Every farm made cider. My Father used to make cider. We used to pick up the apples and knock them in and every day get one on each end of a grinder. My Father would have a big press with two great screws and a great dish in the bottom and he have lots of sweet oaten straw and he would put the cheese about that high, and straw all around. Then start again with the pummy (pomace) till he was about three feet high. Then stick a hatch on the top and then screw him down then out it would come, all the cider sweet, really sweet, we used to make about eight hogsheads a year. My dad had a special measure. Beautiful. Make sure you put in the bung push him down to the corner of the barrel and that told you how many gallons was in there. I would have liked to have had that one. I expect he's a rarity now. Every farmer made cider. And it all tasted a little bit different like wine. Apples all different sorts, one looked like a pear, some were very sweet, some were very sour. Coalbrooks, little red ones. Tom Putt's, Father used to call them. We never used to touch the trees, never prune them or anything. Used to go very year. A beautiful sight in the spring. An orchard all out in blossom. And we had mistle thrushes there. Used to nest in the forks, one of the first birds to nest. Beautiful it was in that orchard. We had plum trees as well, lovely plum trees, they looked too big for damsons.

Then there was "still water". They used to have the still out in the woods and we kept some for the weak lambs. Worked a treat. Just boiled up the apple pulp after cider making. Once the coppers come down and mother tipped the bottle down the drain as they came in the yard. They was looking in amongst the hay, I never saw the still but it did the rounds. Still waters run deep. Then there was an old man down Marshwood Manor who could charm warts, and get rid of luer and ringworm. If an animal was lame you watched it, and when he put a foot down on a clod you cut round that clod and turned it upside down. To learn the charms, a man can only pass it on to a woman and she can only pass it on to a man. My brother could do it but he's long gone. And then there was aller cockle tea *(alder tea)* and feverfew, brimstone and treacle for colds.

I then worked at home for a bit then took on another job. I worked there for two or three years then I went on the council for a little bit. I liked that. I actually helped paint out Beaminster tunnel. Then I went back 'cause they wanted me back on the farm then I went self-employed in forestry work. So I went all over the place doing forestry work. Forestry used to let work out to tender and you had to put in a price. I done well on that. Had my own chainsaws, cleared 12 acres one year of woodland, then plant it. The weeding I used to like. About 100 acres with hook and crook. Good money. Well I didn't mind it, I was used to it. Working for yourself is better than working with someone else. Five o'clock you might still feel fresh and go on another hour or two and earn another pound or two. I'll tell you how you make money. You get a contract sent to you and they ask you what you want to put in for it. I done this once and there was about a mile of hedging near Taunton. Well I didn't want it. On Taunton forestry I thought, if I put in for it they might ask me to do more, so I put double down to price myself out of it and got the job. So that's where you make the money. Its good really, the thing is to price yourself out if you have too much.

Then I done sheep shearing a bit. I used to do quite a few sheep really. Six hundred at one place, 600 in a week. Five days. Tidn't bad is it. About 120 a day. That was my limit really. But you had to work till about eight or nine. But I used to go up there for a day and dag them all out first. So if you know you are going to shear them you make sure you do a good job up behind. Take off a bit round the tails. I had a brother living in Australia doing sheep. He reckoned they do skin the back of them, literally skin them alive. I don't know if it is true.

Then I went down to Forde Abbey 1963. We had a terrible winter and I had a job to get a lot of work. It was that terrible winter 62/63. I think he was an auctioneer they had all the keep for about 40 cows just to feed them and that and Bettiscombe. Snow was higher than this room terrible. But I managed to get down and do them for them.

I started out without a chainsaw. But I soon got one, you had to have one, a German one. They were heavy but clearing you have to have a fire burn. I used to work it out when you take on clearing a wood. What you do is pace out 22 yards, then 22 yards the other. Then get in the middle i.e. a chain by a chain and if I can clear that in a day that is how much to put in for that piece of wood. And 10 square chains to the acre but by the end they had hectares which puts you out a bit. That's the only way to see how you get on. I worked for a lot of different firms. One down the other side of Axminster, a lot for the county council. They've got what they call Dorset clumps all over Dorset, and I went planting up them once right up Weymouth. They got all these burial mounds I planted up the wrong one! I had to go back pull them out and plant another one. Two together I planted up the wrong one. I always remember that I looked at about seven or eight jobs in one day. I went up to a place called Bulbarrow, right up there planting softwood. Dorset clumps I done one at Burton Bradstock. All over Dorset. There's one at Bridport on top of the hill, I planted up a few that was missing there to grow up. So that was that.

Sheep shearing? My brother used to have a sheep shearing round, so I went on that for a couple of years and then he got too old and so I took it on myself. Didn't half work hard that year. I reckon I worked 30 days up till nine, ten o'clock at night without a break. Everybody is after you. When you get a few days of rain, they don't half keep on. You try to please them. There's only a certain amount you can do. Only 12 hours a day can't you. I tell you what, when you go down in Devon sheep shearing the farmers down there are different than Dorset farmers. The farmers down Devon always got a cooked dinner for you. You go up Bridport you get nothing! Don't matter where you go up round Bridport you get nothing, but go down Axminster you get a cooked dinner always. I've noticed that lots of times. I don't know whether they be tight up Bridport or whether they just never done it. Devon farmers you got to come in have a cooked dinner. They are very good down there,

Went down Forde Abbey, did a bit down there and he let me have a cottage, that was the one that I was in. Didn't work regular there, I still went contracting. I only done odd work. Then the Abbey started a big nursery and I got more and more work. So much a thousand. I forget how many thousand I used to do a day. You had to keep going. It is better working so many thousand you can always earn more. So the forestry, the head of the forestry they could afford to pay we contractors 35% more and still be in pocket. They got to pick them up from Beaminster and then get again at four to get them back by five. That's what he told me one day.

With shearing I used to sharpen my own gear. I used to have two lots. Nearly as best working on your own, then you got to pick them up and they are not ready and then you got to stop in a pub for a drink. I rather get on have me grub, then if you want to go to pub then you can go out afterwards. Gamekeeping. I started looking after a few pheasants then I gradually got more and more. In the end I was the sort of keeper without really asking for the job. I love it. I love gamekeeping. It's a lovely job you got to put in a lot of extra time by night but you get good tips which makes up for that. I used to love hunting foxes, don't know why. Not really bloodthirsty. I love the birds and that. Eight thousand is the most, only about six this year. He used to sell about eight or nine days shoot and that used to pay for his own friends and that. We used to have some Germans flying an aeroplane over and we used to pick them up from Exeter for two days shoot. Used to bring some smart women with them. Don't reckon it was their wives.

I used to plant all sorts, mostly Sitka spruce five foot by five foot, larch six by six is 1,200 an acre. I suppose if it is Christmas trees they were three foot apart. There's nine in the middle all the time. We used to sell mostly Sitka spruce. Millions go out down there, you can hardly get them on a big artic going off to Scotland. Used to sell millions of them. I think Margaret Thatcher stopped it, they used to get it off the tax. They could buy a place up there and take it off their tax and they stopped it. That really put paid to it then. I don't think he does any now. He used to grow Christmas trees down there. There's no tenants left down there. Farms are sold off. Farming's gone to pot. I only stopped shearing a couple of years ago.

I used to drive horses for three or four years. I done all the work with horses. I loved ploughing with horses, peewits sweeping down, all the animals. All gone now. Old curlews buzzing and making a noise. I used to work down over towards the Marshwood Vale and going down in the morning to work, all the old curlews were there. And when I been chain harrowing I've had to stop when I've seen a curlew with curlew's eggs and drive one side of them. All gone. I used to go up on Lambert's Castle and there used to be a couple pair of nightjars like cuckoos they used to fly around and I could never find the nest. Well they've gone. Now it's not modern farming because they don't touch it up there. Exactly the same as it was before the war. They were beautiful birds.

Buzzards, always been plenty of those. What they do now, the keeper does, he's got two deep freezes and all through the summer goes out with his .22 and fills up these deep freezes with rabbits. I still fed the pheasants down there two year ago. Go around with a quad bike, tipped it on myself one day. We used to chuck out two or three frozen rabbits by the runs, and they leave the pheasants alone. They eat a tremendous amount of worms, because when they were ploughing, he had about 12 buzzards behind the plough like seagulls. Lovely birds sparrow hawks, plenty of sparrow hawks. We had a rare bird down there for years, don't know what happened to him, a hobby hawk, a hobby. But they migrate in, exactly like a peregrine, in miniature, only a bit smaller.

We had a beaver for nine years and he took a lot of trees down. Take a tree down two foot across, and I had to help them out one day. I think there was an electric wire above and I had to cut em and pull him down the other way. We used to see him, he had his way through an oak gate. Marvellous. I saw him once or twice. I walked up the river when the river was in flood and I walked a whole field and he was swimming on. And then he saw me and I didn't see him after that. He never built a dam. But he used to take out a piece of wood as big as your finger at one go. There used to be dippers, but they've gone. Used to build a nest, got a lot of mink, catch a lot of mink, we had nine one year. Easy enough to catch in a trap, a trap that's legal. Four pieces of board and put him in a tunnel these legal traps are just as bloody cruel as the old fashion. Old fashion one had notches along. These mink, they kill everything on the riverside. I expect they killed the dippers. Nests, I suspect they have they as well.

Never seen a salmon down here, yet at Colmer, I never saw it, a boy brought back a salmon from that little brook. He jumped on him only a little brook a tributary of the Axe right up to Colmer farm. Trout they come up in October you can tickle them but as a boy, see, you don't realise the damage you do. You go as a boy and catch these things, well you shouldn't do, 'cause they were spawning. And the eggs come out. Wicked really but nobody seems to tell boys. I don't suppose boys is interested like we used to be, always going down the copses.

I can remember the red squirrels down there. Colmer Copse before the war there was red squirrels down there before the grey come. The grey squirrel has drove the red out, must have done, I like to see the red squirrel back. I had a theory once, if you could breed tame red squirrels and breed big fierce ones, they could drive the grey out, the only way you can do it, breed a super red squirrel and that's the only way I could see out. I reckon it would be a good idea.

So I used to use horses for years. I used to go shoeing that was a morning's work. I had an uncle down at Wootton. Ride the horse down there, never had a saddle, don't know if my Father could have afforded a saddle. Used to wear a bag on it. Down at Wootton Fitzpaine, but it's all gone now. There's no horses like there used to be. We never had a tractor, my Father never had a tractor till my brother came back from the army.

I sold a lot of pulp once. I used to make heaps of it and sell it to the pulp people. Never seen charcoal burning. Once the foreman come on and he gave me a lot to get out, but you had to carry it out on your backs. We used to send it to a brush factory at Mere and they used to drop an artic off and we used to pack about 12 ton on it and when he was full, you would ring up the haulage firm and they'd come and hitch up and then take it to Mere.

I learnt shearing off of a bloke at Broadwindsor, what was he called now? Broomfield. He had an old engine, like my brother used to have, with four clippers on and you take a heavyweight, a Lister, used to shear different to my brother. He used to shear one side and then turn him over, but he used to do around the top first, then flop them down and do the belly out and the legs and then use the left hand, then swing him back and do the other side. But I found if you both had terrible sheep, two Dorset Horns that hadn't been dagged, my way was quicker, but I couldn't keep up with he very well. We both let go our 52nd sheep together, but if you do it the Australian way and you got a real dirty one, he took a bit longer. But if you took a nice one with a bit of the belly gone, doing it the Australian way, they weren't long about it. I know how to do it that way the Bowen way.

Before the First World War, they used to have gangs, the farmers would gang up, and five or six farmers would go and do one another's by hand. A good hand shearer can do one in a quarter of an hour. They used to have proper white trousers to wear in those days and a bit of a booze-up a bit of a party as well with cider. They used to hire people to roll the wool and that. I've always had people rolling the wool, I couldn't do that, you'd have to charge more. Some people used to roll the wool and not tie it, lot of people just twist the wool, and not put string around it. Had to be the right type of string, wouldn't have binder twine. No. They tell me that if you shear a dead sheep, and the wool packers, wherever they do go, they can tell you that sheep was dead if you shear it. Don't know if you can. But that's what they tell me. I had one die on me. I had one farmer out near Bridport. Horned sheep they're prone to that. I said, "I am going to let him go," the farmer said, "If he dies he dies." Never had a farmer say that to me before. I had one die on me before down over towards Seaton. I used to sharpen my own combs and cutters.

As for pest control you can poison squirrels, take crows' nests out. I am sad to see all the little birds go. I'd like to get a couple of acres of woodland, somewhere. Ivy is the only tree that fruits in the early spring and pigeons, if you shoot a pigeon he has in his crop once about 20 acorns. Now how do a pigeon dissolve an acorn? Must have a hell of an acid in his stomach. Can't hang about in the stomach too long. Acid must be terrific, worse than a crocodile. They reckon a crocodile will get rid of iron.

6 Norman Purchase: Cidermaker, Netherbury Born 1927.

Farming was a better way of life then… Everybody was making and drinking cider in them days. Orchards all round.

I am 78. I was born in 1927 at Laverstock which is under Pilsdon Hill. My Father was a farm worker, Arthur Purchase, he worked for people called Lenthall. 'Bunny' Lenthall was the Father, he lived at Burton Bradstock and he did a book on Dorset Horn sheep. My Father worked there at Laverstock, and then we moved to Broad Oak Farm, they made cider. Cider was part of your wages in them days.

That cider press in Symondsbury, Manor Farm, if you ever wanted to make any cider the villagers could go up there and use it. A communal cider press when Sir Phillip Colfox was there. I think he must have owned it. He owned all of Symondsbury. He even supplied the electric for Symondsbury as well.

My Father was working as a cowman and his Father came from Trent between Yeovil and Sherborne. That is where my parents came from. But her Mother and Father then moved to Moreton near Dorchester. My Mother's Father was a shepherd. We used to go up there on holidays and hurdle the swedes and turnips them days. My Grandfather would go on with five on a stick and I would have one. You had a hole in the hurdle where you put your hand into. We were folding. Used to hack the stumps out of the turnips with a tool that had two prongs. I think he's in the shed now. And I used to come on behind, the sheep would shell 'em out and then after we hooked them they could eat the rest of them. Dorset Horns mostly then in the '30s.

The shepherds used to have the caravan up in the fields with a little tortoise stove, and if the lamb was a bit poorly they used to take them in to keep them warm round the fire. Big wheels, had shafts on them in them days. Farming was a better way of life then.

Went to school in Symondsbury. Everybody was making and drinking cider in them days. Orchards all round. All this was orchard right down through here. Hope Farm. They used to call that the cellar where them buildings are falling down and that is the water wheel up on the road up to the main road which ground up the apples. Water-powered cider. An undershot wheel and there was six hatches and you made up the water and it came through underground to the back of that place. There was a pond there and when the pond was full they had a wooden trough on staddle stones to the barn and then there was a square which they filled up and when that was full up, that give the initial start to the wheel. Thirty-foot wheel. Mr Oliver was a wonderful shot and he used to go round to all these places because he was such a good shot. Lots of rabbits.

We used to catch 1,000 rabbits on 110 acres every year. We used to sell them. Most of them went to Charmouth. The butcher there, he used to take most of them. You see, you used to have rabbit as part of your wages every week. Rabbit, cider and milk. I used to have as much cider as I wanted. Everybody had roast rabbit once a week. Got fed up with it in the end. Wife died a couple of years ago but she loved rabbit right to the end. When I came here there was 110 acres. We had 22 cows to milk

Bridport Fair? One of father's days off, we used to go down South Street with all the stalls both sides of the road. You had the market down between South St and St Michael's Lane. Selling sheep, lambs, beef cattle, used to drive them in those days. Market every week and you had a little market called Geoff's market where they sold chickens and flowers, cheese and butter. Lot of Dorset blue vinny. Most farms round here made blue vinny and they used to sell them all up the streets, great big 30lb truckles like stiltons. I had some

Norman Purchase in a cider shed

yesterday and very good too, very dry. They have to have a certain amount of fat in it. They used to make it when I was up at Hope Farm. We kept the weekend's milk, make it once a week. Butter once a week. Well we'd get enough for one cheese, all according to how much milk we had. Twenty cows, if you had two and half, three gallons per cow, that was your whack them days. They'd sell it locally. We had cider, cheese, butter, chicken, rabbits.

Always used to grow a few turnips and swedes for the calves and then Brussels sprouts. Them days you'd get three sorts, Cambridge No 1, No 2 and No 5 I think it was. Early, middle and late to carry you through the season. Everybody used to grow peas and runner beans up in the field, put up wire netting, to grow peas and sell them up in the market.

Father's wages in 1939 were 33 shillings. You try bringing up six kids on that and we was never poorly dressed, because mother used to make our trousers. Her's got quite good at making trousers, buy the material. The sewing machine I think he's still upstairs now, came from Mrs Lenthall at Laverstock, she give her the sewing machine. Laverstock, lovely sunny spot, nice house. I worked there when I was on the building, I was worse off on the building when I left the farm really. Never had free potatoes, no free cabbage, peas, no free milk. People got half as much again on the side, we had a quart of milk and if I wanted more on a Sunday just dip the jug in a churn and fill up another bottle.

The Army? I was 17 when I got called up. Went into the artillery. Did me six weeks basic training then I went onto 'Heavy Goods', pulling 5-inch guns, 100lb shells. Different to cider. I was put on a draft for India but they didn't want me, they wanted military policemen, so I done a bit of police training. "You got to go to Newhaven. They're moving a lot of new troops out to the Middle East." You cross on the boat, go down by train all across France, Paris, Marseilles, Toulon, then another boat to Naples, Malta, Haifa, then back again. Well I done that trip three times, then I got to Port Said and they said, "you're not going back this time. You got to go to Heliopolis, just outside of Cairo." We would go on patrol on motorbikes or in a jeep. Always in twos. Out to the Sphinx and Pyramids, all round there. Could have done with a drop of cider out there. All they give you is salted peanuts and tangerines. I got wounded out in Egypt. When the riots were on in 1945. Bullet out of the back of a lorry. Broke my leg see, knocked me shin out, and the joint out of my toe. No joke. I was lucky, we was on motorbike patrol, down by the sweet water canal. My mate got it bad in the elbow. I came back to Southampton on a hospital ship; I was in a plaster up to my waist. I went to Park Prewitt Hospital near Basingstoke. I was there nearly 12-month. It was all smashed up sliding bone grafts, hipbone grafts, had the works. I think it was marvellous really. I come out the army in '47 and then went on the building. Built a lot of council houses after the war. Then after a year or two went to Hope Farm.

Nearly every place made cider. People used to bring their apples in to make the cider and bring their barrels. And we'd grind their apples and press them out, water power then. We had an engine after that.

I suppose they were mostly cider apples, proper bittersweets you can't eat. There was Pound apples, you don't see them now so often, the old Crimson King, Tom Putt. I have made Tom Putt this year, Kingston Black, Woodbines and Buttery Door. I have a Buttery Door up in the garden. Going back 50 years what we call Hope Hill, blossom time looking down this valley it was a picture about 20th May. All down through here. It went from here to Slape Manor, both sides of the road. There is a lane there, Hatches Lane, there was apple trees and Hope Farm nearly all that side of the hill both sides of the road was apple trees.

Warren's went as far as Weymouth but Oliver he sold his to Palmer's Pubs. The last three pubs was The Tiger in

Barrack Street, Bridport. There was the Seven Stars opposite the Tiger and The Robin Hood down by the Picture Palace. That was the last three that they supplied, because Palmer's, as the licences changed, they stopped the cider and went over to Whiteways, didn't they, which was horrible stuff! We used to bottle the cider here with champagne corks. Well we used to make the cider and rack it and when the gravity was about 30 *(1030)* we used to filter it, wash out all the barrels take all the heads out of the wooden barrels, wash them out, the fermentation hadn't quite finished, that was sweet. We used to filter it and pump it out into a clean barrel and cork it down and leave it until you wanted to bottle it.

When we bottled it, we never added sugar or yeast, we had to wire them down as it was so powerful. Bottles came from Devenish up Weymouth, we used to get a van load 27 dozen to a hogshead of cider. A bit bigger than a wine bottle. Corks from Bristol because Mr Oliver learnt his cider making at Long Ashton Research Station. Finished now. He went up there on a course, as he was farming. I expect Mr Warren went as well.

People brought the apples in with horse and cart, and we always put them up in the loft. We had a large apple loft and you could get ten ton up there easy. I seen old presses about, but they were all similar, they used to screw them up with a rail, round and round, but then they used straw and would press them down every day for a week.

Cloths were horsehair, we had quite few there, eight slats and eight cloths. They last for years, used to be able to buy them with copper nails, ash usually. It would take 20 minutes to build a cheese – half a ton of apples. To press him out as quick as he'd come down and we always used to press twice, press him down, leave while you pump away your cider, then start him going back and by the time you had finished you had another one in.

Mr Oliver came in 1922 and he had foot and mouth at Litton Cheney, so he couldn't bring no cows down, and he told me that the apples on the farm saved his day, said he made 200 hogsheads of cider. The barrels they used to get them from Bristol, oak ones, some had whisky, tip them out, same with the port, always left some in the barrel. Some was chestnut, come on a lorry two hogsheads and dree hogsheads, then we had 36's, 18's, niners, four and a half. Hogsheads is really 54 gallons.

Then we used to select out what we bottled, a big demand for it. We used to stack them in boxes, they used to be gone pretty quick, lie them down. You've got to keep the cork damp. Some exploded! Bottle it about February time usually, used to go nearly up to Dorchester, Beaminster. Doctors used to have it. Charmouth, where Oliver used to go and Bridport. The postman always had barrels of cider and some of the retired people. We used to take one and bring back the empty, all wooden barrels. To clean them we used to take the ends out and scrub them with soda and water.

Ideal blend? Golden Balls, sweet yellow, mix them with Kingston Black the only apple we would put with Kingston Black. Because Kingston Black, 'twas all right for sparkly cider, but the other used to calm it down a bit and make it a bit sweeter. Woodbine we had up there, Pound apples, we mixed. What we used to do in the loft, we had a loft there, about three times as big as this room and about a yard deep and then they was scattered all over.

We used to buy a lot from France at one time and come across to Teignmouth on the deck cargo. Ten ton loads. Mostly Normandy they came from. I know they used to say the sea was covered in apples when they took off the deck cargo then they had the holds with these great buckets wasting apples everywhere. They would come by lorry. That was in the '50s. I stayed up Hope Farm twenty years.

7 John Gale and Bernie Joy: South West Joinery, Pymore
John born 1938. Bernie born 1937.

Joinery has been more of my life than farming but the tractors is going back to boyhood. Going backwards rather than forwards – John
Father was a Pymore man. I controlled the gates for 50 odd years. You just keep your eye on the river – Bernie.

John Gale: I was born in Bradpole, Middle Street, 1938. Father worked on the gas board for quite a while and actually I was born in one of Jack Norman's caravans. Then we moved up to Bradpole into my grandfather's house. He was a stoker in the Navy and then he was a stoker out at the old laundry out at Bridport. Chief Stoker. I've got a whole list of the vessels he was on in the First World War.

I used to go out to visit him in the old laundry, it was out St Andrew's Road, towards the police station. Bradpole, there was a whole gang of us. We kept together. There was nearly all orchards there. Orchards down on the railway crossings. We used go down and collect the apples in the bags and take them to the brewery in Bridport. They used to pass it on to the bigger cider makers. Some days we used to have horse and cart to take them on in. Well then during the war I can remember where they had the Americans down in the old fish weir copse. Corse they had their tanks and equipment down there then, then it got filled up with Palmer's old bottles and that.

Mother actually come from Cornwall. Her father was a lighthouse keeper down there on the coastguard till he moved back to Bridport. We didn't actually go outside Bradpole very much we had our own little tribes then. We used to have eight or nine of us used to always stick together. Went to Bradpole school and went to Allington school. Left school at 15 and went working for Jack Norman for six months. Bit of everything. I was more or less driving a lorry at the age of nine up on Chilcombe Hill which I shouldn't have done. Tractor driving the whole lot. You could drive a tractor at nine. Then I went on to Netherbury, which was Lower Kershay farm for the Billmers he bought four or five farms all around. Gentleman farmer. Went on there till I was 18 and went into the army. Mostly tractor driving. Started of with the old T20 the dairy tractors the little grey thing, and then we got a 35. Had to get one. We had Kershays Farm which is at Salwayash. Fifty to 60 cows there, then he bought Knowle Farm which he had another 60 cows, then Brimley Coombe, and that was kennels originally and then Knowle farm in Netherbury that was another farm, with a hundred or two odd cows. Mostly tractor work, relief milking occasionally. Used to do quite a bit of dairy work at Salwayash. All machine milked, we had the old Gascoigne portable milker 1951-52, till '57. They collected the milk and it went to Beaminster, and any bad days you had to take it there yourself. We started making silage. We had a buck rake and you'd bring it up and make these big stands and drive up on top of it. Squash it all down, a bit dangerous, so long as the person was shaking it about all right you were OK but if he just chucked it in a heap it would just slide off with the tractor. Mostly sugar beet, we had a few fields of that, mostly turnips, all mixed together and chucked up to the animals in the winter. The Fergie. I could go on places with that we wouldn't dream of going on that now. Up over the top of the hill near Melplash. Used to go over that without thinking about it. The little grey one you could turn the wheels inside out and they were quite wide then. Used to be a bit hairy sometimes. Used to go across the back end of Netherbury which was Warren's farm, he used to make cider, that was quite steep that was a bit hairy, 16-17 year old you never thought anything of it. Warren's was right on

John Gale, "The Fergie", Bernie Joy

the corner, we used to call it the white bridge down on the bottom of Netherbury. When we bought Knowle farm there was three big barrels of cider there. Massive. We tried three out of three and only one was any good, and we had about 50 gallons in each. Up until 12 or 13 year ago you could get cider off of Warren's. That was good stuff that was.

I was farm working right up till 1957 then I went into the Army for two years to Germany and Cyprus. I went in on the Dorsets and I was amalgamated in Germany with the Devon and Dorsets and in between there was the Wessex. So I had three cap badges in two years. The troubles were still on in Cyprus. We were on patrols all the time, Cyprus: Limassol, Kyrenia, Nicosia, we done the whole lot. The whole island. We only seen it by night. We had a few hiccups. We had what you call the "cheese cutter" on the front of the Land Rover, used to go out at night and you could hear the wires cracking, but I didn't take any notice of it. The first few weeks was a bit scary, you are thrown into the deep end, you don't know what it is all about. But after a month you took no notice of it.

Then I came back and went on the land for another month, couldn't take that. So then George Heaver, he used to be the manager for Duncan Tucker's then for John de Savary. My wife used to babysit for his two children, and I got in with them and he gave me a job. And that was 1960 making windows, doors and stairs in the joinery shop, and this was at Pymore. This was when John de Savary moved down from London and bought the whole thing out.

And it went on from there. My wages nearly doubled if not more than doubled. I think I was getting 1/3d in old money an hour and it jumped up to 2/6d and that was a lot of money. I didn't know what to do with it.

I had done nothing of that before. At school I had done metalwork, but woodwork I couldn't. I left there not even thinking about woodwork, and Jonathan my woodwork teacher and a bloke called Pope. I met Jonathan six or seven years ago and talking with him and he was absolutely amazed that I was doing it. It was just another job. I just wanted to get away from farming.

You had the machine shop. Everything was done for you and all you had to do was glue it all up. We are doing both jobs now machining and fitting. 1960 right up till 1973.

Pymore Mill? I met my wife down there. My Mother-in-law used to work in the mill, my Father-in-law was the engineer there. Mostly rope and twine. I got a box of twines left, original box, probably the only one in England. If not in the world. People say they made nets here but they didn't. They used to do ropes. They had long rope walks, but they pulled that down, we found a rope twist where you put the rope on and turn the handles. We found one in the river when they dredged it. We harpooned it and dragged it out. The whole thing closed down in '72/'73. They imported a lot of the flax, we found a lot of these flax seals from Russia. I found them with the metal detector. They got the date on and Russian writing. They came into West Bay and it was stored at the back. They had all the flax machines, the spinning the whole thing. My Mother-in-law moved over when she was 14 she came up from Wales. My Mother-in-law she was in the hostel working at 14 and later she took over the hostel looking after the girls and she was there till late seventies, '74, I don't know the exact date. There were about 130-140 working there. We got a large picture of all the staff.

Carpentry: Some timber came into West Bay. My father went on driving for Bert Bolton's. And he used to go down and a certain amount of timber was delivered at Pymore, more then. Of course we were making doors, windows and everything and he decided to stop the joinery side of it and went on to kitchen units. Kitchens only. I went on to kitchens and then at a certain time I went on to jigs and maintenance and that was when I met up with Bernie and we were doing a similar job. And we went from there. We were made redundant, and my name came up and Bernie's name come up and so we got together. We put the money in together and we had a little workshop at Pymore then. They give us a workshop free of charge for a year plus electric to get us going and that helped. Then these new developers came in and we had a month to get out. We moved to here. But we were better off here. We done better when we came here. More people could see us passing by on the road.

It is funny, we have gone away from builders. We do more for the private person, and they say, "we want two or three windows," and they say, "do you know who can put them in for us?" So we just make them and the person comes to pick them up. Mostly people moving in from up country buying up the old cottages up and a lot of them have got plastic windows, so they take them out and put wood back in again. They certainly helped us. That's when all these new laws come in, it gets a bit hard. I think this was a barn for calves. South West joinery since '81. Twenty-four years. The tractors are jointly owned.

Bernie Joy: The river flooded three times. Eight foot one time. It came right through. We had a cloud burst in Beaminster, came through all the fields, didn't touch the river, a tidal wave, you couldn't get in here, the road just like a river. Out my place at Pymore, it took my shed up smashed it against the wall and I had my wheelbarrows and shovels, fishing rods and shoved them down the hedge at the bottom. It was serious. We were out of action for six months. To really flood it, I controlled the gates for 50-odd years, you got to have a heavy continuous rain all day, from morning to night, non stop, but they've had it close out there now.

John Gale: Joinery has been more of my life than farming but the tractors is going back to boyhood. Going backwards rather than forwards. Well I've always wanted a little grey Fergie, a diesel but the 35 came along I just went on from there. I lost control. I lost complete interest in farming, too much getting wet every day, and when you were on a tractor then you were sitting in wet all day. West of England sack over your head, wasn't funny. The seats weren't so bad, bit more comfortable than a 35. Once you are wet you stay wet. None of this going home and change. I was cycling to Netherbury every morning. Had to be in work most mornings at five o'clock, and leave at half past five. If you were wet going to work, you were wet going home. I wouldn't have missed it. I did enjoy it. I liked the boss I worked for, he was a great boss. He owned a shipping company. Jack Billmer. I think he died on the golf course.

Pymore Mill? It's all gone for the worse. All the things that should be there the gearing on the sluice gates, they should have kept them, but for some reason no one knows where they have gone to. They were going to replace them. They were supposed to be for people to look at but they have not done that. Shame really. When you look out the back window we used to look out over a lovely orchard behind us and then across Waytown and all we see now is a big red brick building about ten fifteen foot away. You've lost everything.

Bernie Joy: I was born in South Street Bridport. Parents moved to Pymore when I was one month old. 1937. Slightly older than John. My father was a caretaker at Pymore mills. He had all the keys for every room, used to open them up and lock them up every night when the workers were gone. Mother worked in the factory. It was what they call twisting, it is when they make the hemp into string and put it onto the bobbins. Twisting. All done by machine Second bobbins they would fill up and put another bobbin on. Repetitive work. She never moaned about it. She finished up getting all the meals for the workers, their dinners, tea and that. We lived right in the middle of the factory. Changed a lot now. When we was kids we used to go up there in the dark evenings look through the door. No harm done, but you know what kids were. You went to school and it was dark by nights. We weren't allowed in the rooms when the machinery was going. Mother came there when she was 14. Drimpton down near Chard, Greenham Mill, her parents worked in that mill. Father was a Pymore man. I lived there till they kicked me out, and got it up for auction. It's all wrong.

Going back to the old factory, they was well known for the hangman's rope. They made the hangman's rope. Pymore had the bare hemp, tow and flax delivered to us in bales. All broke up for string. They supplied Gundry's for the nets and the nets come back to Pymore to be dipped and dyed. Some'at like tannelising, dark dye and then they did this army camouflage nets during the war, that was dyed. All imported flax, lorries come in from the station and they unloaded it. Might have come up from West Bay. They had a railway line up from there. I know they had a big warehouse out there. that used to be store and when it was unloaded it was put in there. One room was flax, one hemp, used it straight away. They had a machine with a lot of needles and women didn't work this machinery, only men. They used to pull it out of the bales and put it on the needles and they would tear it up and come out the other end like a rope, and then get split up again to make the twines. During the war, mother used to make these "pull-throughs" for the army, like lanyards. Some had revolvers on them, just the short ones.

I went to school in Bridport, there till I was 16 and started in Pymore mill. I worked in the carpenter's shop. I was there for about 12-month. Then they started getting short of work and went on down Woolaways. I been carpenter all my life took it on from the old man. He was a carpenter and caretaker. He opened up half past five. They started at six and his day work was maintenance, windows and doors, and then lock up again at six o'clock. He had a big workshop. I worked with him. There was somebody over the old man. I went fishing all my life in the rivers. Mostly trout, eels. I didn't like eels, wrap round your hand like a snake. No I didn't like them. There was one old chap who used to eat them. He'd skin them, jellied eel they call it. I never eat fish at all. I catch mackerel, don't eat them.

You had mostly hand tools, old chisels, so many mould planes. Dovetails. Done by eye. Worst part was getting a bit of raw wood and straightening him up, plane it up square him up. It was all right. Used to knock up all the old packing cases and put spools in to send abroad already been dyed, sent them abroad down to the station on the old horse and cart.

When the actual factory closed down, because nylon came in, Gundry's used nylon because they didn't want the string. Gundry's combined. Soon as they took nylon on they stopped it. That was the main Gundry Mill. Used to make the big nets for under the helicopters.

Waterkeeping? When Father went on I took over that. You just keep your eye on the river, and keep the water up for the waterwheel, because it was the biggest one in Dorset. We used to stand on the central shaft and you couldn't touch the top. Over 16 foot diameter. Wider than what this building was, had buckets on him. He used to drive the machines in the building that burnt down. All the old belt drives, and the main cog that come off the waterwheel every tooth was wood. Apple wood like square with a notch on the end, and they made them themselves in the turner's shop. Most of the wood came in logs and they turned them down themselves. Get a log about eight foot long and 12 inch diameter barked a foot from each end and stacked and as a turner wanted them to make new spools or new bearings, or bobbins they could cut them off and put them through the lathe. Waterwheel was used right to the end. To be honest they could have driven their own generator off it, the amount of water went through there. And what did they do with it? burned it all to pieces. Shame. Cut it up with an oxygen set and just dragged it out and scrapped it.

The river? You had Beaminster, they would ring Netherbury, Netherbury would ring Waytown and Waytown would ring us, and we would ring North Mills, and Gundry's and all down. Slape mill was at Waytown. They all had their little gates but Pymore mills were the biggest. You had a six-foot gate on the bottom of three of them. Then you had three, four foot gates and three one foot gates. There was hell of a pressure. Off the main bridge there the depth was 15 foot. You had a back up pond all grown in and built in and that was filled in from a small stream from Salwayash. That would keep a back up and if the main river got low you opened that gate up and let the water through. On the actual waterwheel, you had a set of three gates on one winder, and the more you lifted him up and the more the wheel went faster. So we could control the wheel on that gate. The actual chap who done that worked in the mill a separate lot of gates. The river in the old state, where the main sluice gates were, it used to go round the back to the wheel, where you had a separate set of gates.

Where they is confused now they say Bradpole boundary and Allington boundary, that was the other side of the river but it isn't. I was on Allington side but the house next to him was on Bradpole side. Corse they was talking the wrong river, not the main river, that was the trouble. Lot of change up there terrible. All the old buildings are gone pulled down. Not the same.

Horsepower of wheel? Twenty-foot wide more than that. Photographs? Lost all mine when I got flooded. When we had that six or seven foot of water our downstairs windows, you couldn't see them. May '79 spring bank holiday weekend. It was bloody awful. It was a cloudburst over at Beaminster. I heard this roaring all morning. I was the only one working at the factory all the rest was on holiday. I had to get some samples out. One o'clock you could see it coming down across the fields. Like a tidal wave, wasn't coming down the river, everything in its way it just picked up. Whole factory was flooded, and the boss came into the factory at night and just said open the doors and let it go. Everything went. Bit of a game wasn't it. Had to have new walls, floors, windows, the lot. I was working for Acrowcraft after Woolaways until they went bankrupt, then I went working for Duncan Tucker's up the factory on maintenance and general dog's body and turned out I went into the stairs shop. Making staircases, very interesting I loved doing stairs. When you got a staircase made you got something to show. And it is there to show. I got a staircase to make now all in iroco and that's going to France. Bloke we work for he do a lot of work over there.

South West Joinery: We set up in April '81. Duncan Tucker's and got laid off. John said he'd give us a workshop across the road, electric free. We moved out here in Dec '87 and we was up Pymore 10 year then we moved in here. It was a building for heifers, the main farm was at Pymore that the son run and the old man kept this. Used to come out there, and there was a doorway out here and in here was all like feeding troughs. There was somebody in here doing odd fencings. And when we moved in here you could still see the water line where it got flooded. Not in the actual building, plenty of water outside. I know the main orchard at Pymore but that was mostly cookers or eating apples.

Cooking? John's mother was in the hostel. My mother used to do all the meals that come from Gundry's in these big containers and she had to dish out on the plates for the workers, to pick it up. They would start at six with a break at ten and the main dinner was half past twelve to half past one. The ones that wasn't living in the hostel would come to my mother's place and get their plate of dinner and go on.

Nice cooked dinners. You had like square ovens with drawers like teddies, carrots all different, then sometimes you had a big deep container, that had soup like a field kitchen and during the war, we had the Home Guard out there and they had the lock up for all the ammunition and rifles etc. They would have night duty and all the way round the factory they would put these barbed wire barricades all round the entrances. They was put up and took down in the morning. They would finish around six, not Saturdays. No night shift. Nearest bomb was in Bridport. The Star and one up East Street. Americans were over at Bradpole. The only thing I do remember, if you got out the road and turn left up Coneygar Lane, they used to do night duty up there, the Americans, as they had tanks up there. But they never came into Pymore.

The hostels: Welsh, Irish, Scottish girls. The local women came in but they didn't live in the hostel. About 140-150 working there, quite a factory. Newfoundland, what they call it up at Bradpole, all them houses belonged to the factory, workers in the factory, and up by the Pymore Inn those cottages, and up where John was too.

I have enjoyed working with wood. Staircases. You've got a job to get hold of good quality timber, it is dried too quick. Take some of these old rafters up here smells beautiful. Supposed to be dried coming across on the boat. Softwood comes from Scandinavia. Some of the hardwoods you can't get at all. Stopped supplying it. We got timber merchants put an order in and within two or three days you got the timber. We used to deal with Travis. Our main dealer is Snow's timber, Glastonbury. Bookcases. Welsh dressers are quite interesting. Knock one up and leave him there and people come in and say, "Is that sold? I'll have it." The biggest one I made was seven foot by seven foot high and he had to go in an alcove between a chimney and a wall. He went in there a treat. One went to Honiton Hotel. See all our work is not advertised. All come by word of mouth.

School leavers? They won't take it on in years to come. There's going to be no carpenters and chippies and joiners. Young staff just don't want it. They are starting to push it, trying to. Our biggest snag here is, we are self-employed. You can't afford your own time to show them what to do, you are losing your own time. And that pushes your insurance up. Like the old inspector come in here health and safety. Corse I wasn't using ear muffs, well they are worse than using the machine. You can't hear the machine running. Good for ears but not good for your fingers. I must admit our worst problem is using that saw and some bugger come in behind you. Your first reaction is to turn. Since we come out here we had three times as much work. We have had a couple of jobs out at Pymore but nothing big. Just done some new gates, took their gates down and renewed them. All I do is make the gates and the posts and they get the fittings themselves.

We have retired… when things go all right but when they go wrong it is very annoying. You can go on lovely for weeks and weeks and weeks. Doesn't matter what you touch everything goes wrong. Just as well go fishing them. I go out beach fishing. Haven't been out for a few years; bass, cod in the winter. I am a bit annoyed I used to go Bexington and Cogden, but you can't drive down Cogden. National Trust. And at Bexington the car park is well washed away. Can't drive up the sides. What good is it stopping people going down there. Cod is decreasing. Mackerel is decreasing. The seining was all right watching. See them shoot out and then get nothing. Archie Larcombe, they used to fight each other to get the shoal. But you watch them down West Bay when they pull the sprats in, upon that beach. Mackerel chase the sprats up on the beach. I went down there one night and I had 180 mackerel. You couldn't stop catching them on four feathers, I come home next morning. I sold the lot in the factory. Well I come on the beach, I used to go down there specially on Saturday night. Stay there about two o'clock and use the mackerel as bait, bass or whiting, the odd pollack. Burton was all right, too many rocks loose your tackle. Nice fish out there talked to some divers and they said if you can get over the rocks lovely fish out there.

Keeping mackerel? Mother used to come round with a little wagon they used to get a dozen and tie their tails together and keep them in the stream and Caddy's shop across the road used to keep big tins of corned beef in the water, the drinking water was lovely. Corned beef and mackerel in the stream. Years ago all this water come from the ground, clear and pure, lovely water, now they put this chlorine in. Mother always done them in vinegar. Eat them right away. I don't like them the bones.

Rabbiting? I done that all my life. Got rid of my ferrets last two year, still got all the old nets, purse nets and that. Shooting: Had to give me gun up all these new laws. Rabbits skinned, chop them up in pieces, soak them in salt water, stew or skin them cut them up, stuff them, stitch them up and bake them. My grandfather used to do them in cider. Always had a pot on the old black stove, full of stew, head the lot in, and we used to share out who was going to have the brains, you eat that. Mother used to get the brain out and there was four of us and each one every other day would have them. We'd eat the tongue in those days. A rabbit was a meal.

Nick Poole in the West Milton Cider Shed

8 Nick Poole: Builder and cider maker, West Milton Born 1956.

One of the things that fascinates me most is coming across old cider apple trees and not actually knowing what the trees are. There is endless debate about whose cider is best. It seems to me that there has been a huge groundswell of grassroots interest in real cider.

I was born in the village of Powerstock in West Dorset in May 1956. My father took over a tenant farm on Eggardon Hill, King's Farm, in the early 1950s so I was born and brought up on a farm. The grazing on the hill was taken by the King's House farm which was just opposite. We had everything on the north of the hill about 100 acres plus we rented a bit more along the Roman road on the way to Dorchester which made up to about 120 acres overall. We had all the ground along the edge of Powerstock Common down through the valley going from Whetley to Luccas and back up to King's Farm house and the land above it which runs back up to the road over Eggardon. And then the actual hill was grazed by King's House farm or Luccas farm, whichever happened to have it at the time.

The railway was just north of our land. We could see the trains going past from the farmhouse. It stopped in about 1973. I was in college at Weymouth at the time and I used to catch it every day. I was one of the last people who used it from Powerstock Station and I had this very vivid memory that I would take the timetable for a souvenir, and being a conscientious, honest sort of person, I thought I had better not take it till the last day. And on the last week, it disappeared. Someone else had taken it, it annoyed me a bit as I was the only person using the station at that time. Powerstock station was actually at Nettlecombe. But it was a very good service with only one carriage with an engine within it, and if I was late in the morning I used to run down the hill and walk about half a mile down the railway line itself and they would stop and pick me up. They would always drop me off at Whetley Bridge which was much nearer to home than if I had gone all the way to the station. So it seemed like a very good personal service.

I actually went to do a catering course in Weymouth when I left school. No idea what I really wanted to do and already made the conclusion that there was no living to be made out of farming. All my childhood I had been working at local pubs, washing up, waiting at table, just general dog's body. So catering was the only thing I had any knowledge of at all and so I went and did a catering course at Weymouth College. There was the Marquis of Lorne at Nettlecombe and the Three Horseshoes at Powerstock and they are both still there thank goodness.

My Father was born in Wales in Cardiff. Historically his Grandfather moved to Wales to work in the mining industry, and later as a gamekeeper. He had a piece in the newspaper when he fought with some poachers and with the aid of the local police, it came to serious fisticuffs. So his Grandfather was a gamekeeper and his Father was a butcher. They still had cousins close to West Dorset and just before the Second World War his Father moved back here to run a pub in Beaminster. My Father did an apprenticeship on a farm in Devon till war broke out and then he joined the RAF to fight during the war, he came back to be here in Powerstock after the war.

But obviously the links were there long before that. Parts of our family go back to this parish as early as 1595. On my Father's Mother's side there was the Symes family, quite a large number of them. The Poole side of the family, the first record is a miller in Upwey near Weymouth who married one of the Symes girls in the mid-1800s.

My Mother's family came from Cardiff but I don't think

they actually met till they were down here, funnily enough. Which is a bit of bizarre coincidence. I don't know much of her background.

Earliest memories of Powerstock? I went to school in 1960 in a classroom where the lady had been there since the First World War. Miss Dawe, very strict disciplinarian. You sat in straight lines behind your desks and you learnt your alphabet. I can still picture the first day there writing out a big 'A' little 'a' and a big 'B' and so on. And basically all of us did the same thing in one form or another in various schools. Powerstock school had a pupil population of 30-35 pupils all the time I was there. That school was built in 1860 from stone from the church at West Milton that was demolished by Sanctuary. There was no telephone in the school, no hot water, no central heating. We had to heat the school in the winter with coke fires, one big stove in each classroom, and we just thought nothing about it, just the normal way of going about things in those days.

The farm was about 120 acres overall which we farmed, mostly dairy, the main source of income. We did dabble in sheep once in a while and pigs. When I was quite young about five or six years old we had deep-litter houses for chickens about 1,500 chickens, and as small children it was our job to get the eggs in every day, an horrendous chore it seemed to be at that time. The milk went to the big dairy at Maiden Newton and it was collected every morning in churns on a lorry. If the lorry failed it went to Powerstock Station and went by train.

The bad winter of 1962-63 we were snowed in for at least six weeks without food or any supplies at all. In fact the BBC came in with a helicopter to film us being stranded in the snow and brought with them a team of film cameramen. Macdonald Hastings was there, the father of Sir Max Hastings, and he came along with his camera crew. Instantly they dropped the camera crew off, the helicopter got iced up and could not take off for three days. And although they very generously brought us some food supplies, they turned round and ate the whole lot while they were there. Yes. We were genuinely cut off. It snowed on the Boxing Day night and the snow was still on the ground in May. So it was a really long hard winter and we were very exposed on the side of Eggardon Hill. We were probably snowed in longer than anybody else in that particular area. Steep slippery roads, that just disappeared. An Arctic landscape. The milk? Well again that was fortunate, the railway was still open and all the local farmers for Powerstock parish took their milk on tractors to Powerstock station and the train did manage to keep going. We drove across country with the milk churns on the buckrake, and Father did it everyday. We just relied on small hay bales and we had sheep. Well, I was only six years old then so we weren't allowed outside many days as it was below freezing and blizzarding nearly every other day. I think we did lose some animals, it set my Father back several years financially, at the end of that winter.

I have memories of at least two people when I was very small working on the farm and they had an outhouse where they bunked in, but after that winter Father had to cut back. It very nearly bankrupted him and I don't think we employed anybody much after that period, although he did have young apprentice lads. I think it was an indication that farming wasn't earning huge amounts of money and through the '50s it was quite a successful period in farming and people were expanding and developing but after a set back like the '62-'63 winter it was hard going afterwards.

When I reached my early teens my Father kept saying, "don't what ever you do, go into farming." So presumably he wasn't making a great success of it, and because I had an older brother who was desperately keen to go into farming, there wasn't room for two of us. We both recognised that we were only tenants and there was therefore going to be problems with handing the farm on or taking it over. I just thought I would look for something else to do and that was what I did. I did a hotel and catering management course. I don't regret doing it at all because the management skills I learnt at college actually set me up very well for running my own business in the building trade. When I finished at college I went and worked in a few hotels around the country and spent two years in London. And although it was absolutely wonderful, an adventure to start with, I began to realise that sort of life definitely wasn't for me.

I came home and gave up catering altogether and worked for a while on the farm with not exactly any pay. While I was thinking what else to do I happened into the building trade, literally by going onto a building site and asking if there was any work one day in Bridport, on a building site. I just started off as a general labourer which I did for about two years and then got myself an apprenticeship as a carpenter and basically been in the building trade ever since. A small building firm that employed about ten people. I did do a TOPS scheme which was a six-month intensive re-training scheme, a college course where you went to college every day. And got some sort of certificate at the end of it and worked for a gang of carpenters who were attached to this firm. Three and a half years and I did every aspect of carpentry going. It was a very good way of learning your trade, absolutely everything from first fix to second fix, to roofs and staircases, joinery work, a very good grounding. New construction and renovation work. I actually enjoyed the renovation work more because new work gets very repetitive and boring. The more interesting work was on old properties and just doing them up and I thought that was quite fascinating.

Wages? I started in 1979 at £1.75 an hour. Tradesmen were then on about £2.50 an hour. I was a labourer. It was better then agricultural, probably half as much again. After about three to four years with this carpentry gang and the two years experience, I decided to go out on my own. At that point it coincided with us moving back to West Milton. In the interim I had left King's Farm and got married. My wife and I got our first house, a starter home in North Allington in Bridport, when they were still genuinely priced. It was £17,500 which in 1983 we even had to struggle to get the mortgage but it was within our reach. And it wasn't impossible as it is now for youngsters on local wages. In 1986 we moved back to West Milton which for me was fantastic. I never thought I would be able to move back into my own parish, because prices had gone up considerably, but we were fortunate. We got this house just on the tailend of a recession, house prices had been stable for a while and then they shot up during that year, so we bought into a cottage. A year later after that, I decided to go out looking for my own work. I have been doing this now for 17 years. No regrets. None at all. It is nice to have been able to move back to my own home parish. The first 10 years I could generally have said that I had six months of the year working in my own village here and Powerstock, without having to travel any further, as there are no other builders living in the parish. I think I have worked in every house in West Milton.

Cider is my hobby. Although I didn't have a particular yearning to go into farming as such, I suppose it was in my blood, because when we were financially were able to, we did buy a bit of land, about two acres with stables on. My wife is very keen on horses so we set up this bit of land, and then we needed a bit more land, and we rented another four and half acres. Because we had some land we thought we would do some pigs. I feel that I am playing at farming, but along with this land that we are renting came an orchard. It had 10 ancient trees, very, very old trees.

The irony is that having taken the orchard over and decided to make cider, the first year most of them blew down in a severe gale and actually uprooted themselves. An old boy who was born in the village and used to make cider here up until the late '50s, early '60s, he came round and looked at the field with me and he could pretty well name every tree in the orchard. Mostly Dabinetts, Chisel Jerseys, Bulmer's Norman, traditional bittersweet apples. When I was a boy nobody was making it, I didn't think there was, but I have since found out that there was a small amount being made in West Milton up until the early '60s on Lynch Farm and Crutchley's estate in Nettlecombe which had a big press. It is still there and has recently been taken up again and a local group is using it. They also made cider in the '60s but at that age, it wasn't something I specifically knew about, and it was made purely for the farm workers.

The cider made in West Milton was just for the farmer and a few of his friends. The general public would not have known much about it. Absolutely amazing the gallonage that must have been produced from the orchards that are in Powerstock parish as a whole. A lot of cider sheds and presses must have disappeared. With that number of cider apple trees in the parish you can only cope with so many cookers and eaters, so it must have been cider. It was 1999 I took the orchard over. Although I had drunk cider most of my life, I did not know much about making it. I knew I had to raise some capital to invest in some equipment, so I just went round speaking to neighbours in West Milton to see if anybody else was interested in forming a cider club. Sure enough 20 people put money into the kitty and we bought our first lot of equipment, myself and an agricultural engineer who was in the club, produced a press. The money we raised wasn't enough to buy a traditional press so we made one ourselves which has been a great success. The first year we produced cider, we did I think, about 100 gallons and we were all absolutely amazed that it was very drinkable and very enjoyable. It has been a great exercise in the community because it is has had the strange effect of bringing people together. There are no shops, not even a church in West Milton now. There is no general meeting place, though we have got a very smart bus shelter, but it is not big enough to have a meeting. When it comes to cider-making time they all turn up and they enjoy helping and they enjoy picking up the apples, and it works very well as a community project. All those that have put into the kitty, are entitled to the cider away and we share out after it is matured and ready to drink. We also give a lot of cider to local functions for fundraising events. I give away 40 or 50 gallons every year for that purpose. It raises good money and can be very often a popular drink at these events.

Well, going back to the historical orchards that remain around West Milton and Powerstock and Nettlecombe, because they are all 70, 80-year-old apple trees, they were planted by people who knew what they were doing. They tend to be good quality bittersweets, We have got Dabinetts, Sweet Alfords, Yarlington Mill, Bulmer's Norman all in West Milton. At Wytherstone, they have got Michelins, Norton Bitters. In Powerstock as yet some unidentified varieties. Sharp, all the apples from Powerstock have been sharp, compared to West Milton, Nettlecombe and Wytherstone, which are bittersweets. Even now to this day we make cider in West Milton and they make it in Nettlecombe, and there is endless debate about whose cider is best. You get used to what you drink yourself. It is a very local, a very personal thing.

I think one of the joys of being an amateur cider maker is that you have plenty of opportunities to experiment, in a way that a commercial cider producer could not afford to do. So every year I try and make an effort to keep one or two of these varieties back and press them singly, even if it turns out that they are not very good. I like to know what they are going to do. And obviously we have a great success with Dabinett. We have got an apple here called Golden Balls, a golden bittersweet which I have not done yet, but apparently that is an indigenous variety to Dorset, and I am determined to press that as a single variety to see what that is like. I have tried Bulmer's Norman, not very good. Sweet Alford is good, we always do an early Morgan Sweet, a thin early cider quite interesting to do. Yes it is quite fun to have something else to do than just chuck all the apples in and see what comes out.

One of the things that fascinates me most is coming across old cider apple trees and not actually knowing what the trees are. We found some really interesting apples at Mappercombe, the Crutchley estate beside the manor house surrounded by remnants of ancient orchards, and there were two very good trees last year, though this year they didn't have enough to make it worth while picking up. But between the two trees there they had a very, very sweet apple and a very, very sharp apple. And although we pressed them singly, it tasted just like that, a sweet cider and a sharp cider, the blend was absolutely magnificent. And bottling and then allowing it to condition in the bottle produced an almost champagne style cider with very good flavour. So we are looking to find more trees in the parish. I don't think we have Buttery Door but we do have one Tom Putt, the other one was cut down for a patio...

After the first year we made the cider as a group, I thought it would be nice thing to find out who else was making cider in the area, and I put forward this proposal to have a cider festival alongside this. I am actually chairman of the village hall committee of Powerstock Hut, and we are always looking at ways for fundraising, and so it seemed like a good idea to combine a night of cider drinking with some fundraising. At that time the only other people I knew were making cider on an amateur basis were the Chideock cider club, who came along and supported us, I also found a chap called Norman Purchase from Netherbury, a 78-year-old cider maker who had been making cider all his life and I think there was one other person who came long with one gallon at that first event. We have done it for three years now and each year it has got bigger. The last time we had a dozen cider makers there and more and more people keep coming. Last year we had a small spot on Hugh Fearnley-Whittingstall's Beyond River Cottage programme.

It is surprising that since we started the cider festival, I know of at least three more people who have started making their own cider. It seems to me that there has been a huge groundswell of grassroots interest in real cider. Commercial cider does not bear much relationship to what we drink here using full juice proper cider making techniques. So I'd like to think there is enough of us to maintain the old orchards, and would like to think there is enough of us to maintain the real old varieties, that are not of much interest to commercial producers. I have just planted some more cider apples: Browns, Fair Maid of Devon, Brown Snout, two Golden Balls, Broxwood Foxwhelp, Stoke Red and Dabinett. And with these old varieties we hope that we may end up with some really interesting cider.

Changes in Powerstock? You don't notice these things on a daily basis, but when you stop and look back it is quite horrifying how much things have changed. In 1960 when I started at Powerstock school there were 26 farms in Powerstock parish and some of these farms were very, very small, and only milking a dozen cows. But this was 26 units that were supporting a family, sometimes one or two workers. And in the interim period now 44 years later there are only four dairies left active in the parish. So that is one huge change. What has gone hand in hand with that is that whereas farming was once the main enterprise in the parish with cows walking up and down the roads every day. It now no longer is. You would have known exactly when the harvests were happening. When haymaking was happening you couldn't avoid it. Now it has to be said there is probably the same number of cows being milked, but because so few people are involved, it has no influence on the parish anymore. All the people who live here now in the farm workers' cottages aren't farm workers, they very seldom ever come from country areas. They have moved in and they know nothing about farming, agricultural ways of life and you suddenly stop and think about that and it seems like a huge change and loss of a way of life. It is disappearing daily and not just in this parish, but in every rural parish in England.

Second homes? In West Milton we have 51 houses and 17, one third of them, are holiday lets or weekender's homes. Just call them part-time occupancy. So a third of the village is not lived in for most of the time. It is a huge amount and it is fortunate that West Milton is just one of the villages of Powerstock parish, so we can still have a good local network of community feeling and projects by combining with Nettlecombe and Powerstock and Poorton. But if you took West Milton as an isolated village on its own, it would be dead long ago, because there is just not enough people in the village to keep the village going. Basically the last village shop in West Milton closed in 1971 which was a start of the period of change. Farming started to decline and farm workers' cottages became vacant and they were immediately bought up by retiring in-comers. They had good cars and Bridport was only five, six minutes away, so they didn't use the local shop and the local shop couldn't offer the range of food that they were used to. So it became immediately evident that small village shops couldn't survive and when second home owners came along that put the final nail in the coffin for village shops.

I also help run a folk band that my brother is a part of and another chap who is probably the only decent musician. I have written quite a few songs relating to cider making. Folk songs tend to reflect the things that are important and reflect social history. I have written some songs that reflect the changes that have happened in the countryside here in West Dorset in the 21st century. I'd like to think that someone in a hundred years time would read the songs and think that that was what was happening in that parish at that period of time. We are called Harvest Moon and we only perform locally. I play tenor banjo, mandolin and guitar. My brother is the lead singer, there is another guitarist, a bass player and a fiddle player. We do a lot of Irish traditional fast gigs, and reels and folk songs that sort of thing, some American folk stuff. It is just good fun. We've even made a CD.

9 Richard and Darren Tuck: Thatchers, Symondsbury Richard born 1964. Darren born 1965.

Our Great-grandfather was a thatcher and his Father was the master thatcher in Symondsbury and his sons were the under thatchers. We didn't know this when we took up thatching. Didn't even know there was a thatcher in the family.

Richard: I am 41 and I was born in Chideock. Father was spreading lime until I came along then he worked on the farm, Mother was a housewife. He was a dairyman to start with and then he was a tractor driver. He worked for the Weld's. Father was from Chideock and Mother was from Chideock. My Grandfather on my Mother's side was a carter and Grandfather on Father's side; he died when Dad was young, when Dad was 14. And he did gardening, hedge laying, manual work, bit of building. But, it is a bit of a weird coincidence, when my Father's dad was 44, he died and my Dad was 14. When my Dad was 44, I was 14 and when I will be 44 my son will be 14, so we all had our sons when we were 30. Quite a coincidence really.

The house I live in now was once the doctor's house and the London Inn was up the hill. We used to live just down the road in Foundry Knapp near the Symondsbury turning and it was nice to stay within the parish. We have lived here for six years now. Children went to the school and we have got quite involved, even though I was close to Chideock. I feel I am quite a Symondsbury man now. I was born in 1963 went to Symondsbury School and then on to Colfox. Children are following on.

Darren and I are cousins, our fathers were brothers. I went from school. I helped on the farm, with my Dad, seasonal work and I worked for the National Trust for a little while, as a YTS scheme and then when I left that I jobbed around really. I was one of the people that can really say that I enjoyed my school though I never really achieved very much. And then the thatching job arose. The job came along. I did not do an apprenticeship as such, I didn't go to college but I learnt with a thatcher in Chideock, we both did. We worked for him for 18 years. Quite a long apprenticeship, people say, "how long does it take to learn how to thatch?" You can learn how to get over the problems but you could never say there is a roof, thatch it the same way as you did the last one, because there is always a different problem to get over, which is a nice thing as every roof is different. So I reckon you need to work with a thatcher for five years at least. He took on more people when more came along or more often when somebody would leave, and another one would come in and the bottom one would go up the ladder. Literally. That was a bit corny wasn't it? You start at the bottom and work your way on up.

Wages were not brilliant but then you didn't expect a lot when you are just a labourer to start with. Then you would hope they would go up the more skilled you got. Water reed was already there when we started. I have been doing it for 21 years now. At that time it was mainly Dutch, Austrian. Now it is Turkish. There is Polish, French, Hungarian. To our mind Turkish is the better quality stuff. Vast areas of it out there.

Darren: I was born in Weymouth in 1965, but we were living in Bridport at the time, North Mills. Schools, Bridport County Primary, then Colfox. When I left, my Father had the pub in Chideock, The George, I worked there for about a year, then I got a job in the dentist's as a dental technician. Bit of a change but it only lasted two and half years as I was made redundant. The dentist fell ill. Things fell apart there and I was just looking around, same situation as Richard. Our cousin married a thatcher and it went from there really. Went on for two weeks originally and I lasted 17 years.

Richard and Darren Tuck thatching the back of George Wright's house, Rampisham

Richard: The appeal to me was from the agricultural side of things, 'cause the farmers were then growing thatch straw and we would have to go and help the farmers harvest and stitching up. Being from a farming background it appealed to me. We get a lot of satisfaction from converting a really ropey old roof with elder and bits of trees growing out of it, into a really nice job. The older varieties of wheat reed are better, Maris Widgeon, Squareheads Master. Now we just buy it in. People think it is wonderful when they walk by taking their photographs. Lovely to see the old traditions and we are there covered in dust and mud, 17-18 years. We've had enough now. There aren't that many reaper binders around, not actual working ones. A lot of show ones, just towed around the showgrounds, nice pristine old grey Fergie dragging it around. We go back to the same farms but we keep our ear to the ground, hear who's buying it and who's got some available. It is a case of first come first served. The last couple of years it has definitely fluctuated. Get a bad harvest there's not so much of it about, so supply and demand. Twenty years ago it was £400 a ton and now it is about £625. We try to buy it in advance if the farmer's got enough and we think we are going to be able to use it all. We prefer it organic, we insist on it. It doesn't necessarily have to come from an organic-registered farm as long as the farmer hasn't plastered it with nitrogen and everything else, basically planted it and shut the gate till he's come to harvest it.

We hope the ratio is about quarter to three-quarters good reed, depends how much grass there is in the straw. Could be a third to two-thirds. We usually wait till the finished product and then decide whether we are going to buy it. There are other thatchers who are in the market and if we say no, somebody else will always come along.

There's plenty of work around. We always try to answer the phone. We always say when we can start the job and we don't say we can be there in a couple of weeks time when we know that we can't. And that is one of the things we definitely make sure we do. Then we get ridges and porches.

Lyme Regis is the biggest test of all. Thatch nearer the sea deteriorates that little bit quicker. It is the damp in the winter months that doesn't help. Depth of thatch, not so much at the eave, but as you go up, thatchers strip the eave out and then build the ridge up. It gets thicker and thicker, and we've stripped roofs off that you could stand on the timbers and I am six foot one and it would be up head height. And the bottom reed was harvested three maybe four hundred years ago. Very black and dusty.

Tools? Apart from the ladder, the most important one, the next one would be the biddle, the main tool which is the square shaped bat, called a leggat or a drift. But you don't whack the reed. People think because it is a bat-shaped thing that you give it a good old whack but you don't. It is the control, a gentle tap. Like stonemasons, you just dress it to shape. The skill is in the eye, definitely. And the feel of the roof the pitch, you can feel if it is going in too far, or if it is not going in far enough. If you don't start it right you get problems, and you get halfway up, which is where we work quite well together. If one thinks the other's not doing it right, we'll tell them instead of beating our way through. Saying, "my bit's all right…" We work top and bottom with wheat reed, one or other of us will take the bottom half and the other the top half. If it is water reed we do it in lines. We always work from right to left. So we just follow each other along.

Spars? We use a sparmaker in Symondsbury. There's three really, two of them are working men and they just do it in their spare time. One is mad on it and he loves it. He makes hurdles as a hobby, one is retired and does it as a bit of pocket money and the other is a builder and he does it in the evenings, he does pheasants and that. They charge £90 a thousand, all adds up. There is a knack to twisting them.

It is the hands really, if the spars are a bit dry then it is in the insides of your fingers and the palms of your hands that really gets you. You can get blisters and bleed, but they say you can't twist spars until you've made your hands bleed. But that's what they told me anyway. Twist and suffer. Like you do when you are an apprentice or junior in the gang. If you are an apprentice you do the preparation, twist them into 50, a bundle of 50, tie them up and then the thatcher would use them. Hazel tends to want to spring out and it is natural materials together. We use temporary spars you put them in and take them out again.

Will Best we've had some of his reed. He does quite a lot. Willow we use a little bit but we try to stick to hazel. Coppices, there's one in the Marshwood Vale. Spars they tend to bring back home and do it in the garage. 'Tis only cut into short lengths. New build. We do that as well. Fry's. He's the favourite one, there's others as well. There's no thatch at Poundbury. Well the one we have just finished is quite interesting Lyscombe Chapel, out Piddletrenthide, Lyscombe Farm, Russell's. It was a ruin. We've thatched it and re-vamped it. Only the chapel. There's talk of rebuilding the cottage as well. It was scaffolded right in, right over the roof. Still a lot of sheep there. We were working for a conservation company. This was the first one like this and hopefully it will go on from there. They were very happy with what we have done. It was obviously a listed building and had to be done wheat-reed.

The debate on water reed: the thing that spoilt it was that water reed thatchers came in and put the water reed on the way that water reed should look in Norfolk. Dead straight, dead flat, very sharp corners, whereas if they had thatched it in the wheat-reed style nobody would have minded so much. We always thatch wheat-reed style whether we are using wheat-reed or water reed, because we feel that's how cottages should look around here. But even if we are doing a new build we will have soft curves. I have used water reed cut from the Fleet. I have used some in Abbotsbury in my early days. Abbotsbury spear. That's real good old hard long lasting stuff.

We strip back all the decayed thatch. You could get gullies where the water has gone right in and you have to strip all the old thatch off. It goes to dirt. If it is wet, it is just mush and you can't leave that on there. It dries out and goes to dust. So it is a bit like a dentist, you get all the decay out and then you replace it, fill in the holes to start with, make sure it is all right, fix it back to the timbers and then off you go. Thatch always seems to go in the gullies if it is going to go. Bird damage is another thing. Jackdaws and starlings. They keep us in business. They ask us to put nets on. That keeps them out. Maybe we should say, "no. we can't get the net any more." You can put nylon nets on, the fire brigade don't mind them as much, because they can run them down with a knife but the wire mesh they can't rake it off so easily. Bit more resistance to that.

The side facing the weather is the side that is going to wear first. And that is how we do our ridges. There are three sorts of ridges. The traditional Dorset butt up ridge, you do the north side first, and then the south side is butted over onto the top of it, to make that weatherproof. If you did it the other way round the weather could drive into the ends of the thatch. There is a block ridge which we butt up with the patterns and then there is the pattern turnover, where the thatch is wrapped over the top the ridge, so there is no actual join on the top. Always wheat reed on the ridge.

Travel? We go about 45 minutes from our base, travelling time. Weymouth, Yeovil, Axminster, Kilmington, maybe a little bit further. Very often stay locally. Almost at the stage where we are re-thatching a house, did one in Chideock, but I had thatched the back and then I thatched the front. You go back, ridging every eight or ten years. Rough rule of thumb is 25 years, you are doing well then. Moss can be a problem, usually on the north side of the roof.

Other tools? We use spar hooks to make the liggers that go along the roof, splitting the sticks, so we make them ourselves, and we have shearing hooks for cutting out the eaves and the barges and we also shear the wheat reed down, we don't shear the water reed, we just brush that down. The hook is a left-handed hook, but you use it with the right hand, and it is like a sickle, but inside out. They have to be extremely sharp. I got a bit close to one the other day. Thumb's still there. You have to keep them extremely sharp, the sharper they are the easier it is. They are very hard to get hold of as well. These hooks, Morris's of Dunsford, there's an old chap there and I don't think he's passed his knowledge on, of how to make them and I don't think he is that well. He did have cancer. He needs enough orders, a reed dealer wanted 60. We get our reed from Lulworth. He said he hadn't got time, but it is a shame his hooks are really good. That is a dying art. They sell his spar hooks down at Groves. We have got four or five hooks, we have got one Morris one, he keeps his edge the best. We have got a Finch one, that is pretty good. We came across this chap who was a hook collector, a bit of an anorak, his marriage had broken up, we thought there is no surprise there. He had all these hooks on boards, we wanted four hooks, but he wouldn't split the thatching collection so we ended up buying the whole of the thatching collection for the four hooks, but they are good hooks. So we did pay an arm and a leg for them but we need the tools. We said we don't want to look at them, we want to use them for what they were originally made for. They were made to be used.

We use hang ladders, the spike ladders. Scaffolding, health and safety, roads are busier now. You used to stick a ladder in the road and as long as somebody was stood at the bottom and could ferry the traffic out round, but now it is non-stop. Even when we first started we could put a ladder up in the main street of Chideock, but you can't do that now. Twenty years down the line. Next job is traffic lights, in South Perrott right on the bend. The scaffolding is right out in the road. No problem with traction engines these days. Sparks catching the thatch, but somebody caught fire to a load of straw the other day. Some idiot hung out the car window as a tractor was going through Chideock and they actually set light to his load of straw, but luckily the tractor driver had the sense to keep going and stopped up on the Chideock hill and unhitched his trailer. The whole lot went, but if he had stopped in the middle of Chideock. Phew… Quite a dangerous place Chideock. We've managed to survive there for 20 years. You learn don't you.

Darren: My Dad is a member of the cider club. Not quite so involved now but he was for about 10 years. I used to go out there as a boy, 15, 16 year old, good fun then, all the old boys. Still quite a few characters out there now, but times change. A lot of people moved into the village, since I have moved out and it is a different group altogether, not real locals, a mixture of newcomers, but what they do is very good, raising money for charity and that. A great idea for a social thing, but I can remember going there as a boy and seeing the old boys as they slowly had more and more cider and as they were making the cheese up, they started chucking the pummy at each other just like kids. All good fun, and then they would sit down and have bread and cheese afterwards, the same old stories and reminisce. It was quite good. Still happens now.

Richard: Our Great-grandfather was a thatcher. Grandfather was Frank, Great-grandfather was Jim and his Father was the master thatcher in Symonsbury and his sons were the under-thatchers, Jim being one of them. We didn't know this when we took up thatching. Didn't even know there was a thatcher in the family. Dad just sort of said. For my Dad, history is history, but unless you ask them you don't find anything out. No they don't like to talk about the past too much, they just get on with everyday as it comes. They are forward looking. Either that or very forgetful.

I wouldn't push my son into thatching, I definitely wouldn't. It is not an easy life. We get by. I don't like to think that I'll still be thatching when I am 60. We'd love to take on apprentices but the thing that is a bit of a hiccup is the insurances. We have had people ring up and ask if we would like to take on people for work experience. Boys, girls when they come out for a couple of weeks in summer from school. Year 10 I think it is. And we said yes. Well then they said, "what about your insurances?" But because Darren and I are partners our insurances aren't quite as high as if we were employees. Public liability insurance, we looked into taking a lad on for a couple of weeks, it would have cost us £700-£800. Well it was never worth the hassle. It would be nice to be able to and as time goes on, if we get so busy we need to take somebody on, then we will. There are so many new-build and in seven or eight years time they will want some work doing on them. Just under a quarter new-build. They are building an estate. We haven't been abroad but we have been to West London, Chorleywood, Pinner, the Loudwater estate, St Alban's. A customer in Bath, Milton Keynes of all places. I never went to that one. I got married. Loughton right in the outskirts. Mostly water reed up there, new roofs, water reed. Pricing up on squares, 10 feet by 10 feet. Hasn't changed much. Trouble is these plans are all in metric. So we have to convert it without tripping up. We often go into Bradfords and order three metres of four-by-two. But they accept that. They know what we are on about. And I am sure we are not the only ones. We are trying to change.

We are lucky that the farmer we buy the wheat reed from, he stores it and so we go and take it as we want it and the water reed we have it as we want it from the dealer. He's in Lulworth. Yes there is definitely a shortage of good wheat reed. Farming has become very mechanical and there are less people working on the land. Very labour intensive harvesting. And threshing is not a two man job, six is what you need and spread out over a month, a month of good weather is what you need.

We know of two reed combers, Packhams have got one that is three, Huxters have got one, Dave Symonds has got one. Bert Dibben used to have one. He passed it on to somebody and he adapted it and had a conveyor belt to take it straight into the bailer, which was nice as that was the dirtiest job, getting in underneath. We do the reed and the baler. Pitchfork it in. But under a Dutch barn is not always so good, the dust hangs in there. It is always nice to have a bit of a breeze, blowing away.

Thatching? We do it because we have to live, but really it is the transformation, the biggest thing. It is definitely seeing a nice bright yellow finished job. That is what it is all about. We take quite a few photographs before and after. That is where the most satisfaction is. Saddles, eyebrow windows, Devon is a bit more rounded than Dorset. I don't think they tend to strip so much off. That's why they tend to look like that, they tend to build up a bit. South Somerset is very, very similar, then as you go towards Wiltshire they put the fancy spars around the eave and that as well. A bit more decorative. The Dorset one is more practical, more straightforward. We do rick thatching on people's roofs, haven't done one for a while. Last as long as a ridge, a bit of a false economy. A chap at Chideock, George Bartlett, used to have that done on the front of his house. "That will see me out." He kept on living. We did it three times, he lived till 95. Poor bloke, so he might just as well have had it done properly in the first place. Lot of thatching is word of mouth. Boards help. We do advertise a little bit. Parish magazines are good. Probably the best ones, value for money. £35 will get you one week in the Bridport News that is a year in a parish magazine. And the thatch stays in the village for the next 25 years. Quite often you are on a job and somebody comes along can you come down and have a look at mine. Then that goes on and on and on.

Darren: My Father was a works manager in Bridport Gundry's, netting, but that is all gone and split up now. He worked all his life in netting. Started as an office boy and worked his way up to the board of directors at the end. So he did very well. Often went abroad. America and Germany. He can go back a few years on netting. In the later years he was on the sport side of things. Edward's sports they are still going now. Football nets. He was made redundant. He was in there 28 years. The roping industry, then he moved back to his place of birth Chideock and took over the George Inn. Back home only 150 yards up the road from where he was born. The pub was just about dead in between where my parents lived and where Grandma used to live, dead in the middle.

My Mother was Weymouth. Born and bred and she worked in the North Mills factory then. That is how they met and married obviously. And along came my brother and myself. I took up thatching exactly a year after Richard. What are we now August? I started in August '85. So we have over 40 years combined.

My Grandfather was in the Navy, they met through Weymouth/Portland he was more from the east coast. One of 11 and his Mother was one of 13. Not many of them left. He was a captain. And in his later years he was on tug boats in Weymouth. He's long gone now. We have put the nets over corn ricks, drapes everything you can over them on the nets to keep it down. Good use for an old fishing nets, cargo nets.

We just need some new apprentices. An insurance company that isn't going to charge us an arm and a leg to take somebody on. Once you have employed one that is it. Just taking that first step. We are not sure if we can warrant one yet.

You have got to have a good sense of balance. And as you get older you think more about it. You get up on a roof and you definitely become more careful. We use aluminium ladders now. We are more safety conscious now than we were ten or 15 years ago. We get sunburnt. It is as bad in the summer as it is in the winter. The heat drains you. The heat can be very draining. In the rain things get a bit slippery. Better than being in an office. Hideous, hated every minute of it. Stuck inside. I worked in the lab.

Richard: I have been part of the Symondsbury Mummers, for about six years now. You have to live in the parish of Symondsbury. That is the qualification, or work in the parish of Symondsbury. You get asked and I did and I was very cagey about it to start with. No secret handshakes but you wonder when you see some of the things going on. But I started off. Played Room, not a very big part and right at the beginning and then they asked me to. Roughly 10 people. The old boys got their part and that's what they do. It is only the younger ones like me do the other parts. And I don't mind doing it. I asked Dave Warren who plays Doctor, he used to play the Egyptian King as well, and so I asked if I could play the Egyptian King. So then Dave swopped. He does Room and I do the Egyptian King. The main performance is New Year's Day evening at the Ilchester Arms at Symondsbury.

First of all Father Christmas comes on, then it is Room, the Egyptian King, then the soldiers come on and have a fight. Then the Doctor comes in and he revives them. Then that is that part of the play over. Then it becomes Farmer and Wife, but Father Christmas always plays the Farmer. Farmer comes in with a hare, his Wife wants to roast the hare, he wants it fried, they have an argument. He kills his Wife. Doctor comes in and revives the Wife. Then once again the Wife comes in riding a horse. Farmer says: “Let me ride the horse,” she says: “Bet you can’t.” He tries to get on the horse, horse kicks him, he knocks the horse down with his stick, kills the horse. Then they bowse up the horse themselves. The Farmer and the horse. And then the horse, they reckon he can tell fortunes and so the crowd is then involved in that. And then we sing a song at the end. It all lasts about 45 minutes to an hour. And have a great laugh doing it. It is a great local entertainment. I have always found that if you are up in front of the old boys they won’t give you any help. If you have forgotten your words they say, “what? Are we doing a different play tonight?” They won’t remind you. If you are struggling you just struggle. That is it. There is a contact. Father Christmas. He is the contact. The Symondsbury one doesn’t change unless they decide to add a few lines of their own. Originally they went round to different people’s houses, large houses and they would do it. We don’t raise a huge amount, people do put a few quid in the pot. We have done some for charity. The mumming is good fun and the crowds all seem to enjoy it.

10 Michael Stoate: Miller, Cann Mills, Shaftesbury Born 1962

Being a miller is something I really enjoy… I just love going to all the European countries and trying the local breads.

My name is Michael Stoate and I have lived here all my life. I was born in 1962. My Father was a miller and I am the fifth generation milling. My Father was brought up in Bristol. Grandfather had a mill at Temple Back, near Temple Meads on the back of the canal. They had barges coming in on one side and trains on the other. The mill was electric and the barges came from Avonmouth. Some of the farmers talk about the grain coming from Persia and India, full of mud and soil and it was washed in those days and went through a wetting process. It was very big and built in 1912. The grain silos were one of the tallest points in Bristol and a lookout was put there when the bombers were coming over. I think the grain silos got hit at one stage. A lot of the flour went down the West Country on the trains. That was built from scratch and before that they were at Watchet on the Somerset coast. And again they took advantage of the sea and big sailing ketches took flour over to South Wales and came back with coal. They even took sheep over to Wales. So five generations ago we were milling flour in Watchet, very near the paper mill. They were using some imported grain then. Originally it was water power there and then a steam turbine. Started in 1832 and then in the 1880s the roller milling system was put in. Then there was a fire there and the mill was destroyed and they were running out of capacity. Then Bristol took over from there and that was where my father was brought up. The business had got quite big then and incorporated several members of the family. That started in 1912 and then in 1932 Spillers purchased it but they carried on trading under the Stoate name till the '50s.

All flour. One of my customers, Oxford's down at Alweston, he came down with an old Stoate's invoice from 1950 and it was paid 1957! My Grandfather had pretty well retired by then. He had five children but two were in milling, my father being one and Uncle David kept working for Spillers. My Father was born in 1919 and he had his training in Bristol and then the war broke out and the flour changed during the war. He was in the Navy. He started off in the Eagle in the Mediterranean I have seen the pictures of it and it looks a bit Heath Robinson. Then he was on Coastal Forces and captain of his own motor launch. Forays across the Channel. Quite hairy that sort of thing. MTBs? Not too sure where he was based, did some of the North Atlantic stuff too. So he travelled around a fair bit by the sounds of it.

Then after the war in 1945 he came back and worked for two years with Spillers in animal feed mills. Barry and Grimsby. But I don't think he enjoyed working for them very much. During the war flour changed colour and got more like wholemeal, they were trying to waste less and that made more sense, and they were putting calcium in, they were putting chalk in. Specification is still here today and by law you are still supposed to put all those nutrients in it. The big mills are keen to put it in because chalk is cheaper than wheat… and they got the set up for doing it.

When milling changed from stones to rollers, the flour definitely got whiter and finer. It is called a gradual reduction process. Whereas with the stones it gets ground in one pass, with the roller milling it goes through various stages of rollers set at different distances apart. On the first break rollers it only gets cut into about four different fragments. And as you break the grain a few little bits of dust get sieved off, then it goes down and down and down, until you get to the finest. If you do it all in one pass everything just shatters then it is difficult to separate out, but if you do it gradually, it is easier to separate. Then you can re-mix and to get the whole meal if that is what you want to do. And they tend not to put the wheat germ back in as it is worth quite a lot of money on its own, and it is very high in oil which shortens the shelf life of the flour. Either you pay a premium price in a health shop or you buy stone ground flour which has got it all in.

I think Father just wanted a small country mill. There were two he looked at, one in Anglesey and one here. Thankfully he chose here. It could well have been a tidal mill up there. He ended up here and this was an animal feed mill then. 1947. Ev Miles's mill at Melbury was still operating for his own use, French Mill and Gears Mill had stopped by that stage. So a lot of it was grain brought in by local farmers, ground, then given back to them. It was totally a feed mill. He had a coal round, coal in sacks and just a merchant really, animal feed and fertiliser. Then there were loads and loads of small holdings and they needed their animal feed, their coal and their fertiliser. One delivery and it was all done. I know at one stage Father had to take the local water board to court, because they were going to put a pumping station in between here and Melbury Mill and suck it out of the stream. All five mills on the Stirchel are listed in the Domesday book.

It is an amazing stream of water, it is so consistent. You look at the stream it doesn't look very much, but it is just consistent. It is not enough to turn the wheel but you build the head up in the pond. By the morning it will be full again. By the dam you will get four or five feet but by the island it is only six inches deep. Within a night we get enough water to run the mill for 10 hours. So it is almost ideal. So all five mills used the same water. It is the diameter of the wheel which gives it the power. You got the buckets and the leverage of the water in the bucket. Just open the sluice and away she goes. Generates about 12 horsepower. Quite respectable in medieval terms.

In 1954 the whole place burnt down to the ground and that was quite a major problem. It was a diesel engine. He had a hammer mill and the diesel engine drove the hammer mill, and it blew its gasket. The whole lot went up. Tisbury, Shaftesbury and Gillingham fire engines all turned up. I think as a family we have burnt down two so far. I don't know whether that is good or bad. We certainly pay the insurance premiums. It was quite a tragedy at the time and so Father rigged up some temporary equipment to keep going and had to put up something pretty quick and so that is why it is modern prefab 1950s functional. Not very pleasing to the eye but I don't think I would be doing what I am doing now without that building.

I have got five sets of stones. A lot of work when they are all running at the same time. I have got four in the main water mill and tend to do all the same thing together. You get to know the stones, some are better for other things, if I am doing rye there are two sets of stones which are better for that. Just the geology of the stone. The same stones, they are all French Burr and some have just got natural holes in pockets and they just cut the grain up better. The Burr comes from the Paris basin, sadly the quarries have mostly been built over. I have probably got enough to see me out. I have got one set of composite stones installed fairly recently in there from Denmark and the early ones weren't very good. We had a pair of Dreadnought stones in there and Father in the '70s, he started moving away from the animal feeds and started doing flour, and he put a set of Dreadnought stones in running vertically. They make a meal, but they don't make flour. It is quite coarse. He used them for a while and then took them out and used French Burr. French Burr is a limestone, geologists tell me it is a primitive limestone. Very, very hard, almost flint like, it just holds its edge really well.

French Burr came in about 1790s. It would have been Derbyshire Peak stone and the same sort of stone was quarried in Wales, and that would have been the standard

Michael Stoate at Cann Mills

mill stone. Fine for doing oats and barley and soft wheats, but as soon as you start putting hard milling wheat through it the wheat grinds the stone. The stone wears away very quickly and particles of stone end up in the flour. The better quality milling wheats tend to be very, very hard, particularly the imported ones. If they are too dry you dampen the wheat down, moisture content ideally 14-15%. As soon as you go over 16% you get into an awful sticky mess grinding it. You grind it and it sweats, and you get sweating in the machine. I buy locally when I can and as the season goes on I go further afield. Where are we now just about to go into April and we are getting it from Pewsey. I have Canadian grain coming in all the time and I blend Canadian with English. I do the wholemeal, brown, the white, a malt star, rye flour, self-raising flour and spelt. So that seven that is all the organic ones, and I do three non-organic ones.

Yes. There was quite a bit of overlap between animal feeds and flour, Father used to employ several people. He used to have a miller here and two or three drivers, and he used to keep a couple of hundred pigs as well and a few Portland sheep as lawnmowers. By 1970 I think it was, he stopped doing animal feed and so he probably had been doing a bit of flour for four or five years leading up to that and then he was out on his own. Ralph Coward in Donhead was growing his Maris Widgeon wheat then and it wasn't called organic then, it was all compost grown, so that's how it started. Father used Ralph's wheat, and whatever quality it went through the mill and George Anstey in Shaftesbury would take it and make bread. Thirty-five years later it is all the rage. George Anstey would buy the flour. Just then some of the hippies were coming out of the trees and they would open health food shops. And a lot in Bristol, Herbert's bakery and two wholefood shops called Stoneground and Grain Store and Fodder Foods, loads of them.

Food yards rather than miles, and the supermarkets weren't touching any of that stuff then and so it was more the alternative market. It grew. Oxford's were quite an early one. He knew the stamping ground and so Bristol was logical. In the end the van was going up there twice a week. But they weren't terribly good at running businesses, these hippie wholefood type shops and as the market grew and other shops started opening and supermarkets started doing some of the health food lines and extending the flour range. Essential, they amalgamated. It was called Harvest and Nova Whole Foods, and now they are Essential Trading and we have been dealing with them since they begun. They have been very good customers over the years. A big business now.

I was born in 1962. I have an elder brother but he was more interested in ornithology and taxidermy. I left school and did an engineering course, mechanical and electrical engineering, the choice was to go on to university or come back here and apply it. I chose to come back here and apply it. I really enjoy that side of the business. You require it every day. Obviously we have gone backwards in the type of machinery we are running. The Bristol mill was state of the art when it was built, one of the most modern mills in Europe. I mix new and old technology here. I won't deviate from the millstones but applying the power to them and conveying the grain and the flour anything to make life easier. There's not a huge amount you can do. It was a fairly gradual process taking over from my father. I think it was 1990 when my father officially retired. But he had certainly taken a back seat well before then, and it must be a really difficult thing to do, handing the business over, but with a bigger concern there's a slot for you. A sales role, a technical role, but when it is a one man band you take the whole lot on and you have your own way of doing things. That is moulded over the years, but he seemed really good, he gave me the run of it.

I worked out with a firm of millwrights. I learnt a bit travelling round the country repairing old mills. Chisels and redding. I started off with the old mill bill and tapping away. And there was a stage when we used Kango hammers but they are a bit brutal. We have moved on from there. Now it is angle grinders with diamond tipped blades, dressing stones, it is the sort of thing you never stop learning about. I am learning more and more about stone dressing as time goes on. Each stone has different properties even though they are all French Burr. They all behave slightly differently. Roughly speaking every 18 months you look at them. You can get a few hundred tons through in that time. If you read some of the books they say they need dressing every 50 tons, well I am very glad I don't have to do that. In one day on one stone, on the small set run off the water, they will do just about the ton, and then the others the four-foot stones, they are doing about a couple of tons potentially. It is a job to get hold of them, anybody with some could probably name a price. They are heavy up to three-quarters of a ton each.

I have a pair of callipers for lifting the stones joined by a bolt. Always been here just got them from the shed, and I dropped my first mill stone a few weeks ago. The bolt that holds the callipers together decided that it had had enough and it dropped about four feet and the floor of the mill is four inches of reinforced concrete and it just punched a neat little hole straight through the concrete. But luckily it didn't damage the stone at all. Not a habit I want to get into, so now I have a modern high tensile bolt.

In 1976 the water decreased a little. I think we only lost an hour a day. Big sponge. Daily routine, get the mill going then the grain, and there is always moving grain around, through the cleaner first and then blended. When it comes in I test the moisture content, and I tend to buy it on analysis. And if it is from a local farm, I like to bring a small bag back and analyse it. There are about five or six organic farmers within a 15-mile radius. They used to go for thatching straw, Maris Widgeon. They are now growing Paragon, a spring variety. All varieties quite intensively bred and so their disease resistance is not so good as the old varieties, so they hang around for a few years and then they change the variety, keep swapping. I feel the flour all the time, and if you are sieving it you feel the bran too. You get to know the bounciness of the bran. Still hands on and constantly doing sums in your head, monitoring how many bags an hour you are getting out, just to check that the machinery is running at the optimum rate. And when you have got all five stones going and a lorry tipping grain and customers coming down, there is quite a lot going on. The weather doesn't effect the grinding very much, more in the grain storage and conditions at harvest. If it is just a damp day, doesn't make a lot of difference.

I think we are the only mill working commercially in Dorset. A chap ran one for a while at Upwey, but I don't know whether more will open. I don't personally go to farmers' markets but I supply quite a few cottage industries and they make all sorts of things. Scones, pies, biscuits and cakes. Loads of little cottage industries buy the flour then sell the produce at the farmers' markets. It has a knock-on effect. The flour mostly goes to the South West. We have got a van that is going out all the time, we are up to London once a week. I go directly to some bakers, artisan bakers, wholesale bakers who mostly supply restaurants and hotels. There is a real market for that up in London at the moment. A lot of the bakers in London are ex-chefs. They are ones that have specialised in the baking and some of them have given up the cookery bit and gone on and taken completely to bread. There's a chap called Dan Leppard who started off as a photographer then he went into cooking and spent some time in America baking. And now he's the man to talk to, a baking guru. He doesn't come from a long line of bakers, but he is involved in Sugar and Spice and is involved in the consultancy business helping people set up bakeries.

Bakery courses here, in their third season. A chap called

Paul Merry who is Australian and had his own bakery outside Melbourne for 15 years. He built the bakery himself and the oven out of mud bricks and specialised in wood-fired ovens and traditional ovens. The bread ovens were made out of bricks and steel door, and this one's cast out of refractory material clay. It is a French one, and he will just put it in as a different element of the bakery course, in addition to the electric oven, but based on the Italian bread making techniques. Traditionally these are all done in a wood-fired oven. Well you heat the oven up for three four or five hours then scrape all the ash to the side then put your bread straight onto the tiles, and you get that delicious crust.

That is the future at the moment. Huge enthusiasm for going back to basics, the primary sources of food and reducing food miles. And these bread machines they have helped us and a lot of local people come down here to get their flour, largest percentage of bread machines last for three months then gather dust and go into the cupboard next to the ice cream maker probably. So some people appreciate what bread making is all about and some then come down on a bread making course and take it a stage further. He runs about 70 days for courses through the year.

In a year we probably put through about 400 tonne a year through the mill. So that is quite enough for me. The business has got more specialised. The Bristol mill was mass producing white flour. That was quantity and now we have gone for quality. Being a niche business that is the only way you can go really. No point in making mainstream flour.

Being a miller is something I really enjoy, it is hard work, no getting around that. Physically it is hard work, but I don't mind that, it is nice to end the day, thinking you have put something into it and the power is on the doorstep.

The windmill was a hobby of Father's. A transitional period with animal feed to flour, Portuguese. I think when the mill was designed, a prefab concrete building, it was designed to take a third storey. So if Father wanted to expand he could plonk a third storey on top, but when he pulled out of animal feeds he realised that wasn't going to happen, and he already had a love of windmills. He enjoyed sailing, he travelled to Portugal a lot, and during the war he stopped off there for a while. And when he got married they had their honeymoon out in Portugal. We had a house out there for 30 years. We started going out there as children, 1970-72 and just sold it four or five years ago in a very rural area and saw so many changes. I just love going to all the European countries and trying the local breads. And a lot of these countries are slowly losing it. It was a choice to sell out in the '30s, and probably it was the right choice, really, because the family had got the milling as big as they could get. That way they could sell out.

Trouble with restrictions, they started poking their noses in at one stage and I told them that we were not abstracting water. And so they muttered about charging us for taking the water out and so I mentioned that I might charge them for putting it back in. Green energy. There are grants available.

It would be nice if there was a locum miller. I used to shut the mill down for two weeks in the summer and a week in the spring, but I haven't done that for ages. I think I only stopped three days last year. I don't work weekends. There are these standing orders, so over the last couple of years I have increased the capacity of the mill. So I am hoping. I do have a bit of help, At the end of the day there is so much bureaucracy with health and safety you just don't want to go there, so it all relies on myself. Which is a bit dangerous. I am not allowed to be ill. I ruptured my Achilles tendon about four years ago and was in plaster for nine weeks and I think my consultant would have thrown a wobbly if he had seen me going up and down ladders and grain bins with this plaster on. Farmer's lung? I wear a mask all the time. I remember, as a child doing animal feeds, you couldn't see from one end to the other.

11 Graham and Norman House, Bakers, Maiden Newton
Graham born 1962. Norman born 1937.

Yeast is a highly comical thing to look after. The best dough you make is like a virgin's breast. Firm but yielding… Saturday morning is Range Rover morning.

Graham: My name is Graham House, my Father is called Norman and my Grandfather was Walter Evan House and that is why our firm is called W.E. House. My Grandfather was working here before the war as an apprentice with the baker who owned it at that time, a bloke called Freddy Garman. When he saw war was looming, he decided that he couldn't go through all the rationing and the difficulties of wartime again so he asked my Grandfather if he would fancy buying the bakery and running it himself. Corse this wasn't easy at the time as he was just a tablehand. He had a wife, my Grandmother, two small children, my Father Norman who was three and his sister who was five, at that time. They were renting the property next door. It was just staff accommodation, and my grandmother said: "Yes we should try it and we will go for it." So he took over the business on 10th May 1939 with no previous experience of running a business and with war about to start. That was good wasn't it!

I was born locally in the Dorchester 1962 and I was always groomed for this job. When the school bus would draw back into Maiden Newton from the local comprehensive I would have to get off the bus and come straight into work. At that time it was cutting sides of bacon, because bacon was cut on the premises. There was very little pre-packed bacon in those days. I used to pack the dough cakes, and help my father weigh up for the next day. So I was always being groomed, ever since before that time, when I was too tiny to reach the boards in the bakery and I had to stand on bread tins, so that I could reach the boards in order to work. And going backwards, when I was no good in the bakery I was encouraged to stand in the corner and remain silent or go and play on the coal pile. Before that time in 1968 when the oven was converted to oil, there was a couple of tons of coke in the coal hole and I liked to run up and down the pile. They were so busy they didn't have a chance to stop me. After I left school at 16 I came to work here and I have been here ever since and I am 42 now. Twenty-five years. Lived in the village got married and just moved up the road, always been village life.

Daily routine? Well on a weekday my father comes in and the first thing that he will do is switch the prover on. The oven, because it is on a time switch, will have already heated up to its operating temperature, an old steam tube oven, we never let it go cold, but it will have just stoked itself up. It is electrically operated, oil fired. Heats up to baking temperature and then during the night it falls away to about 350°F or 360°F. Any less than that, the brickwork cracks up and steam will escape. Sundays we just keep the burner ticking over. On Sundays we have cooked people's roasts in the oven. We certainly used to do people's turkeys and they were a total nightmare. Somebody would say mine's not done and mine's overcooked. And then they weren't sure they got their own back. And you lost your Christmas Day. I know in the past we have dried people's eiderdowns over the ovens all that sort of thing.

So the first thing he would do is start up the large dough machine and draw the water to the correct temperature. He starts at quarter past six on weekdays and five o'clock on a Saturday. If you are a town baker you have to start earlier but as we are a country baker our customers are tolerant. Our customers know it is no good coming in here before ten o'clock for a certain loaf because they know it won't be ready, which allows us to start later. He then lets the water into the mixer and the mixer makes the dough and then he puts

Graham and Norman House

all the pies in the oven which have been made the previous afternoon. And so he starts those cooking, and when they are baked, the dough is ready and proved, that then goes into the oven 450°F is the optimal temperature. Proving takes 30-40 minutes. So then you take the bread out of the oven and that coincides with the shop opening. The smell is brilliant. Good PR.

That is at eight o'clock. Then you carry on manufacturing during the morning, make the lardy cakes at noon which are then retarded, which simply means that you keep them cool till the next day. And then you can put them in the prover so that they can puff up. Then everybody has a lengthy lunch break from two till 4.30, then we come back at 4.30, prepare pies and weigh up for the next day and get all the dry ingredients ready. And it saves time the next day, and so all you have to do is put the liquids in. We get our yeasts from the bakers' buying group. In days gone by there were firms like DCL, Distillers Company Limited, they used to bring our yeast. It is much more centralised now. You can use different yeast but we simplify it and use the same yeast for everything. The flour comes from Shipton Mill which has Prince Charles's Royal warrant on it and cheap Continental flour which comes from Germany, through BAKO simply because it is cheap. Yeasts come from Pinnacle, a company in this country. Comes fresh like a block of putty. We just keep it in the fridge. Yeast is a highly comical thing to look after. After a while it starts to gas or dry out. We get it once a week, but as soon as something goes wrong with your bread production you start suspecting your yeast. We have had a good run lately, but in days gone by we always had two yeast companies, DCL and BFP, British Fermentation Products, so that we could play one off against the other. So if one person's yeast was poor the other one's was likely to be better, but now it seems much more uniform. Could even be computerised. Yeast is a living plant, there are millions of yeasts. Hopefully wild yeasts will have all been screened out. You often see that on wine bottles "wild ferment". Good name for a nightclub.

I like the family and the village aspect of it and Norman likes the pure baking, producing. There is very much a social element to it. I very much enjoy village life, you are well known and the kids come down from the school two or three times a year and have a look round. It is very nice a real feeling. If you live and work in a community you are lucky. You don't put on one hat when you drive to work and when you drive back you take it off. When you are actually in the community you are just Graham the baker all the time, which is nice. People don't take advantage of that. It is lovely. I used to live in Toller. The post office and pub have gone, it's just somewhere to live. It can be fun. I have said the wrong thing on the odd occasion.

When the dough has been mixed, you then leave it for 10 or 15 minutes in the mixer to have its first prove. Then you knock it back which means you punch all the air out, then throw it out onto the boards then scale it. That is done by hand. Each scaled piece is then moulded into the correct shape of the loaf then put into the tin for a final prove, which will take 30-40 minutes, whereas in the tin it rises to the correct level. Then you can set it, which is putting it in the oven with a peel, which is that long wooden paddle, that is setting. Fifteen minutes later you draw, which is the opposite of setting, you draw it out of the oven and tip it out onto the wooden rack there, for it to cool, otherwise it goes all soggy. Then whack it round the shop and away it goes. Walks out on its own. It is as easy as that.

I think we get through a tonne of flour a week. We are doing about 250-300 loaves a week and 500-600 loaves on a Saturday. We do wholesale drops to a couple of shops locally, and of course in days gone by we had a very busy bread round, but nobody has a bread round these days. It has gone in the last 10 years. Certain stories about rivalry between bakers in the village and families that would take 12 loaves each time you would make a call and certain families would take stale bread because it was cheap. Say a loaf was 12d you would sell off your stale at 2d. They would buy your stale bread, they had so many children. The protein content is the same whether it is stale or not. A pint of beer and a loaf were always the same price and six eggs. Six eggs is 50p. A loaf is a pound and beer is £2.50. So it should be £2.50 a loaf. People in the country like white bread. If you have brown bread you are poor, if you have white bread you're well-to-do. Still the case. So people in the country will have white bread but with the introduction of the malted loaves, granary and multigrain loaves I would like to say 50:50. I would say we still sell slightly more white than all the brown put together. That's the change in people's taste, but the change of people's buying is the bulk. People are eating less bread, much less bread. They don't need to be filled up and as the nation becomes more affluent they eat more meat. I have got one chap who was a farm worker and he has eaten two metric tonnes of our product in his lifetime. He always had Walt Houses's bread as he calls it and now he has retired. He was a tractor driver and he comes from that old tradition of high bread eating, high fruit and veg. Very little meat. Cold on Monday. Rissoles on Tuesday.

Pasties and pies a vast increase. In days gone by, people had their sandwich boxes. They had their sandwiches during the day and the wife produced a cooked meal at night. Now I am not sure if the wife still produces a meal at night, but certainly people don't bring lunchboxes out. We draw on an awful lot of trade from people dropping in for a late breakfast or elevenses or something around teatime. So those traditional meals have come to us. Women are just not able to produce lunch and tea. They can just do one cooked meal, but they are often out working themselves. We get a lot of trade from men.

Lardy cakes? A lot of people, when they see the cakes being made, I can't understand people. I am shocked. I am amazed. "Look at the lard in there!" I even had a customer who asked if there was any animal fat in a lardy cake!! And I was dying to say: " Madam, no, of course not," but I couldn't say that. There is a hell of a lot of lard in a lardy cake. That is why they are so tasty. People are drawn to fat and sugar. The other change in people's buying habits is that in days gone by people bought everything in the village. And indeed you had to register at the shop to have your coupons during the war, But the vast majority of people's purchases goes out of the village into the supermarkets. That is fair and reasonable, they have got bigger packs and they are cheaper. So how we have been able to survive is moving down the more speciality food end of the market. People are prepared to pay more for fresh local foods. Like local honey, local cheeses, air-cured bacon, all fresh local foods. The bakery is good, bakery still works, but we have had to specialise to survive. More delicatessen type operation. We don't have a guaranteed take from the village of staple food stuffs.

There's the Premier stores and the garage which has opened a Spar shop and all they are doing is packaged convenience foods. And that leaves us with the fresh foods. We slice our own ham whereas with the other stores everything is shrink wrapped, bar coded and dated. Thankfully we have got a Post Office which is just a post office and that is how we would like it to stay. So it is good.

So I am the third generation here. Yes that's right. Well my mother and my father work here and I do, and I have one brother and he made the decision, even though he used to get roped in at Easter and Christmas, to help. That almost helped him to decide that he didn't want this as a career and so he moved to Bridport and he is building the pier at West Bay and so that is what he does, he works for Voisey-

Axminster Excavators. It's a bit like working in a goldfish bowl, working in a family environment. But of the four of us, three of us are in it. There are helpers in the village. We have in total 18 of us working here, but some are just children who come in on an "as and when" basis. We have a lot of students. Most of the young women came to us as schoolchildren to help out after school or on a Saturday. Pack some buns on an Easter. Then get married, have their children then come back to work here. Part-time work suits us all very well. They do say 15-20 hours a week. They are in the village, some can't drive. When they have got young children they are available, so when they say little Johnny is sick, they can go to him. And they just walk home and prepare their husband's tea, do a bit, then they are there when they come back.

This road outside here is our lifeline. People talk about a bypass for Maiden Newton, but if you do that, it will kill our trade and certainly shut one of the shops for sure. That road brings hungry men and the ladies that are shopping in the village and workers into Maiden Newton. Including Wynford Eagle and Toller Fratrum, the population is 850 souls. The good thing about Maiden Newton is that because we have such a good range of facilities like the hardware store, train station and the school, all the valleys come down to us. Hooke, Toller, Frampton, people from Sydling, Cattistock. The geography helps us, it funnels them down to us, the roads come down the valleys and it is always noticeable. We have lost our butcher which is now the fish and chip shop. On a Thursday morning the bank used to open and that was always our busiest morning, people would come from other places then go to the butcher and baker.

I think Maiden Newton is a small town. It is a place that people come into. We have our core of villagers, who are not desperately loyal but they are there. If they are passing and they have run out of sprouts, they will come in, then we have got people who come in for services or simply to pick up specialist foods. Saturday morning is Range Rover morning. They all come they have got their second homes and they have all come down from London and first call into House's thank goodness. It is the only morning we can sell croissants. We don't make them on any other day than Saturdays when the Range Rovers come in.

We have had many debates on this. Do they take local housing away from local people or are they much more prepared to spend in the community? They come in and they just want to spend here in the village, they don't want to go off into Tesco's they have had enough of that. They will spend. Tesco vans, they come in here and buy pies from me. Sometimes they even come in here and ask directions to people's houses. And I am thinking, he is just a driver. We are not trying to impact the weekly grocery take. We want to do the specialist goody buyer, a croissant, some local butter, you can't find those things in Tesco's. The daily loaf. The subsistence buyers who buy fresh foods, they just pop in. Statistically village bakers are disappearing. We have ensured that a business like this could go on by specialising in foods that people want to buy. Augment bakery with other fresh local foods. Yes I think it could go on. I think if you were just a pure baker you would have a struggle.

Geography? We are just beside the River Frome. It is to do with the valleys. That hill stops people, very few come over the top. They tend to move to Dorchester. Most of our customers come from upstream. They are following the watercourse, they come down from Hooke, Toller, Halstock, Corscombe, those sorts of places. Railway station makes a difference. We get quite a lot of medical people. They can get to hospitals to Yeovil, Dorchester and Weymouth. Rented accommodation is always snapped up in Maiden Newton. If you are renting you are going to want to use public transport and you would use that line.

Norman: This part of Dorset is very sparsely populated. George Anstey in Shaftesbury he went on and on he was 76. Village bakers aren't going to be many left in a minute. Fifty years ago village shops didn't stock a lot. I can remember stocking the first cat foods and dog foods. They had the scraps from the table.

I am 67. I was born on 9th April 1937 and I was born within the village and my name is Norman Evan House. My Father worked for the previous owner and come 1939, war was imminent and the owner said I can't face going through another world war, as he had been through a previous world war. It was pretty difficult as they took the men away from their work. So my Father bought it as it was. Pretty risky, my Mother had a very hard time, she had a young family. My Father was born in the village and my Mother was one of the local policeman's daughters. She worked at the local corn and cake merchants. My Grandfather worked on the railway. It was quite an economic venture. Bridport line which carried all the goods and the main line. My Grandfather was a lineman, I don't think he was on the platform. I think there was a lot of maintenance. Totally different then.

I was only a boy during the war, but I think bread was rationed afterwards. I can remember the huge amount of Americans. Very generous. My Father used to supplement his income by repairing bicycles. They seemed to be mad on bicycles. He opened up the double doors and repaired bicycles which is quite funny. They were all stationed away from the villages, the camps, there was a huge one where the Clay Pigeon was. Very exposed. They used to bicycle to go into the villages. Most people had white bread. We didn't make a brown bread we only had Hovis. We didn't do wholemeal, wheatmeal or granary. Flour came from Avonmouth. Yes I can remember my first apron was made out of a Canadian cotton sacks. During the war they increased the extraction rates. We had the shop that has always been there. Very little fresh veg, people grew their own. I think any little business has to keep developing all the time. We took the door that is open to us. So we try and do local hams, honey, three honey suppliers, four local egg producers. A choice of local food, if you can manage to find them, sourcing them, that is the thing. Not so easy.

I like the baking best. I like the hands-on baking, that's the bit I have always enjoyed. The milling has totally changed, like dust now. They rupture the cell that increases the water consumption, and we used to get big holes in bread. They used to say the baker's wife is pregnant, that was the old joke. The best dough you make is like a virgin's breast. Firm but yielding. Don't put that in!

Never known having local flour. Did go down to a mill between Crewkerne and Bridport and he had a little mill, and he let me have some flour and I made some bread for him, just as an experiment. This was a small village, but it came out OK. Just like a housewife's bread, a bit sconney. The pies and pasties that has increased with people's income. They are better off, Passing trade increasing with the volume in traffic. In the 1940s and '50s very little.

Bread round? Used to go round three times a week. We had one van. Yes. The immediate villages, up the valleys, Toller Porcorum, Toller Fratrum. We have always been very small commercially. People always paid the same price. Unheard of charging for delivering. Often you would have a grocery order as well. We stopped delivering about three years ago. Bryant's gave up David Bryant his health wasn't very good. Crabbs up at Halstock.

Village bakeries? A bit like the whisky trade in Scotland where you have the vast commercial trade and the few malt distilleries and I think it will go that way. They are always light years ahead of us. It is a job to tell. The savoury trade must almost be equal to the bread trade now. People eating proportionally less than they did. It was part of the staple diet. Some people round here, meat was two or three times a week. Stale bread. If you had some over. I think that is where the fallacy came in. "New bread gives you indigestion." Not a grain of truth in that. Mother wanted the kids to eat up yesterday's before she served the new. If you are price conscious you don't buy from a small baker. If you want quality you spend your pennies where you wish.

Water meadows? Never known them working as such. Known them further down the valley and Toller Fratrum. On the Frome. Oh, yes I can remember them. It was a complex irrigation system. Andy Eliot they have bought the meadow. There's not many who would know how to do it. Yes I can remember them clearly. When I was a boy they had gone into disrepair and what use to happen, the water drained back into the river and some trout would be in the pounds, and the little brooks. And so of course as it drained you could get hold of them. Yes of course during the war we used to catch them anyway. We get eels. Never used to eat them. Never fancied them, used to give them away.

As a kid we always used to fish, fork them, tickle them, stab them. Have an ordinary fork and sharpen the prongs. Take one out and you'd have just the three and lash it to a stick. We used to go out at night. We only got brown trout, but it goes for a fortune this fishing. We got fishing rights. From this bridge for a quarter of a mile went for £20,000 a few years ago. It goes for a fortune, but that is private. There's some lovely trout in there but the salmon only come up as far as Dorchester. They do get there, I have seen them, once or twice. River salmon specially in the floods.

NB: Since the interview was recorded the business has been sold, but it is still baking excellent bread. Norman has retired and Graham is working for Eldridge Pope in Dorchester.

Will Best silaging, Manor Farm

12 Will Best: Organic dairy farmer, Manor Farm, Godmanstone
Born 1947.

We were the only commercial organic dairy farm in Dorset for 10 years. In a way we were the experimental farm for the whole of Dorset. An organic farm is a fantastic place to live. It is just humming with bird life.

My name is Will Best and I was born in the Dorset County Hospital, the old one, 25th October 1947. Both my Grandfathers were doctors and my Father was heading into following his Father as a doctor and he failed his part one medicine at Cambridge. But by an extraordinary fluke, totally unconnected, an old lady in Wales, would have left her estate to my Father after her son died. And it was all to down to politics and religion and all sorts of amazing Welsh stuff, and to cut a long story short, my Father's solicitors were bought out of the inheritance for quite a nice sum of money, which in 1930 went a long way. So my Father was able to abandon trying to become a doctor, which he wasn't getting on very well with anyway, and he went to Stuart Tory up towards Blandford as a farm pupil. He looked around for a farm which was this one, Manor Farm, Godmanstone, which was 150 acres. Initially he rented it and bought it when the old lady died. This was 1934 and he set up a herd of pedigree Guernseys. He hunted and he was on the council and he was church warden, lay reader, lay treasurer of the Friary at Hillfield. He was also a magistrate and chairman of the district council. He helped found the Dorset Wildlife Trust and had quite a broad life. And as long as the farm paid its way that was enough.

No sheep. It was the Guernseys before the war. He claimed that he doubled the arable acreage the first year he was here, which meant that the mangolds were increased from half an acre to an acre. But in the war it was all change and they had to get the plough out and the binder and the Fordson tractor and start growing arable and potatoes. They were all in the Home Guard. We had Italian prisoners of war and it was all very busy. After the war we carried on with arable as well as the dairy. With 150 acres you could make a good living, certainly in the '50s, not a problem really. They showed cattle, won prizes at the shows and sold pedigree cattle.

The milk? In the '30s, possibly the '40s, there was a man called Ockey Collins who had a milk round in Cerne and he used to come round and collect milk, because father was one of the first tuberculan tested herds. I don't know if anybody pasteurised it or not, but apparently Ockey Collins used to collect it and do a little milk round. I don't know if that took all of it. Certainly as long as I remember it went over to Bladon Dairies at Milborne. They used to make cheddar cheese over there, you could ring up the milk factory and they would bring you out a cheese on the milk lorry when they came to pick up the churns, and it was really nice cheese. He never got more than about 35 cows and he reared all the heifers, they sold a few pedigree heifers and so on.

With the advent of war the top ground was ploughed up for corn and there were some potatoes. You see we are on the chalk but it is amazing what soil variation you get across the chalk. Some of it is clay with flints, not a heavy clay, but a serious sort of clay. Then there is browny, black loam, which they call the boy's ground, which is very easy working stuff. A doss really. And some of it is a kind of sandy clay without stones in it, just a few acres, and they grew the potatoes up on there.

Some of that was always downland in the pre-enclosure time, may or may not have been ploughed post-enclosure but certainly since the First War would have been back to grass. And some of it was downland for ever in fact. Pigs. We had pigs down in that yard when we were kids, there may have been skimmed milk from butter making and then there weren't any. So maybe they just had a few in the war.

After the war this farm really stayed in rotation and Father, he got a bit between two schools. He was friends with Rolf Gardiner and Peter Joyce and those pioneers. But he wasn't really committed enough to go down the organic route. On the other hand when things through the '50s and '60s, when 300 units of nitrogen became the thing, he wasn't ready to go down that route either. So he was a little bit lost in between in a way.

I was born in 1947 and we lived in that house over there as kids. I have moved all of 50 yards. The first memory I have got of my entire life is the sun reflecting off the bonnet of our first new tractor, which was a David Brown Cropmaster and it was 1950. So I wasn't even three and I stood out there, it was bright red, it came off the road and I was so excited. So I was a bit into farming already. The marvellous thing about it was that it had a double seat. The thing about the Cropmaster was that it came out in the late '40s, and this was designed so that the farmer could run his farm with it and also take his missus into town. It had a really fast top gear, about 25mph and had a double seat and was unique in that respect. The interesting thing was that before the war farmers had cars, but they didn't have tractors. They certainly put the hay sweep in front of the cars, but this was trying to turn it the other way round. We had one Fordson, a secondhand one that appeared during the war, and that lasted until, I can remember riding on that one, not driving it, so that lasted until sometime in the '50s.

When we had the Fordson, the horses still did a bit and I remember when I was small, and by this time we had the David Brown as well, and there was one horse left. And the only person who worked it was my Mother and she went out turning the hay with it. It wasn't really needed any more, but she was the last person to actually work a horse on the farm. Her Father was a doctor and he married the daughter of a wind miller, a man with a windmill in Buckinghamshire, Wing. Grandfather had a stroke when he was only 50, he worked incredibly hard, because all the work they did for the farmworkers, they didn't get paid for. There wasn't any money for it, so any money they got, was from looking after the gentry basically. But he was a committed sort of person and would do anything he could for the farm workers. And he was always out in the middle of the night delivering babies. She reckoned, he used to go out on his rounds in a horse and trap. She was 13 when he died. She said it was overwork… but anyway they rented the house, which was from the Rothschilds. And they kicked Grandmother out and she had to find somewhere she could afford. And so she came down to Dorset, to Spyway at Askerswell. My aunt still lives there now. And so they were country people, horse and dog type people. My Mum trained as a nurse at St Thomas's and did some nursing at the beginning of the war.

I have got another cousin, another great-grandson of the miller, who works in Essex, he is in the milling business, because some cousins still live up that way. But I don't know enough about the family and the mill. The funny thing is I went to Wing to have a look and there is a petrol station and it has the forecourt and the bit where you go and pay, it looks a bit odd. And then you suddenly realise that it is the bottom bit of the old windmill, all the rest has gone and you can see the shape of it.

Well, you see this tractor, I was talking about the double seat. And Father did all these other things, didn't do a lot of farming. Well there was this guy called Fred Moxon, who was like Father's foreman. And I spent a lot more time with him than I did with my own Father. I used to sit up on the double seat and he'd sit there and smoke and I would steer and work the hydraulics. This is aged about five. So I knew how to do all the jobs. And it wasn't until I was about 10 or

11 that I was left there on my own. But I did kind of learn that side of things at an early age. I think the big shock came when I was sent off to prep school aged eight. Cold baths and the cane, real old traditional prep school, Latin and all that. But, it was down near Langton Matravers, they have still got one or two prep schools there now. But this one doesn't exist now. The extraordinary thing was that we had the Empire and cold baths and all that, and astonishing snobbery, allied to the fact that all the food was organic, cooked on the place. A wonderful kitchen garden, an orchard and no tinned food. Wholemeal bread and this is in the '50s was absolutely unheard of. And so that must have been good for me. No Mother's Pride. I loved this hairy bread and salads with spring onions and everything in season. I wasn't really aware of what was going on at the time, but looking back, it was quite unusual. They just had a couple of gardeners, an orchard and just grew all the veg in the garden. I don't know where the meat came from, beautiful beef, cut really thin. They certainly had got the organic philosophy and this is one of the interesting things, there was a strand in the 1930s, '40s which actually inched towards eugenics and that sort of thing. Really quite right wing, I think it was a bit on that end of things. We were British, the upper classes and our job was to "rule the empire" and we had to have the right food to do it. I am sure there was an element of that. These two guys, two brothers who ran it, were sons of a canon in the Church of England. So we had a lot of Book of Common Prayer, King James Bible which I love to this day. I go to church and I don't open the Prayer Book. "Dearly beloved, etc..." It is just in there and I am hugely grateful for that, we didn't have any alternative. Just drummed into us. And endless running, we used to say: "Can we have baked beans sir?" "Absolutely not." Nothing out of a tin, only real food. It was quite interesting and endless rugby and cricket which I loved. I got into rugby. Sunday afternoon walks over the Purbeck Hills. Wonderful so it was a mixture, some fantastic things and some really rather horrendous things. This class thing... ooh. I couldn't understand it, because I spent my holidays with the farm workers and their kids. I couldn't get my head round that. I lasted five years there and then off to public school. The food wasn't like that at all, the emphasis on sport and Latin was about the same and the snobbery wasn't quite so bad, but the food was Mother's Pride and you are so hungry at that age. The sport was great, Shrewsbury and more beautiful country. Used to get out on the Welsh Marches and so it has always been the beautiful country that has kept me.

I wanted to play cricket for Somerset first. But that didn't quite work out. I wanted to be like Vic Marks but I lost the plot in that respect. I can remember coming back during the school holidays and first thing I would do was go and see Fred Moxon and see what he had been up to on the farm. And the second thing I would do was walk the farm and think to myself when it's mine I am going to do this, this and this. Fred taught me a huge amount. He was wonderful with animals, he was one of those people if someone had a dog they couldn't control they would give it to him. He lived in Forston as a kid. His father was a gardener and a farm worker they tended to move around a bit in a small circle. He rented a dairy when he was a young man at Frampton and Southover. He worked on the building for Fry's and then he came in here. He was brilliant with horses, cattle, cows, any cow that was kicking the guts out of you, five minutes with him and she was quiet as anything. Dogs if they couldn't handle them they gave them to him and within a few days they would be following him around. And he enjoyed the arable side and all that. He was a big influence.

Then I went to Cambridge. I didn't particularly want to go. I was a fairly docile person and if you passed the exams they pushed you off there. I read agriculture and I hated it up there. I had never lived in a town before. All sorts of buses and cars everywhere. Everyone says Cambridge is beautiful. Well it is, but it is still urban. And of course in those days they never had enough accommodation, so you lived in backstreets in digs with a landlady. I had never lived in a street before, you stepped out straight onto the concrete. It was flat, cold. Yeah. I was a bit lost up there. Sugar beet and heavy clay. Putting wheat in with huge great clods, "one for the rook, one for the crow, one to rot and one to grow" with these crawlers and these icy blasts blowing past. I wasn't really at home up there. I probably sharpened my critical faculties. It a very academic, theoretical type of degree. We did a lot of soil science and animal physiology and botany which at the time seemed tedious and it was damned hard work. We had lectures six mornings a week, practicals in the afternoon, essays to write. Perhaps I took it a bit seriously. I was bright enough to get there but not bright enough to swan through. It was quite hard graft, a bit of a treadmill. No organics, absolutely none. Barley beef was just coming in and all arable rotations with no stock, just coming in. Big tractors and the hedges were going. It was the prairies, the gung-ho stuff. This was the future.

And I remember we went out to a farm. An old-fashioned farm with a Polish chap looking after these cows. Lots of straw and the cows laid in an open yard, lots of straw, and they reared all the beef up to big stores and composted this dung and put it on the land and they grew wheat with a crawler and they had some pigs and it was in rotation. Good old-fashioned farming. And we went there and our exercise was to tell the bloke how to farm. And of course what we were supposed to do was tell him to get rid of the cows, do the beef indoors so that he finished it double quick time and pour artificial on the land to grow big crops in a continuous arable rotation. And I remember a big laugh because when we arrived on the bus we got off and I said: "Look at this. A real farm!" So I obviously had some understanding of what was going on in British agriculture. The other students all laughed. "There goes Will being unprogressive. Ha ha ha," and we did all the business, the linear programme to show that the boring system was going to be more profitable so that was what you had to do and I think I argued a bit against this monoculture, short-termism, but not a lot. I didn't know a lot. They should have been aware of soil erosion, it used to blow a bit on the Fens. They took the hedges away and it just blew and up on the Brecks the sandy stuff. No it was quite interesting.

I can't claim to have discovered organic farming and got my whole thing worked out, but I did develop a degree of scepticism. I remember my economics lecturer, he said: "Will, what are you off to do?" and I said, "well I'm going to farm at home, we have got 200-odd acres," which we did then. He said, "you know what you are going to have to do, you're going to have to specialise, and dairy is probably the best thing down there, and so you will have to have 200 cows." so I said, "yes Mr Wallace. Thank you," but I didn't believe it. My Mum died at the end of my first year and Father, really, it knocked him quite hard, he was getting towards 60, and he didn't want to farm it any more, so he said, "well if you want to farm this farm Will, just the minute you've got your degree, you come down and get stuck in," which I did.

And he sold his herd, laid off his dairyman and I came in with a clean slate really, and Fred retired with him. You kind of think you have to leave something for your kids as a going concern, for them to take on, but as a matter of fact there were no debts and he helped me. All I did was get some bulling heifers and put them to bull, and I took on what machinery he had left. He helped with the basics. I got going without too much debt, a little bit of borrowing but you didn't need a lot of capital in those days. There were people in those days who went farming as tenant farmers.

Came in with cows, sold the milk before they had the first cake bill and got rolling. It was a different world. There were no quotas, nothing to stop you, you just rang up the Milk Board, put it in churns and they came and took it away. So it was a good way to start. No refrigeration. We had the old water cooler then we stuck the churns down by the road and they stayed out in the sun till midday until the lorry came. And they had the sniffer at the factory. They used the milk up straight away and Bob's your uncle. Pick up once a day. It varied a bit and then you had to go down and pick all the empty churns back up. Spent most of the time filling churns up, because you fill up a 10-gallon churn pretty quickly. We had a little breast parlour with a pipeline. Yeah that was how we got going and I was incredibly lucky in as much as not only did I get involved with Pam but she agreed to come in with me from the word go. I was 21 and she was 19 and we had our farm. We bought some land. Our neighbour wanted to sell some land next door and we bought that with the enthusiasm of youth and making a few mistakes, we hit into it really. Very soon we had a family.

What I did was this. I increased the arable. I intensified using more of the old nitrogen, they would have been proud of me in Cambridge. Don't want to give myself too much credit. I was a little bit sceptical, I still operated a bit of a rotation. Having said that I can remember fields we had in arable for 10 years. Putting more and more stuff on, cows got mastitis and we gave them all this penicillin. And I mean you didn't even have to throw the milk away then. The vets just gave you all these things to whop into them and steroids if their foot swelled up.

Combining? We got the kit, got an old combine and assembled a few tractors. We did it, still got some of the kit now. Then in the '70s we went into the Common Market, prices doubled within the year. It was bonanza time and I was able to put in a herringbone parlour and put in a nearly new combine, put up some housing. I had had them lying out before then. It was quite extraordinary. It was boom time and the corn boys were really going mad and they were growing these new varieties that grew phenomenally, but they got all these diseases. They were aerial spraying fungicides, great blue clouds coming out of the sky, dropping aerial fertilising, nitram landing on people's gardens, burning all the straw and the smoke choking everybody. It was at this stage that Pam and I, but Pam to quite an extent, said, "hey this can't be right. This can't be how we are meant to farm." And so we started fiddling around with lucerne that fixes nitrogen and peas and we got some sheep for the golden hoof and she started studying homeopathy and all sorts of things were happening. We didn't really know at that stage about organic farming until we happened see a notice for a Soil Association meeting in Taunton and we were amazed to find there were all these other people who were organic farmers of our sort of age, youngish people.

Because about 1980, years tick by in farming, so anyway we decided we had better become properly organic. Lawrence Woodward came down from Elm Farm, helped us put up a conversion plan, to get the thing going. And so we put in these clover leys where we had this arable, and nothing happened in the spring. The clover grew and gradually with getting the muck in the right place and letting the soil breathe, gradually the fertility began to build. In those days it was all softly, softly approach and the advice was to convert a third of it first. And then move on and do another third and then another third. A long process, but by the time we had done the third, it all seemed to be the right thing to do, so we just did the rest as quickly as we could. It must have been 1983 that we officially started conversion and '86 when we were harvesting organic crops and in '88 we had organic milk. Which meant that the whole farm was organic so it did take five or six years of conversions.

Nowadays there is much more knowledge and it can be done much more quickly. Sheep certainly helped get these leys going, manure's the stuff, and when you got these leys not doing much, you could put the sheep on. Then take them off and let it recover a bit and gradually it would cover up with clover. We used Flexinet. When you see how those fields grow stuff now, you have to remember that literally they didn't grow anything without all these inputs. So it was sort of scary, you expect something off those fields and you don't get anything. Other things did quite well. The fields that hadn't been hammered with corn, more in grassland, they had quite good organic matter in them, natural fertility. So if you ploughed them and put a crop in something grew. And of course in time it improved so much those rye grass leys, you get a dry summer they just gave up. But these clover leys, you can't stop this clover growing. And I should have said in the early years in the mid '70s, we took on a lad when he left school as a sort of apprentice. Thought he would do a couple of years and move on and he kind of dug in. He was a local chap and by the time he was 18 or 19 he wanted to take over the milking from me which he did. His name is Phil Hansford and he's still here 30 years on. And when we got into conversion he was pleased because he loves birds. He's a good gardener he's a country boy, he understood it. He studied homeopathy and he's really absolutely brilliant at it. And uses it exclusively with the cows and has written a little book on how to treat cattle with homeopathy. Amazing really, so we learnt all that.

We were the only commercial organic dairy farm in Dorset for 10 years '88 till '98. One or two of the older chaps were very, very cross with me. People like David Foot and Bob Saunders who had grown up in the hard times when farming wasn't productive and wasn't making any money. They welcomed the intensification after the war and they could really grow crops. Things had got profitable and their memories, the old days weeding and hoeing. They thought I was letting the side down and were quite cross with me, though Bob Saunders, a year or two later, came round the farm and he was much more positive. There was no market for the milk, but a lot of the others of my age they watched over the hedge with a lot of interest and I thought they must think, "what a mess that place of Will's is compared to our tidy thing." But they do make quite encouraging remarks sometimes. We have always had a lot of farm walks. The neighbours don't need it, you can see it anyway. My neighbour here gets on top of his hill and gets his binoculars out. In a way we were the experimental farm for the whole of Dorset. And one of the nicest things that happens to you is that when you go on the farms of the people who came here, and some of them are quite distinguished organic farmers, and they came here when they were thinking about it perhaps 10 years younger than us and had a look round and thought, "well I reckon we can do this," and rang us up a bit, picked our brains. They are established. The leading people now. And that is kind of encouraging. We were lucky. We just weren't prepared to go along with all those chemicals and antibiotics. It was no way to farm.

Initially we just sold the milk to the Milk Board. But you have to remember the price of the milk was the same as it is now. In real terms it was about double. We could sell the corn, we could sell the wheat for good money for bread wheat. We could sell the straw for thatch which we started doing in '86. Still do that. Still do Maris Widgeon and a bit of triticale as well. And the lambs we sell privately. Half lambs for freezers. Cluns funnily enough. So people sought us out for the lamb because they couldn't get organic lamb otherwise. And we had a few pigs and did sausages and stuff, so all that was getting a premium. But the milk was going to the Milk Board. Then Unigate got in touch from Totnes and said we are doing a bit of organic milk into Plymouth and they sent a lorry up here every other day. But it didn't work. They didn't get their sales. When it went into Plymouth it bombed as they say. Totnes was all right. And a chap we were a bit friendly with up in Sussex established Busses farm yogurt. And so he said, "why don't you put in a yogurt plant down here?" But we didn't want to do that we weren't ready for that at that stage. So he said, "all right I'll collect the milk." So his little tanker came down from East Grinstead. But that didn't work too well, because he had a mixture of black and white and Channel Island milk up there for his yoghurt. And when he made it out of pure black and white because he didn't have an evaporator and it was too runny. But at the same time he got asked by Waitrose for liquid milk. So he said, "if you put in a pasteuriser and a carton machine, I'll draw it up for you and tell you what to get. I'll market the carton milk for you." So we did bite and decided to go for it. This was a couple of years later, by now, '91.

So we stuck all this in and by the middle of '92 we started churning out the first Manor Farm whole milk in little cartons. And off it went to Waitrose and to one or two shops in London and these guys up in Sussex did the marketing and distribution we just had to churn it out. But there were all sorts of dramas with their company, in the end they went bust. So we had to take on our own marketing, and that was quite an education. The first time we went to Waitrose to see the buyer, I was absolutely scared stiff. Absolutely no idea what to do. Somehow winged it. That was the thing. They didn't have many other places to turn to. The Percy Brothers, were doing their thing down at Honiton and they were doing Tesco's and another chap called John Jones in Wales was doing Safeway's and we were doing Waitrose. And then Sainsbury's came on and Percy brothers got that. They built quite a little empire down there and expanded and were quite forward thinking. But anyways the market grew in the '90s and we put a separator in and we started doing semi-skimmed and cream. And then we were buying in milk and basically grew out of our set up in the corner of the cow yard. We were doing about a 1,000 litres a day, so it wasn't big. But then we had to start buying in. Our yields weren't that good. So we were under 5,000 litres per cow, and I always like to keep a mixed system, grow our own cereals, not have to cram too many cows on. Mill and mix, we have the same mobile one we've had for 35 years. That solves the problem. It has changed hands a few times. Jim Farquarson runs it from Pimperne now, but it is basically the same thing. We use our own cereals and buy in a bit of protein. And then we had to buy in milk, which was very difficult because it didn't exist.

We slightly lost our way when we should have been expanding the business but we couldn't get the milk. Then suddenly all these people went into conversion and then there was loads of milk. The conversion was subsidised. And then there was suddenly loads of milk and we had lost our foothold in the market. Waitrose had had to go down to Honiton to get milk as we hadn't got enough and we got a little bit left behind. But it was still growing. We had started to do stuff in London and couldn't really cope here on our little set up and to cut a long story short we ended in the autumn of 2000 with Coombe Farm at Crewkerne doing the job for us. And since then we have doubled our sales in the five years, doubled our turnover by concentrating on the marketing and distribution. And with the farming we have got this partnership over at Toller with the Chaffey's, another 50 cows over there, that milk is going into it and also some Childhay Manor milk, Tim Frost's farm. Coombe Farm manages the organic dairy there and so we have some of that milk. So it is all Dorset Organic Milk.We know all the cows and the herdsmen. Fully traceable. Completely traceable. Tabs on everything and happy with the way the management happens. Coombe farm are very professional. Tanker picks up the three farms, tips into Coombe and then we go and collect. We do all the distribution, with vans charging around. All along the South Coast and up to Bristol and up to London.

So we have gone from this total dependence on Waitrose to I don't know how many customers. Ninety I suppose. Organic shops, farmshops, restaurants, pubs, people who go out and sell the cream at farmers' markets. We are on the green end of the customer spectrum, the people who know all the environmental issues and look at things basically in a similar way that we do. We get a lot of stuff about, "how do we rear the calves? How do we avoid upsetting the mothers when we take the calves off?" Lots and lots of stuff, email queries. The website certainly helps. We use biodegradable packaging and we do it because we are concerned. It strikes a bell with the customers and the brand works with them. A lot of running about, it's a fiddly little business. We do cream, full milk, semi-skimmed, skimmed, cream both in pots and catering sizes. And it's butter next. That's going to be the next project.

Organic corn? We have only got 11 acres of Widgeon this year. Sometimes it's up to 20 and we have got 20-something acres of triticale, and the rest is oats. We feed the triticale and the oats, we roll them and feed them. The wheat if we are lucky will go for milling. We have got an old reaper binder, we have got two both dating back to about the war, if not before. It goes well and then we get lads to stitch them up. We do 10: four each side and one on each end. We have always done that and when they are ripe we pitch them onto trailers, elevator and build a rick. We build the ricks in the corner of the field we are doing. Find a flat bit and then in the autumn and winter Dave Symonds comes with his thresher, he comes from Chideock. He's a thatcher. We pay him in bundles of reed and sometimes if he has got enough of his own we pay him in money. And thatchers come and collect it from here, and sometimes they are desperate for it, and sometimes they don't want to know. Bert Dibben used to come the first couple of years. He was amazing, he lived it. You are lucky to get £700 a tonne now. And if you look at the increased labour costs you ought to be on about a thousand, the problem is all this water reed that comes from Turkey by boat and they slap that on. We have got some who are proper wheat reed men and they do it properly. Pete Symonds, Dave's brother, John Butler over the hill, here at Buckland Newton and one or two others. Ian Hobday at Cattistock.

I try and keep the price fairly steady but harvests vary sometimes. There seems to be loads of wheat reed coming out of Devon and sometimes there doesn't seem to be any. And so unfortunately it goes up and down. Very often more down that up. We put tarpaulins on. The thresher comes late autumn, he comes twice. Do some, then go up to Sherborne. Do some then come back down again. Go back and do some of his own. The grain, Maris Widgeon is bread wheat, the problem is you get a bit of vermin in ricks and it is very hard to clean their droppings out and so unfortunately you can't sell it for human consumption, which is a shame as it would make lovely bread. Years ago we had quite a complicated arrangement when that nice chap was running Upwey water mill, lovely water mill, renting it from the Meechs, Norman Day he came up and collected the wheat. Bagged it up in West of England sacks and he put it up his sack hoist. He sold some of the flour and we had some of it back and it was dropped up at Leigh at Fudges and they baked this wholemeal bread for us and our daughter designed a wrapper and we dropped it round the shops. Manor Farm organic bread. But unfortunately the mill got into a bad state of repair and the owners wouldn't do anything about it and Norman had to give up. So we still would have the problem with Environmental Health saying, "sorry mate you can't have rat shit in the wheat. You can't sell this for human consumption." They must have done in the old days. Brown bread. That bread I had at prep school...

The future? Environmental scheme payments has got to be worth looking at because I can't see any point really in commodity farming. I can't see how anybody is going to make any money, because it is the globalisation thing. So if you are into the local, quality, added-value type food and combining that with going for the highest level of conservation environmental payments, that has to be the way forward for anybody in a relatively small scale. And of course it is hugely satisfying because you are actually doing something worthwhile. You're maintaining this beautiful bio-diverse landscape. An organic farm is a fantastic place to live. It is just humming with bird life. You are doing your bit for the carbon because you are growing your hedges and your trees and not using fertiliser. The manufacture and transport of artificial is a huge producer of greenhouse gases. The food is of high quality and its good for people. So you are half way there because you know what you are doing is worth doing. And then you have got to make the economics work. Single farm payment is a bit of a joke. The Government wants to hit biodiversity targets, they want to hit global warming targets and they want food to remain cheap. Quite honestly a lot of British farmers are going to be doing the biodiversity and the global warming targets and the cheap food will still come from I'd rather not ask where.

I don't think many of my friends in Cambridge are left in farming. They are consultants and one is an MP. I honestly don't think very many of them are still actually farming, which is rather ironic.

Emily and Mike Davies

13. Mike Davies: Cheesemaker, Woodbridge Farm, Stock Gaylard, Sturminster Newton Born 1939.

My son and I do the milking in the morning as we have always done for many years. Real hands-on. We are very self contained in all senses of the word, which leads to the great character of the cheese. The skim gets used primarily by Emily in her soups.

We're busy because it is Easter and the South West Food and Drink Fair in Exeter. Which is good, not knocking it. Just keeping pace at the moment. Got a little export order to America and Canada that has just crept up these last months, had it good for Thanksgiving before and then it was quiet. Now they have really come back on.

I was born in Walton on Thames 1939. I came to Dorset through my Father being in the Royal Navy and he was stationed at Yeovilton in Somerset and I was very lucky. I was starting my farming career when there was a farming ladder. Started at Farm College at Cannington which was renowned for its cheese making and dairy farming course. Then taking a herdsmen's job and seizing opportunities as I saw them and was able to have my own tenanted farm in the Blackmore Vale, which was just here at Woodbridge Farm. Nobody in my family was farming but with my Welsh connections there must have been farmers way back. I rented the farm from the Stock Estate off Colonel Yeatman. We still rent but we are making a good living off it thanks to the cheese and the soup, I might add.

The farm now is 650 acres. We run about 220 cows and nearly 200 followers and most of the work is still within the family. We have a chap who milks in the afternoon but my son and I do the milking in the morning as we have always done for many years. Real hands-on. Over 30 years we have bred the cows very carefully and that has been due to my son. We are totally enclosed, an enclosed herd, which is nice and he has brought in quite a lot of Holstein influence and we have quite a good yield per lactation. We keep the cows longer than a flying herd. I would hope that it was over five lactations. When we first started it was the good old British Friesian and now of course when the Holsteins came in they were referred to as hat racks being very tall and spindly and not a tremendous confirmation. But over the years with the American influence, Italian and French influence we have got quite a good looking animal producing a lot of milk. We are very self-contained in all senses of the word, which leads to the great character of the cheese.

Blue vinny was obviously made in Dorset for many, many years, hundreds of years ago, and the demise would have come with the Milk Marketing Board, when people were given a ready market for their milk. So they weren't going to bother about making fancy cheeses. Also with the last war the semi-hard and softer type cheeses were banned in any case by the Ministry of Agriculture. I would have thought one or two of the old cheese makers would have been asked to make some, but they must have made it secretly. It was banded around for quite a while, passing off as second grade stilton. To some extent it publicised it, because the fellow who was operating the scam kept it quite secret as to how he was doing it and this gave rise to people hunting for the blue vinny. So ironically the publicity worked.

We started nearly 25 years ago now, just in a very small way making it in the garage in very small moulds. Every Saturday morning we made 20 gallons into five, four-pound cheeses storing them in my wife's walk-in pantry and interest grew from day one. We went to the ministry and got the recipes which varied slightly. The one thing about blue vinny was, and still is, it was made from milk that was hand-skimmed, some of the fat had been taken off. We keep that to this day, we still hand skim. We are allowed to go up to 3% which is a low fat cheese.

A few problems, such as turnips to keep the milk up in the late spring. The cheese all collapsed because of the added oil in the cheese, and thrown in for good measure the smell of turnips and the taste of turnips, which we should have known about, I suppose. And then a little bit of aggro from the environmental health people who weren't terribly helpful in the early days and have become more helpful since.

Milk is taken from the morning's milking which is lower in fat because of the sheer volume, kept warm and brought down into the vat where it is left to settle for about two hours. The girls then proceed to take off the cream. We then add the rennet, which is vegetarian rennet from the local laboratory in Castle Cary. And then we put in our starter in powder form which is manufactured for us. Two or three drops of blue in 1,600 litres is all we require.

This is where the tales come of dragging mouldy harnesses through the milk and old farmers' boots round the outside, spiking with copper rods, storing on damp flagstones with hessian bags over them. Very, very few and far between they went blue. We keep our own residual culture going as it is rife in our ripening room at the moment. Skim the milk, add the rennet and starter. Then leave it for about two hours. Then cut by hand with the American knives. We get pieces about the size of walnuts and the girls have got the curds and whey. They stir the curds and whey and when they feel it dragging they know the acidity is building and they know that they must stop. All by touch and hand, then left overnight. In the morning the curds have obviously matted together. The whey is drained off and the curds are cut into blocks heaped each end of the vat and salted. Ground by machine then packed away by hand into the moulds. We have two sizes. We use a stainless steel rod. It stays in the cheese mould for about four days. The weather affects us, especially if the weather is thundery. It will affect the milk and being unpasteurised it will have an added effect. Very difficult to keep the conditions just right in the summertime when the cows are out to grass.

The maturing process takes from nine to 15 weeks. Short compared to a Cheddar. About the same time as stilton. We have a market right over the country. A lot of course going to London. We are very lucky because we have a summer trade. In the summer people want to have blue vinny and Dorset Knobs. A good summer trade along the coast line of southern England. The cheeses leave here as truckles. These pieces are being prepared here for the Exeter Food Festival which is this weekend. We have several wholesalers we deal with Hawkridge, Longmans, Coombe Farm.

We don't take all our milk, we only make about a third of our milk into cheese. And then the rest goes to Barbers of Ditcheat for cheese, the skim gets used primarily by my daughter Emily in her soups. Traditionally cream and butter would have been made from that. That was the main idea of thing. Blue vinny was made just up the road at Hill Street. It was made at Cook's Farm, Stalbridge. I think most dairy farms in Dorset made blue vinny at certain times of year. Vinny being an old English word for blue veining.

The future is a niche market and so we want to keep it that way and so we don't want to go berserk in expansion. Obviously with pressures on dairy farmers at the moment it is very tempting to expand but over the years we have just built it up steadily. On average about 18.5p per litre is what dairy farmers get. Making it from unpasteurised we had a few problems with the official but of course it is very silly, because the milk from cows now, with all the hygiene rules and regulations, milk is cleaner now than it has ever been. And I have drunk unpasteurised milk all my life.

The soup came about because my dear daughter Emily was going to take over the cheese business from me because I have gone past retirement age now and that was working well. Went to market and brought back some pieces and decided to make them into soup, not knowing what to do with them other than throwing them away. And that has really taken off.

Sweet maize silage and sweet grass silage keeps the milk sweet and makes a sweet cheese. That's why it is so much easier to make it in the winter than in the summer. The milk varies from each field. Varies with being in the Blackmore Vale with the various stratas, the clay, the stone brash and the mixtures of different grasses, and the way the cows eat the grass off that particular field. It does vary from one field to another. We are making about 30 tonnes a year. We employ myself and two girls and that's about it. My son and son-in-law are supposed to be helping me but I don't see very much of them! They are in the soup kitchen all the time, very conveniently…

Clive Sage and his new pedigree ram

14 Clive Sage: Shepherd and sheep shearer, Monkton Wyld Born 1964.

Farmers' markets: We are doing Taunton every Thursday, Poundbury once a month, Bridport we are doing second Saturday every month. Buy direct from the producer. Learn where your meat comes from, and make sure you get what you want.

I was born in 1964 in Axminster, four miles away from the farm. Eventually I got planning permission to build Wyld Meadow Farm, which was part of Father's land. New farm buildings and a dwelling. Just in Dorset, a 400-year-old boundary hedge just up here. A frontier zone, we need a passport to get over the road. Somerset is close by, so it is pretty much three counties and this gives us benefit, on the farmers' markets side. We have a lovely view of Charmouth down the valley. This is pretty much the head of the River Char, the springs start pretty well below us, and straight down to Charmouth.

Father was born on the Mendips, right on top and when Mother and himself got married, they decided to come down here and started a little dairy farm. His father was a farmer and he helped him out with a few cows. They started with a 60 acre farm and rented that for a good few years and then they had the chance to rent Higher Pound Farm and then took on Ridge and Lower Pound Farm.

After Bicton Agricultural College, I had a year and half travelling and eight months in New Zealand where I learnt to shear sheep. Part of that was milking on two dairy herds, one was 560 cows and the other was 650. I saw that as a bit of a factory line, and decided that that wasn't for me. When I came back from travelling I managed to farm sheep. I also went off to do some contract lambings for David James at Sixpenny Handley. I used to go up there and do a shearing round. Ewes and lambs, the most we ever did was 20,000 across Dorset. And that was myself and two Kiwis with Alan Derryman, the God of shearers, 20,000 the most we ever did, I did that for several years, and then I had two Kiwi brothers, probably some of the best shearers I could find that were over here, and went on shearing for David Fagan, a world class shearer. I was away from the farm so much… I was leaving at six in the morning and I wouldn't come home till nine or ten o'clock at night. So I decided to concentrate on my own farming and started my direct selling. I took on rented land wherever I could in the Lyme Regis area, lots of little horsey paddocks and bought some Dorsets off Father, and went up to Wales and bought some ewes up there, Welsh mules. But the Dorsets, I have increased those, and ever since then I have stayed in a closed flock, for disease reasons. It was quite a big decision. Father wouldn't let me rent any of his land, but he was prepared to lend me equipment to use on the sheep, with handling facilities.

I was running a flying flock and took on whatever paddocks I could, all round the Lyme Regis area, four or five acres here, there and everywhere, and I spent a lot of time running around. It was nothing for me to be seen running my sheep through the centre of Lyme Regis with my sheepdogs. There was the odd occasion when my sheep went walkabout into people's gardens. I remember one occasion when it was like the Grand National, they went up into a cul-de-sac. And I was too embarrassed to go up there so I sent my dogs up there, and all I could see was these sheep jumping over these privet hedges all the way down through and on a Sunday. All these people came out with their gin and tonics and sherry, and stood out in the front of their houses, laughing and giggling, as the sheep jumped over their hedges. I was expecting them to shout at me, but they were very polite. Light entertainment, never seen sheep run up their cul-de-sac before. They are probably my customers now.

Then there was Wyld Monk Sheep Services, did that for five or six years. A good name for people to remember. Something a little bit different. Then I took on bigger blocks of rented land, gradually built the flock up and when I took on the rented farm I dropped the contract flock management and kept the shearing. We did the shearing for several years, then dropped the shearing and concentrated on the marketing the lamb. It was a case of having to diversify. Father gave me the opportunity to take on this land in 2000 and I had the planning officer out here and he said, "it is an Area of Outstanding Beauty." And I pointed out to him that the reason it was an area of outstanding beauty was because past generations had looked after it so well. And he said: "Quite right. Quite right, Mr Sage." So I went round and saw the neighbours, and I didn't get one objection and had the full support from the local parish council.

We went to visit our first farmers' market in Poundbury in Dorchester. It had just started and there was no one selling lamb there and we asked the organisers could we bring along our lamb? And they said fill out the criteria form, and before we knew it we were trading there and at Bridport. That was the first two markets.

Our flock? We are up to 600 breeding ewes and we've stayed fairly consistent there, I've always had a few suckler cows Angus and Devon cross and I've played around a bit with those and up until last year I always used to sell off store cattle. A year and half ago I put in my own cutting facilities here on the farm, because we spent a lot of time running around, using external butchers. They were telling us when we had to have it cut and how we were to have it cut, and our customers had certain requests and I couldn't fulfil their orders. So I thought let's bite the bullet and put in our own processing facilities. This was the next step on and we were doing a little bit of mail order but we were up to 20 lambs a week. And we were stretching the external butchers we were using. They were pleased to have the work from us, but there again, they weren't terribly obliging, their own work came first, which you can understand, so I paddled my own canoe and built my own facilities.

Having this at my own back door is brilliant. I have customers that come here on a Tuesday and a Friday every week. We can supply hotels, restaurants and send out mail orders. And we help other local producers out by buying their products.

Farmers' markets? We are doing Taunton every Thursday, Poundbury once a month, Bridport we are doing second Saturday every month. That is the market that I help run, as Director of Dorset Farmers' Markets. It is a market that is building. And the demand is there for local produce, food miles and all the rest of it. We are selling something in the region of 90% of all the lambs we produce locally. So with regard to food miles that is very good. And really when you look at sustainable farming, Defra use me as an example of one of their best farmers who has diversified, in that I am creating work for local people. One chap full-time for me, a butcher part-time and two packers that come in part-time. We don't compare ourselves with supermarkets or butchers, we just work on quality rather than quantity. We want 100% satisfaction from our customers. Trying to get lambs there every week of the year at a certain weight, at a certain grade. We have to do three lambings to supply the market, all the year round. With a Dorset, it is unique in that it has this breeding quality to lamb at any time. We have been quite fortunate and over the last three years we have won a gold medal in the Taste of the West Food awards, that's something we are very proud of. Marks for packaging, taste, aroma, texture.

The Ram? Every year I try and go to the Dorset May Fair, something that has been going for many generations. The

Dorset is one of the oldest breeds of sheep to this country, it is unique to Dorset and it can breed out of season. So I always try and buy one or two pedigree Dorsets just for new bloodlines coming in. Some years I buy ram lambs, some years I buy shearlings. This year I was well-chuffed with the boy I ended up with. A poll Dorset from last year's champion ram from the Trevilley Flock at Delabole in Cornwall that made £2,500. They have brought some new bloodlines in from Australia, a bigger, leaner, meaner carcass. I paid 560 guineas. I bought the reserve champion Texel at the Exeter a couple of years ago and unfortunately he was killed by the other rams last year. I always buy in.

Venison? I have got a game licence, and sell a little bit of roe deer from the farm. I have stalkers who come in. There's 500 acres of forestry right beside us and that mainly goes to hotels and restaurants. We buy in bronze turkeys from a local chap at Combe St Nicholas near Chard just four or five miles away. And then we get geese from Mr Dunning at Gooselade Farm, East Coker. It all works out. And then we get top quality free range chickens from the Ark Chicken Company. If I could sell everything direct from the farm it would be marvellous. Farmers' markets are here to stay and the great thing about it is the support from the local community in that we are regenerating towns, and it is almost going back a generation. Here in the village there used to be a butcher and he used to take his stall down to Lyme Regis and I just feel that I have just taken over where he left off. People, with all the food scares, want to know more about where their food comes from. All the time the labelling is getting stricter and stricter. All this is playing into our hands in that the more publicity we get about buying quality products and buying it direct from the producer, and traceability with accredited markets and promotions from people like Hugh Fearnley-Whittingstall, the better it is. Buy direct from the producer. Learn where your meat comes from, and make sure you get what you want. And if you are not happy tell them so, and you can have that feedback with buying it direct whereas if you go to a supermarket chain you haven't got a clue where it comes from.

More and more people are using our name on their menus. It is a knock-on effect. For instance we supply a chef who won restaurant of the year in the South West last year. He promotes our lamb, Ian Simpson from the White House in Charmouth. We also supply the Victoria Hotel in Lyme and the Chideock Hotel, who have won gold and silver awards this year.

The beef we hang for three weeks and the lamb is hung for a week to 10 days and we do a certain amount of mutton as well.

Ron Woodrow and Simon Berry, Beaminster

15 Simon Berry and Ron Woodrow: Butchers, Beaminster
Simon born 1971. Ron born 1940.

I moved in August three years ago. So I had to go to see my bank manager rather swiftly and take the plunge… Ron knows what he is doing.

Simon: I was born in Portsmouth in 1971 and came to Dorset when I was seven, to Netherbury. My Father was working for a sheet metalwork company in Bridport. In Netherbury then there was a pub and a post office.

I went to school in Beaminster and I started butchery in Bridport in Rawles. I had a Saturday job after school. I did pet mince and horrible little jobs behind the scenes. Dog's body job then. You don't see much tripe these days. People used to eat it. Not a lot of people ask for it any more.

My Grandfather was in the army and used to collect fossils, and that was why he came down here. He used to polish them up and sell them. Mum's parents used to live on a farm at Symondsbury, but Dad's parents came from Portsmouth. At the age of 16 I left school, was a few months in Rawles and then moved to Frampton's, here in Beaminster. That was 1986. Then I was learning everything. Started on a YTS. Pay not very much but it did go a long way then. I had a motorbike.

I have only been here across the Square for two and a half years. Cutting up is all right. You start with pet mince and then you start to bone things out, learning how to handle a knife so you don't cut yourself. Learn on different bits and pieces until you can handle a knife. In those days we hung meat for a couple of weeks. We did buy a certain amount of local and then went over to Scottish beef. Not much mutton, pork was local, lambs were all local.

Game when I started. You'd have had to draw it all yourself and pluck it. We'd get through a side of beef a week. Normally we tend to rely on local abattoirs, Norman's in Bridport or Snell's in Chardstock. People are looking for more local meat, less fat. Sell quite a few sausages. Make them all ourselves, do a few different types, beefburgers or pork and apple.

I moved-in August three years ago. Frampton's was being sold and this shop came up within two hours. A butcher's called Hymas and Hymas, and so I had to go to see my bank manager rather swiftly and take the plunge. Big step to take. You don't know until you try it. Seems to be working out well. People like to know more about the meat, where it has come from, how it was slaughtered. Frampton's used to have a slaughterhouse years ago.

Ron knows what he is doing. Bones, we have to pay to have them taken away to be incinerated. Offal get through quite a lot liver, lamb's kidneys go well. Next door is a deli. I am 34 and the future's looking good, touch wood.

Ron: My name is Ronald George Woodrow and I was born in Curry Rivel in December 1940. Father started off in a greengrocer's shop, then he became a baker, then he became a butcher and Mum was a domestic worker down at Stoke St Gregory. Grandad Woodrow was a plumber and he had an accident when he was very young man and when my father started working he was the only bread winner. He provided for the family.

My Mum's dad he was an interesting chap he was called Ishmael Jeanes and died of tuberculosis because they were brought up on Sedgemoor. The damp. They lived down at Stathe, a little village just the other side of Curry Rivel and he worked for the Great Western Railway and he had withy beds because the willows grow on Sedgemoor. My mother when she came home from school walked three miles from school and then had to strip withies at a brake.

Father used to say, "come on girls there's a wad of withies waiting for you." And they did that after walking three miles from school. Hard work and then during the winter months Sedgemoor would flood and they would move all their furniture upstairs and weren't able to go to school because they couldn't get out. Every year it would flood. They didn't have the resources to pump it out like they have today. It's different altogether now. They move water from one moor to another and pump it out bit by bit.

My father and my brother and myself were in partnership in the butcher's business in Curry Rivel. I left school when I was 15 and came into work in the shop. Before that I was cycling five miles home from school then making sausages doing all the odd jobs, to build the business up. The business was sold in 1981. Father had a serious accident with two cattle and mother died when she was 54 which was rather tragic, but we were married in the village and we had our family. It was 1981 when my father retired. But we had already moved to Yeovil in 1976 we were involved with part of the church which was happening there.

Then I went to work for Graham and Stuart Loder in Union Street in Yeovil, and this was in 1981. Had a week in Madeira before starting the new job. I enjoyed that work but it was completely different, town shops to village shops. Speeded up a lot more. We were country and we worked a lot of hours not 8am-5.30 pm as in the towns, more like seven to nine o'clock at night sometimes. Five, six days a week used to have one half day off a week, but then that speeded up when we went to work for Graham Loder as their business was expanding. The trade was colossal and when I look back now I wonder how I ever coped with it. It was amazing the volume of meat going through. They did six carcasses of beef a week, 10 or 12 pigs and 15-20 sheep a week. And that was going through one shop. My job was serving in the shop and they employed four people down the back on one side and a deli side on the opposite side where Stuart was employed and two part-time ladies to serve. I stayed with them about seven years and left in about 1987-88 and went to Parson's in Cheap Street in Sherborne. I was with them 13 and a half years and they had a slaughterhouse that I was involved in. I used to do part time slaughtering and they would employ me the rest of the week in the shop. I saw the carcass right through, we did that at Curry Rivel as well. We knew all the farmers round the village. We used to get the beef from a farmer at Buckland Newton for Sherborne. We bought direct from the farm. They started off buying from the market but that gradually dwindled down, the cattle market in Sherborne, we used to go in and buy sheep on Mondays have them back and I would kill them, 25-30 sheep that was my Monday morning job and then they found it was easier to buy them direct from the farm. We had sheep from Coram's in Leigh and beef came from John Hiscock. These were Texel cross the sheep and Hereford cross Friesian. I went 13 and a half years for Parson's, then an advert came up for this butcher's in Beaminster, which was owned by Stephen Froy, this was Frampton's. But he wasn't a butcher he was a chartered surveyor. He took the business on in 1994 and it was making money, so he kept it going and then I met up with Simon in October 2000. Simon was already working there and we got on well together. Simon knew the run of the shop, a bright lad; I got on well working with him. I was there two and a half years, then Stephen Froy sold the business off. Simon had a few hours to decide whether he took over the other butcher's shop Hymas and Hymas. I worked till March the following year and I have been with Simon ever since. So I have been 18 years working in Dorset as a butcher.

I also took on part time work at a farm shop a place called Pitney. Which is out near Langport, Walrond's. All his own meat. I helped them out for three years. It was on my day off. I had Wednesdays off. In Beaminster at Simon's the meat comes from Snell's at South Chard. They are excellent. They are a small local abattoir, nice people to deal with. They would buy direct from farms. Starting from the slaughtering side of it, it is a bit of a messy job, you use a saw to cut the animal in half, and with BSE you have to take the spinal cord out and you have special knives and then we let that settle overnight then the following morning split that in half again, so you have two forequarters and two hindquarters. And we would take that from the slaughterhouse down into the refrigerator and that would hang till the following week. A week to a fortnight is long enough three weeks is too long, because you waste stuff through hanging too long. The idea of hanging it is good. It increases flavour but bigger abattoirs go through the processing very quickly and you don't know how long it has been hung.

The slaughtering side of it is very hard work physically, a messy job, horrible but I enjoyed it. I enjoyed seeing the end product, from being alive and then killed then sold through the shop. I used to like telling people in Simon's shop exactly where it came from. That is the essence of good quality meat. And the pork came from Darvill's farm at Toller Whelme and that was very good pork. Lambs came through from Snell's.

I think as a butcher personality comes into it quite a bit your customer becomes a friend. That helps to know people, what cuts they like, used to put back orders for certain people. Myself I like a nice piece of rib on the bone for beef and rolled shoulder of lamb and anything in pork. I think the best sheep you can get around this area is Dorset Down and Dorset Horn but the only problem is that they do produce fat very quickly, so within three or four months you have got a lamb that is fit for slaughter. There was a farmer, Peter Mead from West Coker, he had a Dorset Down pedigree breed and his son is continuing it. High-class pedigree. In Curry Rivel a chap called Anthony Lang produced Dorset Down as well. These are good breeds. Beef was red Devon cross or Angus cross Friesian would produce a good beef animal. A side of beef could easily weigh 300lb: 130lb for the forequarter and 170lb for the hindquarter. The easiest thing is when the guy comes from Snell's and you got them hanging up in the lorry you can get your shoulder into them, if you got them hanging up you can easily deal with it, same with the pig, same with sheep.

Secret of butchery is sharp knives and cleavers. I used to pick up knives that Simon would discard and sharpen them up. If you got an old whetstone with water, that is one of the best things to do. You had a hand one. The electric ones are high tempered and take a lot of the tension out of the knife. So you don't use them very much, I use oilstone as well. The secret is to steel it, learn how to get a steel going, and then you are all right. And then occasionally put them on an oilstone or a whetstone. I had knives when I started working in Parson's they gave me a new set and I have still got them they are made by a Swiss firm. You need a boning knife for boning out a large knife for cutting steak and joints and then a cleaver and a meat saw.

Wooden blocks are still used, they used to use boxwood that doesn't splinter. They are expensive, very nearly £900. Each block is set so that they fit together. Some butchers still use sawdust, it is still legal to use it, it absorbs the grease on the floor. Sawdust is still used and for cleaning boiling water and soda.

I enjoyed working in Beaminster, the people were very good. Didn't take you long to know people. We used to say, "meat to please you, pleased to meet you." Lot of people come down have second homes, more busy at the weekends, and some bought quite a bit of meat to take back to London.

You got to have a sense of humour being a butcher. One lady said, "how many kidneys have you got?" "Two," I said, "like you." That brought a smile to her face. Another time in Curry Rivel one lady said, "I will have a sheep's head but leave the feet on." Used to sell sheep's head and trotters, a lot more offal. In Parson's we had 15 different types of sausage and they sold ever-so well. A bacon and leek and garlic sausage used all the scraps of bacon in it. Same with faggots. We did dog food in the tubes.

Meat is not that expensive really, other things have gone sky high. It is a lot of work in preparation. That animal has to be brought up two and half years old then sent to the abattoir. The over 30-month rule has just been released. Going back to Curry Rivel we would have cattle that were four or five years old some of them. They had been down on the moor and left down there for about two years and then the fatstock markets, Langport, Ilminster and Yeovil every Christmas but all that has gone. It is a shame they have taken the markets out of the towns which is not good.

A pleasant run into Beaminster every day 15 miles from where I live, you could go across Halstock and Corscombe, a lovely ride at this time of the year. Any time of year. It is beautiful really. I like Beaminster I was thinking of moving, that was on the cards. I might finish up there I don't know. Lovely place.

Sadly Ron had a bad car accident in the summer of 2005. He is still in hospital as this book goes to print.

16 Peter Cariss: Beekeeper, Shipton Gorge
Born 1940.

I think it is fascinating the way that a nectar source is conveyed by the waggle dance to the rest of the bees. I was absolutely hooked, I really was. The trouble was I didn't go to a beginner's course till I had got 35 hives.

I used to have 15 cows, but I have never been a dairyman. I went to an auction that I was assisting on and came out with a cow and she gave seven gallons a day and I hand milked her, but not for too long. It was terrible really. Every possible container was full of milk. And I ended up buying four calves and putting one on each quarter. Tea?

We can't be truly organic. Bees fly too far. The nearest I get is, I sell a lot of our honey through Modbury Farm. Tim and Julie Garry, their Jersey herd is organic so I can say honey produced on Modbury Organic farm and neighbouring farms.

I was born in Birmingham, 1940, so I am a townie but I was evacuated within 10 months and I was brought up in the country. Shropshire, I lived in Shropshire, I moved back into Birmingham. When I got married I moved into Gloucestershire and I farmed 250 sheep. Then I went up to Tenbury Wells where I had 15 cows. My father was an auctioneer. I think most town people have got some country ancestry but the town and the country have become terribly separated. Different sets of values. I tell you what is interesting, the selflessness of the beekeepers. I fell over a stile with a beehive in the middle of the night and they were furious with me that I hadn't asked for some help. And yet in the city everybody seems to out do the next person.

Sheep was the first: Chipping Campden. I started with Billy, Twinkle and Tuppence, three bottle-fed lambs. In the end I was taking an awful lot of sheep on to sprout fields when people had finished picking sprouts and I was fencing them at weekends. But that wasn't my job, that was my hobby. I was an auctioneer for 40 years, from 1957. Residential property, investment property, chattels, furniture and antiques. I once sold a collection of Royal Worcester porcelain in about 300 odd lots, and that was in the '70s.

I came to Dorset 18 years ago. My in-laws lived in the village of Shipton. I commuted for a while and the family were here. I had 11 offices straight through the Midlands. Eventually it all went pear-shaped. I didn't start the bees, it was my son, James, he was at Colfox. And he had chickens and then he had ducks and then he had bees. He had a hive of bees and then he went of to university and so I had to help and he decided to become a post graduate and is now doctor of biochemistry. I was left with the bees. I was stung… I had them in the garden.

The extraordinary thing was, there was a Mrs Dommett, Lorna Dommett, she still has the launderette in Bridport. She had a little honey shop, South Street, just behind the launderette. She sold honey and she sold beehives and that is where James got his interest. I went there to get some bits and pieces and she asked me if I would join the local beekeepers' association, four or five years ago. But I wasn't very interested in bees. I had seen bees at clients' houses. Never took any real notice of them. But I went to a meeting of the West Dorset Beekeepers' Association. They have got hives at Parnham and Ken Bishop who is a real Dorset man, he is the county chairman, he said there is a swarm somewhere here about. And there it was hanging on a tree and he popped it into a little nucleus box. And then I saw the bees fanning to call their friends in. They send out a scent, quite fantastic. I was absolutely hooked. I really was. I thought they were fascinating and lo and behold down the garden I had a swarm about a month after that. Eight days later. I know now why, I had two little casts, so instead of having one beehive, I had four and of course you get curious as to how it is all working and they are absolutely fascinating. They were about long before we were and I think one of the most amazing things is that if they want a queen, they can make a queen and a queen bee is just like any other bee, except that it is just fed differently. They make a big fuss of it. Then when they have capped it over and fed it well with royal jelly, the rest of the bees scarpered off. And they go into a little swarm, not far from the hive. Sometimes lasts an hour, sometimes lasts a week. There was one the other day at Berwick Farm and I thought I'll go and have a quick lunch and come back. Not a sign of them when I got back. It is extraordinary how they do it. But if they didn't do it that the way, and they had a forest fire, the bees would be lost. So they have their own way of spreading about and mine are better at it than most.

I started with my son's hive. Then I split it up and got four. Then I was told you can only move a beehive three feet or three miles. If you moved it six feet they would just go back and perish where they had just been. So I knew Bernard Fry at Little Bredy and I took two hives over there, far enough. Then I got honey to sell, I knew Tim Garry. He has got the farm shop so we had some bee hives at Modbury Farm. Then just up the lane at Berwick Farm, then farmed by Keith Rixon, who found James some hives and equipment and shared his knowledge. Berwick Farm was bought by James Wyld at Puncknowle Manor and he said, "why not have one in my garden?" So I have got them at Puncknowle Manor. Then I had them at Chilcombe House by invitation of John Hubbard, and with Mike Fowler at Hammiton. And then after that we couldn't keep them in the garden, as my wife and daughter got stung and the dogs got stung. So I moved them out of the garden to Icen Farm which is up the hill here. I haven't got any beehives at all at Higher Sturthill except the ones I make. And then my mother died and I inherited an orchard in Melplash and I took beehives there and to Mapperton House. Lady Sandwich was keen to have some beehives. I only went to Mapperton House and Melplash Court because it came out in a circular from the beekeepers' association. Then in this last year by invitation of Rupert Best, I have now got 18 hives at Hincknowle.

Orchards aren't particularly good for beekeepers, the nectar is distinctive, but not particularly rich, but apples depend upon insects to pollinate. I don't think the townies in London appreciate how valuable the beekeeping industry is, they say it earns several million for the economy. But they are cutting back on the bee health programme and they are cutting back on bee inspectors. Under EEC regulations, the chemicals we use have to be bought through vets. It is amusing to think, "will the vets come and look at the bees?" Although I have a good vet and he keeps bees, I don't think many vets want to go into beehives.

Ian Homer in Litton Cheney is the Ministry Bee Inspector and his wife runs beginner courses for beekeepers. Very nice and generous. I think it cost me £10 for a series of eight or nine evenings and with slides and demonstrations and all sorts of things. The trouble was I didn't go to a beginner's course till I had got 35 hives. The saving to Defra is about £250,000 but the cost to the country would be vastly more. That is my political slot.

My orchard has got trees in a sequence. Two rows of Dabinett, I then have a row of Chisel Jersey, then have a row of Michelin, then two rows of Dabinett then a row of Browns then a row of Yarlington Mill. All for the pollination. Behind where George Wright photographed the hive I thought it was a little crab apple tree, but it isn't, it is a pollinator for Rupert Best's trees. Christopher Vye planted and it is very well organised. I personally think that bumble bees with a nice warm furry jackets do as much pollination as honey bees do. But honey bees are an insurance.

Peter Cariss in Rupert Best's orchards, Hincknowle, near Melplash

Bees tend to take a little time to settle to a particular location and I found that at Mapperton House where you have got lime trees they settle down very much better in their second year and good true country folk knew this, that they do better in their second year. They know their way round better. I think it is fascinating the way that a nectar source is conveyed by the waggle dance to the rest of the bees.

The other thing that is fascinating is when bees swarm. That swarm that you fail to catch, that swarm will have moved off when scout bees will have come back and found a nice little home such as they did at Chilcombe. John Hubbard's house is four storey, it needed a 42-foot ladder to terminate some bees which had got in underneath his Cotswold slates which I admitted might have been my bees. They needn't necessarily have been. Very rarely do they set up home within two miles of where they were or they defeat the object of what they are trying to achieve. So they might have been somebody else's bees, but I doubt if they were.

Distinctive flavour is important in honey. We have beekeepers who want apple blossom honey and get very upset when somebody grows some oilseed rape which distracts the bees from their job when they are trying to make the pure honey. Lime honey is distinctive but I haven't had enough experience and tend to mix the honey. This is the first year with 50 hives so some of them might not produce much at all. I ought to get 20lbs of honey per hive on average. But there are recorded instances of people getting a hundredweight off one hive. Which in my case would be very useful.

A hive consists of a brood box of 11 frames and a dummy board in which there is the queen, the workers and the brood in cells. And that is the private department of the bees. Private in that you don't want to take much out of there. Occasionally you want to take a frame out of there for another hive but you don't take any stores of theirs. Above that you have a queen excluder to stop the queen laying in the combs above, and you have 11 combs above which are shallower frames. The reason that they are shallower frames is that when you actually have that box full of honey you have enough to carry. You are able to put a second or a third super over there. A lot of beekeepers, me included, over the year let the bees have a brood and half, so they have one super privately for themselves which they fill with brood. Occasionally the queen comes through the queen excluder and spoils your honey by laying in the other boxes. That is the general principle upon which we work except for the fact that last year, knowing I was going into the orchard at Hincknowle, I had some queens flown in from Greece, an island 17 miles off the coast. So you get a pure-bred bee and go to Mr Bickerstaff in Liverpool and he puts it in the Royal Mail and posts it down to me. I use those queens to set up those nucleuses, like that little box there. But the bee inspector thought I would do better with local bees than bees used to the Greek sunshine. I make sure all the time that the bees have plenty of food for themselves. They consume a lot more honey than we take. We only take their surplus. I am not sure what the percentage is. Some produce a large surplus and others produce very little surplus at all.

You have to avoid bees robbing other hives. When it comes to the autumn I need to feed my bees to make sure they have enough to last them through to the spring. The difference between a honey bee and a bumble bee or any of the solitary bees or a wasps is that honey bees stay awake in the winter as a colony. Although they maybe confined to the hive, they need to be fed which is why they store so much. Whereas solitary bees only the queen survives the winter and this is why there is a good force of honey bees for pollination in the spring. But is an extraordinary thing that they know to gather as much nectar as they can to turn it into honey. One of the clever things that bees do is they concentrate their nectar to such a point that it isn't going to go mouldy. Then they cap it with wax so that you end up by having a very long lasting product. I am told it takes six pounds of honey to make one pound of wax so it is obviously very important.

Propolis is simply a sealing compound which bees get from the sap of trees which they use to seal all the little gaps that might mean that they have a damp winter or the earwigs get in. Bees vary. Some produce an awful lot of propolis and makes it very difficult to manipulate the frames. They really do stick everything down. I am amazed at just how much they can produce. But they gather propolis rather than the wax which they make. There are beekeepers who make more money out of their wax than they do out of their honey. Beekeepers want wax for their foundation, because we give the bees a printed sheet of wax with the size. You can get it printed with the size of the worker bee cell, which is traditionally what most beekeepers buy. But you can also get it printed the size of a drone cell, males, and you can therefore encourage the breeding of drones. I haven't told you how drones come about. Workers are the product of an egg which is fertilised, but the queen has the unique ability to lay in a larger cell, an unfertilised egg. She can control the spermatozoa and lay an unfertilised egg and turns out a male. We had, in recent years a nasty problem of varroa mites and we treat varroa mites with Bayvarol or Apistan. But such is nature that they are becoming resistant. There is a preference for varroa to go into drone cells, because drones take a little longer to hatch. The shortest time is the queen at hatching. Drones take longer than a worker to hatch and so you can produce drone broods as a means of entrapping varroa and then you destroy it. Quite clever.

I sometimes put a shallow frame into a brood box for the sole purpose of getting the bees to build brace comb in the space, which is often for drone brood, and you can then break it off. The males don't count for an awful lot in a bee community. In fact the bees decide in September that they are not going to let the boys back in and you see horrible tussles on the flight board. They refuse the men entry and they spend the winter as one queen and the infertile workers. We say infertile workers, yet when it comes to an emergency, when there is no queen and no queen cell there, possibly because the beekeeper in a clumsy moment squashed his queen, then the workers will start laying.

Well it has developed over millions of years. I think I am right in saying that they have found in fossilised amber, trapped remains going back ten million years and so it was a long time ago they developed their special systems. But the extraordinary thing is the way in which the queen decides things. The queen measures with her forelegs the size of a cell that her workers have made and they must be thinking they want me to lay unfertilised egg in this one. So it is a true community that is working not individuals. It is very clever. To quote Ken Bishop his famous words are: "Bees follow a pattern but they don't do anything invariably." And you can get caught out. But they follow a pattern, they have logic. One of the most amazing things on their foraging, they will go along the hedge that way then follow it at right angles that way but when they want to go home they will go as the crow flies. We are told that they are orienteering from the sun but they must allow for the movement of the sun and the time of day. But then we can only move a bee hive three feet or three miles. If you took that bee hive 3 miles away and a week later put it 20 feet away from where it was the bees would have forgotten their flight lines and be quite happy. So they don't have a very long memory.

The thing that worries me is that most of the beekeepers who I know, who have been so very, very helpful only keep two or three hives. Bee farmers on the other hand tend to have 500 hives plus. There are bee farmers in France and particularly in the States and in Australia who run 3,000 hives. I am not sure of the economics to be honest. I have economised. I had to work very hard when I found those swarms in the garden. I went to Bradfords got some broken pallet and made hives. Low-cost housing. The trouble with pallet wood as I now know is that everything is so heavy. The Western Gazette had some hives advertised the other day, £250. They were made of cedar wood, lightweight, functional. Mine are more upmarket decorative and sturdy but heavy. I like to have a sloping roof. I think they look nicer. I like them to look smart. Woodland green is my colour this year.

In a hive? Fifty thousand. A very strong hive will have 75,000. Many of my bees have been swarms that I have caught. The association lets you know or you let them know if you are interested in swarms. I once spent five hours up a chimney in Powerstock getting a swarm which was very foolish waste of my time really. The trouble with swarms is that they have that swarming tendency and if you are not very careful they are off again, like tearaway kids.

The thing that can spoil it all is the bad tempered hives. Which is why people would like to breed friendly, easy to handle bees. But then you might have other problems. There is a retired solicitor Mr Lyall: “It is only the bees that sting that produce a lot of honey.” They can be absolute shockers, I have had them. I haven’t been able to get out of the veil up to half a mile away from the hive and they have followed me in the Land Rover. Some at Burton Bradstock seem very charming, and I hope they stay that way. Although you have got protective clothing they will find a way through. I have had them come up the blouse and I have had 50 stings on one occasion. You carry an Epivax, self-injection is as bad as a bee sting. I carry Piriton tablets, because I had some bees underneath electric pylons and we think it was because of the pylons that they were very bad tempered. Not so bad tempered now that I have moved them. All the characteristic comes from the queen and they may well have superseded the queen and got different characteristics. But I had a dreadful time, I was putting together nucleuses, which means in order to make it work and introduce a new queen, you get a frame and brood from three different hives. You can imagine you have got to open three hives and put them together pretty quickly and put an air freshener on them to get them thoroughly confused and then slip in a new queen in a little container. Then she eats her way through the candy and joins them. But she has slave bees with her and they try to protect her. Anyway I was doing this and the one hive went for me and I was stung some 50 times. I knew I couldn’t have driven the Land Rover. I was in quite a state. Luckily it just passed. I started to walk for help and fortunately it was quite a long walk and I got half way there. All the fuzziness disappeared and then I had to go back to the Land Rover and they were looking for me. They are not stupid. Got to admire them, everyone that stings dies. The ultimate suicide bomber. They are incredible in their support for the unit.

The swarms are wonderful to handle because they haven’t got a hive to protect. I haven’t done it, but you could catch a swarm without a veil. They are the easiest things to handle and they are absolutely delightful they are very exciting. I love swarms. The only way that you get trouble is that when you shake it off the branch and you get one stuck down the neck. We use smoke. The smoke is as if there was a forest fire. They think they are going to have to evacuate and so they fill their tummies with honey before evacuating. I am told that where hives have burnt they have found the bees inside the hive, so they haven’t actually gone. But their natural instinct is to fuel up, pack a lunch and it calms them down which is why you can handle them when you smoke them. Some bees don’t even need smoking. Other bees the smoke seems to aggravate them very greatly.

One of the problems with the honey is that if you are out there collecting off the boxes, you are not extracting the honey. You need a very good wife. The honey comes in on a frame, hopefully capped both sides and by judicious spacing nice and fat. Preferably without any grains of pollen in it and you use a capping knife. I have got an electric knife that slices the wax off. You then put it into an extractor and by centrifugal force you spin the honey out. Because we only have a small four-frame extractor which is a tangential extractor, you have to do one side and then the other side. You have to start it slowly otherwise you will break up the comb. Do one side slowly, then the other side slowly, one side fast then the other side fast. Otherwise you find that the whole thing can start to break up. Our frames are wired. The honey collects at the bottom of the stainless steel extractor and you have got a tap. It goes through a filter into a stainless steel bucket and is then allowed to settle to let the air bubbles come out. You then bottle it from there. Oilseed rape honey is a problem because if left in the hives, it crystallises in the comb. So we have to extract that early. This year I don't think I have got any rape honey. It was noticeable that Mappercombe did not grow as much rape.

Wax I have not been very clever at. I bought a double glazed window pane. I put that over a stainless steel box made out of an old dishwasher and that we use as a solar wax extractor. The problem is that in old brood frames there is a lot of cocoon skin from where the grubs, the young bees have been and you don't want that in the wax.

What impresses me most about bee keeping is the selflessness of country people and beekeepers. What in any city is often a closely guarded commercial secret is in the country new information to be shared by all. I am sure it is much more of an English trait, the proper way to behave. It is true that to find a fool in the countryside you have to take him there.

Roy and Mel Warburton, midday

17 Roy Warburton: Publican, Shave Cross Inn, Marshwood Vale
Born 1945.

I can remember coming in here as a kid, always coming in here with my Grandfather and my Uncle and that. So I have known all the old faces in the Vale since I was a nipper. I just hope this place remains as a pub for generations to come.

I was born in Weymouth in 1945. My Father was in the RAF and my Mother was in the Land Army. We lived at Stoke Mill till 1947 and then we emigrated to Waytown. My Mother's parents ran the mill, I can remember it flooding a lot when I was little. Grandfather was a miller he just milled flour and cattle feed. I was only three or four years old but I can remember it. When we moved to Waytown I used to help my grandfather with the milking of the cows. He used to make his own cider and when my grandfather was down here from 1926-1947 they all used to go to each other's houses drinking cider. Bluntshay Farm, across the two fields, less than half a mile I should think.

My Mother's side of the family. I've got them dated back to before 1800 as living in Whitechurch Canonicorum. They actually moved from Whitechurch to Baltonsborough in Somerset, then they went to Godney, then Staple Fitzpaine near Taunton, Bishopswood and come full circle back here again. My Grandfather started work as a baker in Ilminster and when his first wife died he moved back here and married a lady from the Vale. His sister and brother-in-law had the shop and post office up in Marshwood from the 1900's. His family were millers in Bishopswood, Keat's mill just opposite the old pub. All my Grandfather's side were from the Bishopswood area called Goodland. My Mother's grandparents were from Whitechurch and before that Combpyne and from Colyton before that, and then from Beer. My Mum was brought up from the age of six in Marshwood so she's been here a long time and my Uncle the same time, they were all brought up at the bakehouse in Marshwood because her mother died of TB when she was only six years old. They moved over here and my Grandfather married another lady from the Vale and moved to Stoke Mill.

Stoke Mill stopped in the early '50s. I don't think it was used very much after my Grandfather moved out. He only rented in from the Moores. He did mill flour, probably for the biscuits, flour and cattle feed. The baking was done down there originally. The mill and bakehouse at Stoke Mill. My Uncle was 90 a couple of weeks ago. The mill was on one side of the lane and the bakehouse was on the other side. I don't think they baked when my Grandfather was there, as it would be in direct conflict with his brother-in-law up in Marshwood. That's where Moore's started off down there.

My Mother, when she left school she was a nurse in Crewkerne, then when war broke out she must have been moved over to Maiden Newton, that is where my Father was living in Cattistock. So that's obviously where they met. After I was born we lived in Cattistock and Waytown. I went between the two sets of grandparents.

When I was four we moved to Germany I can remember that quite clearly, walking round Germany. Hamburg, just piles of rubble, piles of red bricks, I was over there for three years. I think we came back in 1951. Still great piles of rubble, not much construction work going on at all. I tell you another thing I came remember, the Berlin airlift. I can remember me Dad taking me to work when they were loading the planes up and bawling my eyes out because he lifted me up into a Dakota and I was only a little tacker, four years old, five years old, and he lifted me up into the back of the plane and said, "right you're going with it." And I remember crying me eyes out. I got very vivid memories of those planes going off every ten minutes. My Father was on engines, an air frame and engine mechanic. I can remember the planes lining up on the runway one after the other, maybe 50 planes in a line. Unbelievable. Loads of photographs me Dad left me of all the different planes. Crash landing and not getting off the ground. He was full-time in the Air Force. Travelled round quite a bit but I always used to come back here for summer holidays. I always came back to the bakehouse in Marshwood and Christmas always went down to Cattistock.

Here at Shave Cross we are in Marshwood. Stoke Mill is in Whitechurch. I used to stay down here all through the summer holidays, go round with the bread van, go round the farms, deliver the bread, help make the bread. They were still using horsepower. Two horses, two horsepower. Four-legged ones. I can remember them pulling the hay in with horses. Used to go out in the fields, I was eight, nine, ten right up till the time I left school. I used to come down here every summer, so I knew the Vale quite well. I can remember picking the apples in October putting a great sheet down under the tree, used to climb up the tree and knock them down. I remember going up with a saw with two pieces of rope on the end of it, like a chain, two eyes on the end. Climb up the tree, and the men used to stand at the bottom with two bits of wood wrapped round, pulling the saw round the limb till the branch broke off. Basic pruning. Cider presses. Jack Rendell's at Kitty's Farm, Bill Dare over at Great Bluntshay, Alan Pitfield at Prime, and Grandfather had one at Stoke Mill, and he had one over Waytown as well. All cider. He used a free-standing mill with a big handle, green, about four feet high a cast iron thing. The one down at Bluntshay was mechanical. My grandfather used to make it at Myrtle Cottage just on the junction to Oxbridge, most of the fields had trees in them. Blossom time, beautiful down that valley, I remember it, I remember it well. I used to go ferreting. When I was four or five I used to have two or three ferrets and a dog, and put some nets out. I remember killing a load of chicks one morning and got a bollocking for that. Day-old chicks.

My first primary school was Netherbury and I used to walk from Waytown to Netherbury and it seemed like it was a bloody lifetime to walk it. Cos your legs is only about nine inches long, and I used to walk on me own a good mile and a half. Me Mum used to walk up to the 'Hare and Hounds' which is about 100 yards and then I went down a steep hill and climb up the other side all the way to Netherbury. And then on the walk home she used to meet me half way every night.

We then moved to Middle Wallop. My Dad was there for nine years, seconded to the army, he had good knowledge of helicopters, so when the army took over the airfield they seconded him across from the RAF and that's how he got B.E.M. for outstanding achievements with helicopter aviation. From there he moved back over to Germany. I started work at 14 and a half in Germany where I worked in a garage for three and a half years, repairing vehicles, motorbikes and cars. When I came back from there we spent six months living back in Marshwood again, waiting for married quarters, in Bury St Edmunds. Then I worked in a firm up there called T.H. Nice and we used do all the Greene King brewery lorries on a rotation. From there moved to St Andrews in Scotland, worked there for three years. I left there when I was 21 then I moved back down to Marshwood again and lived there with my Aunt and Uncle at the post office and helped make the bread on Saturday nights. The bakery stopped in late '60s, say '68, then Mother's Pride started supplying them, we still delivered bread but it was Mother's Pride.

Then when me Dad came out of the RAF, they took over the shop and post office in Marshwood and I went to work in Bridport and used to come through the Vale here in the morning and after that I worked in Yeovil and got married. Married 24 years to my first wife, and I been with Mel 21 years, I was married for 10 of them to somebody else before I got divorced… Well I have been a mechanic for the most of my life but a friend of mine started a car transporter firm up in Yeovil, Roger Bastable, Abbey Hill. Well I was a director of that company until he sold it out. And then in '83 I bought my own business and built all the new workshops and body shops in Axminster and then I was doing that until my son died in 2000 and I lost the plot for a couple of years then. My wife inherited some land in Tobago, so we went over there, designed and built a house so I spent quite a bit of time out there.

This pub was shut for a year. When I was married to my first wife, we used to come in here a lot then and I can remember coming in here as a kid, always coming in here with me Grandfather and me Uncle and that, so I have known all the old faces in the Vale since I was a nipper. And it hadn't changed at all, except there used to be a door there and that bar had a partition along it and there wasn't a door on the front, just two benches and we used to sit on there. Crisps with the blue salt bags in and proper shandy.

I bought this pub because it is a unique bit of history really for this valley. They were trying to sell it as a house and I thought we stood a chance of reviving it because of my local knowledge and everything, and it is just a lovely building and if it was changed into a house it would be lost forever. The history of the pub, since I have been here I have been documenting everything I can get my hands on. I got virtually all the landlords back to about 1500. I been in the Record Office in Dorchester and I got dates back to 1325 when it was listed for different things. The pilgrimage, whether it is true or a myth is not certain, Shave is a derivative of *sheaga*, which means a small hill, and this valley was full of trees, and there was only two routes to walk through it and this must have been a high point as all the rest was marsh. Also pilgrims used to stop here on the way to Whitechurch Canonicorum. The shrine is still active. There are only two churches that have got the saints remains still buried in them. Whitechurch Canonicorum and Westminster Abbey.

The pub was closed for over a year. We had loads of sagas buying the place, but we eventually bought it. We had to apply for a licence which took three months and went back over to Tobago and waited over there, and came back Easter 2003. We opened 10 days after we come back, went to an auction and bought all the bits and pieces we needed to start the kitchens up. Most of the furniture in here we brought with us, the dressers, the clock, that's my Grandfather's clock. I can remember that all my life the clock from the mill, his wedding present, moved less than a mile. Never been worked on since I have known it and it keeps bloody good time. Bought all the chairs and the fireplace. We use as much local produce as we can, the beer is Branscombe. When they started brewing they were mates of mine and the other one is a Dorset one, from Weymouth, the Dorset Brewing Company. And we just stick with them. Got fruits de mer for somebody tonight, crab, lobster, langoustine, mussels... went down on the beach couldn't get any seaweed so I got some samphire grass instead to dress it all up with.

I love my vehicles. It's my life, my vehicles. Nineteen vintage cars, four vintage motorbikes, some modern cars, Mercs, a vintage Vauxhall, just a whole shed of them. We got four part-time people and two full-time, myself and my wife all work here. Colin the chef is from British Guyana which is now Guyana. Which was British Guyana when he was born over there. We do all Caribbean food and international cuisine. Caribbean Dorset. We got Taste of the West Silver Award last year, West Dorset Camra in 2004, and won the Regional Pub of the year for the Wessex region. That brought us quite a bit of publicity.

This has always been my home. I just hope this place remains as a pub for generations to come. We will do our best to keep it like it. Never going to move. Next place I am moving to is up Marshwood cemetery.

Mark Harris at home, Farnham

18 Mark Harris: Hurdlemaker, sheep shearer and old soldier, Farnham
Born 1912.

I been a hurdlemaker all my life. Corse I made a lot of sheep hurdles, especially as the older ones have died out.
Italy: Serious fighting? Oh Christ yeah. I never expected to see this place again. Well it was like anything else, you just thought if you could scrape through. We were burying our own mates when we landed.

I was born just below the pub in 1912. Been here all my life. Ninety-three in July. My Father worked with a horse and cart, driving people about, no buses about much. He did have a small holding of about 30-odd acres off the estate. The General, used to hear talk about him. My Mother, they was farmers up Rookery, near the Larmer Tree gardens. Grandfather was also with horses. I can remember when I was about five year old, horse and cart and bakers down here where they used to bake the bread, when I was a nipper. No butchers, people used to kill their own pigs and that then. Years ago a lot of people kept a pig, fed him on scraps, potato peel and waste and that. Used to kill a pig. There was a slaughterman down the village, corse you wouldn't be allowed to do that today. Had to be slaughtered and salted and then hang the hams up in the open chimney corners, in they big open fires. Used to have they hams hung up with newspaper round them, keep for ages up the chimney and that was rashers when you cut them off. Old thatched cottage, bricked floors, used to have to get down on our hands and knees and scrub the bricks, and do the hearth. And the bakers still baking with faggots after the war. I were a hurdlemaker all my life, used to tie faggots for the big house down here, but they gone over to this steam or whatever.

The First War? My eldest brother, I lost two brothers during the First World War, the eldest one he survived but he was wounded badly he was in hospital for a year and five weeks. The Dorsets. And the first thing I can remember seeing him, my Father's friend drove me and my Mother to Wimborne to see my brother lying in hospital and the first time I know of him. Two more joined up, both killed when they were 19. I can't remember about the second one at all. The third one he was two year younger, corse I would have been five year old and I just remember him, but the second one I can't remember at all. Weren't old enough to remember him when he went, and the oldest one went to hospital to see him. I had the dates off the stone down the churchyard. The oldest of the two there was no trace, the other they traced but his body was never found. It hit my Mother quite badly. I was one of 12. There was 11, but the youngest I remember, when the second one got killed and the one that I knew, the shock, she was breastfeeding, the shock went to the milk and caused his death, so I understood.

I started work when I was 14 year old, 1926. Worked on the farm for a bit then went self-employed, straw tying, hay tying, sheep shearing. My Father was a contract sheep shearer and his forefathers, my Great-grandfathers, but it is finished now. But I was one of the last ones to carry on, just the hand shears. He give up just after the war and bought an engine and I got that engine now in running order up to the steam fair. They had me on the radio on about him last year, had him up the steam fair when it first started 30 year ago when we were using him then for shearing. Corse we went over to electric towards the finish. Used to shear over at Chettle up till a year or two ago. My Father, my brother and they used to shear sheep by hand. After the war sheep started to come back in. Eventually we went over to the electric, much easier, smaller and you could put him in the back of your car.

With the hand shears them days. It is grass sheep now, nothing on their legs, nothing on their bellies, they only got it on the sides and back. And years ago it was them other breeds like teddy bears. Dorset Horns, Dorset Downs and Hampshire, some of them Dorset Downs, the young sheep they couldn't see out, like teddy bears, we used to do by hand. Shear all up and round there and the chops and under there. Anybody can do straight work, but we used to do 35 or 40 teddy bears by hand. Of course we did do them a bit quicker when we went over to the engine, but nowadays anyone can do straight work. 'Twas always getting round them corners which took the time. I give up those sheep over at Chettle at 76 year old, 17 year ago. Only done few pet ones since then, finally gave up the big flocks at 76. We were shearing with electric.

I went self-employed tying straw and hay. Then I took over hurdlemaking from me Uncle and I weren't allowed to do anything, only knocking the knobs off. He didn't let I have a go. He amused me just get they rods ready, knock the knobs off. Anyhow I fetched. I saw how 'twas done and of course over the years I picked it up and kept me eyes open. Oh yes I started bidding for an acre 'tis cheaper than it is now, a penny or sixpence a perch, or a shilling, that was at first five yards each way, but they stopped the sales in 1972. The auctions were held down the Museum Hotel here. What they used to do was, have different names for each wood, then they had the names for each block, they put down to go there, mark it out. A gad straight out from one track and somehow they finish up straight through, measure every 11 yards and put a post in and that were lying straight up through that wood. And they did put in these big woods and the name of the plot, they put the number, shave a bit of bark off the corner, marked out, the size on there and you go and have a look at it in these catalogues. Then buy it down the pub and the bits you set your eyes on someone else would have it and you had to step in and buy a piece you weren't so keen on you know, or else you finish up with nothing. It went to the highest bidder. The most I ever see there was 70 odd but that weren't all hurdlemakers, lot of them were visitors to see what was going on. I suppose there were about 30. Some buy the wood that weren't hurdlemakers, for clothes pegs, bean poles etc. There used to be 20 odd hurdlemakers on the estates round here and now there's none. None at all. I made most of them in the wood. Ern, he bring them back and make them at home.

Sheep hurdles? Well it is a job to describe it, got to put the bottoms in, so they don't fall off particularly for sheep hurdles, when they are out in the field. They do pitch them forward see and there was made different from a barn hurdle, they was three foot high and you had to keep the bottoms up for sheep hurdles because they would force them into the ground. Two shores for the first hurdle then after that one for every hurdle. They pitched them all out you see, then put the sheep out, but they had enough hurdles to make another fold in front, so that the next morning they turned the sheep out of that one where they had been 24 hours into the next one. Picked them up and carry them forward and pitch them up for the next fold. Now it's all runners for sheep, electric wire. A whole field they be running in, and so they had to be bound both ways, two-thirds of the way up and because they were moving every day, they would pull them out of shape. They are stronger, they just make them as tidy as they can, thick as they can. Ten sails in a sheep hurdle, a garden hurdle only nine. Some of them only seven but that's laziness because they can't be very strong. Only done it so they can make them easier but they are not worth buying.

There's different types of hazel some glassy and some good, some go round, some like a corkscrew when you spin them. Seven-year cycle, there's older than that on the estate. Some don't make strong hurdles too young. Not only that, you wouldn't get six foot sails out of it. Seven year old, you want six foot six to make a hurdle. Got to have the points down the bottom and an inch or two on top. You got to cut them longer if you want to get six foot of work in them. You want six foot six to play about.

How many would I make? All depends on the weather. Paid by the dozen. Eleven shillings a dozen and now it is seven pound a foot. Six foot long 40-odd pound for a six foot, £20 for a three-foot hurdle. A lot of hurdles were used for the First World War.

The Second War? I ought to have been killed before I went abroad. Got bombed out of a trench. September 1940. I joined up in July 1940 and within a fortnight they started bombing the barracks, bombing the barracks to hell they were, Caterham. On the 1st September they moved us, we were in some blocks three storeys high and they started knocking the barracks down. They moved us out and only occupied the bottom of the three-storeyed buildings. Many were killed. Went there for a month. 1st September. These high buildings. We ought to have been higher up but we were in some huts on the cricket pitch. 1st September the siren went. They were expecting the invasion 1940 this were, they said: "Two squaddies go to the ammunition store to take a box of ammunition down. All the rest of the others in the trench." Then it was my turn with the other chap and they rushed out to the trench outside and we had to go to the ammunition stores. And when we got back the bombs started falling on us. We were last in the trench. Half underground and half out, dirt up on them. The next thing I knew it were only a 50-pound bomb, come down on the top of the trench, cut straight in half. If I hadn't had to get the ammunition I wouldn't be here. And t'were only a 50-pound bomb as luck would have it and it had 11 blokes. I were up out of the trench and the first bloke I went to help his leg came off in my hand. Bloody hell.

Anyhow that was two o'clock and after it were all over, we patched up the trench. And that siren went again that night, and we went out in the same trench what were left of us. Patched him up you know and they got us back in before the sirens stopped. Only just got back in. Then next day we were in these huts and we had these boards about that high *(two foot)* off the ground I thought it were a bloomin' plane crashing down on us. I went to dive under the boards and all the shutters come down, BANG! When I come to I didn't know t'were next morning. Victoria block had 50 blokes in it and part of the cookhouse were all down and that bed boards and blankets and bodies all over the sports ground. Found me next morning, you didn't know what was going on exactly, so dark and that. We couldn't go to have our meals, not all in one go. Went in there one day and they started bombing and we were jumping out of the mess windows and all sorts, I were knocked down that night. Got bombed out of there.

Later on I went to Italy. The invasion of Italy. I had a septic arm at the time, a boil up here, still got the mark. I were in company headquarters, they were up on the hill in Italy, we couldn't make no advance. This was company headquarters and I had to get the food through to the others. Only a stone's throw away across this river and we had to supply them with water. We had to go over the bridge to give them water. And we were over there one night and the bloody Jerries come up the road on the bridge and got through behind us. We were in the yard over the other side of the river in this farmyard, and this tank and that, were rumbling along the back there anyhow they got further away from us and we come back over the bridge. Oh it was a hell of a story it was, '43 this were when we invaded. Salerno. We couldn't get inland. All the heavy stuff were out to sea, they what should have been on the big guns and that, I remember we give them rifles to fight with us. I was only an ordinary guardsman. They wanted to make me corporal. I wouldn't have it. I was in Italy right up to the end. They got the two battalions the 1st and 2nd Coldstream guards together and picked out half of them to come back and the other half stayed there. I was in the third battalion.

Serious fighting? Oh Christ yeah. I never expected to see this place again. Well it was like anything else, you just thought if you could scrape through. We were burying our own mates when we landed. Wrap them up in a blanket, they had their discs on. Bury them there and then, till we got far enough inland. Then we had a proper cemetery and they dug up them bodies look and put them in the cemetery. Oh Christ. Ah. Burying our own mates. That were worse than the '14 war, corse this last war we were on the move, not in the one place too long, longest place we were in was Cassino. I read there were 105,000 killed there. I don't know how many attempts they had. The Poles took it in the finish because they overrun Poland in the start. I read a book about it from the library.

I was in a position look where I could see their gun on the hill and they could see me. And the second time I were up there, I were in this one forward trench. They dropped one right on top of him. You do your business everything in the trench. Lot of people very interested cos I was up there. It were mud up to here last time I were up there. I pulled out a night or two before from a position not quite as close as the back of that house. Lay down on the bricks with my overcoat and the one blanket I had, and an insect bit down there in the hollow part of the ankle and I scratched it and it went right up here turned to a bloody abscess right up my leg. And they got me out of that trench that night, mortaring over us. I did not know how to keep up, 'twere dark and I was ready to be taken prisoner. I were travelling for nearly a week, and only had me kit. Went right back down to Salerno and went to the field hospital on the Sunday night and they gave me a bed. MO said: "Crickey you look beat, have you been in a war?" I said: "I am afraid I have, I am in terrible pain." And he said: "You're a stretcher case." Got down to Salerno next morning, corse somebody opened it and then I was right as rain. You know.

But that night when we got out of that trench see, we had to hang up in another place for an hour or two and we had to cross over where Jerry could see us in daylight. Anyhow they moved us right forward into this village and all they said was get them under ground level if you can and where it had been raining, it had froze. Bloody icy the bottom of the trench and it was all a mess. I got hold of some stones I put them in the ice and I got down on that ice and went to sleep and how I got up next morning I don't know. I stopped in the village, first hospital place, First Aid place and they went on and I had to go down the road to our headquarters and I was still walking in bloody agony. I got down there and it was getting daylight, went round to the cooks where our rations come up from and corse they had pulled out and had gone on down the road somewhere. I suppose anyhow as I said, I got down to our headquarters and they made a cup of tea and I went down to the sergeant, the RSM and in there the quartermaster sergeant, and he chewed my head off as I was in such a state. Hadn't shaved or nothing. He didn't give I a chance to explain anything. We were right up at Cassino. I was up there on and off for six months, they wanted me to train as a sniper.

Wounded? The nearest I had were shrapnel. We were in a place like Win Green. We tried this valley, to take it, they shelled us down the valley, and pulled us back. And they then decided to go up what would be one end of Win Green. 'Twere about two mile long because he had guns trained on both valleys, they decided they would go up over the end and lay a smoke screen. Lifted 100 yards every minute and these smokescreens were going over our heads all the way along and then exploding in front of us, so they couldn't see us. But they got the guns on us just as we were approaching the bloody end. And I dived down, there were a bank there, I dived down, then whip, I know it were bloody close. And then afterward this bloody shrapnel cut through the back of my trousers right here. Never touched me flesh. Anyhow after the shelling we got up and looked over the bloody brow and I could see Jerry and there were some cornfields down in the bottom, hyled wi' corn. I can see it if it was only yesterday looking down over a steep bank like a stickleback and I could see this Jerry laid up against a bloody hyle. He had his bloody leg shattered, and one of our blokes got a rifle and shot him there and then down over the bank. And I thought to myself that's bloody cruel, he couldn't do no damage. They get trigger happy. Well then we started getting our wounded out and buggered if they weren't firing on our stretcher bearers. The buggers were 'til we caught them.

The sergeant major. Hill 270. We took he. He had to be taken two Saturdays after we landed. He had the VC, Sergeant Major Peter Wright. I had a septic arm at the time when they took the first prisoners off the hill. See them out, me in charge of them, cos I couldn't dig in as I had a septic arm. Twenty-four hours time they sorted the last wounded off the hill. And then they sorted my arm out. I was evacuated back. I were out for a month or two. I went back convalescent. And had him in a sling for five or six weeks in Egypt alongside the Suez Canal. Then I went back just before Christmas '43. Hill 270 was just after we landed. Third Saturday. It had to be taken before we could get anywhere, to get heavy stuff in from the sea. We lost a lot. There were some joined us from England the night before, cos we came off the one hill what was leading up to it, to take this other hill the next day. We had to go through the Scots Guards that were in trenches part way up. And there was some fellows joined us from Salerno just come out from England that we had left behind a few months previously. I didn't see no more of some of them. We had nine left. We were made up to strength that night, we had nine left out of 120 and the other lot what was on the other side, the other company they had 50 left out of 120. Wasn't all killed. Some killed, some wounded. Sergeant major and this gert big bloke. We used to call him Tiny, his boots were 16's, bloody hopeless training cos he were such a big bloke and heavy you know and we had full kit on and when we were training they mid push you in the bloody river. Anyhow Tiny he put the first Spandau nest out and then the Spandau had him. The sergeant major took over, chucked a grenade in the next Spandau nest and went onto the third and done the same there and eventually got to the top. But they hung on with the 50 that come up from the other side, and that nine.

I had my life saved more than once. Lost a lot of friends. Yeah. I was on duty when the tanks got bombed, on a hill and we had to go up and dig in between these tanks all along. It was a moonlight night. I can see someone stand up a bit on the hedge in the moonlight and I was on the end of this bank and the others a bit further back couldn't get out. I were right on the bloody point. Anyhow I let rip at him with this automatic weapon I had, a Bren gun, and I never had 'em. But next morning when we got daylight, I said to the chap, they said we had to do hour on and an hour off, the others could get out bit further along. I done an hour all right, then I woke him up, (what the hell was his name?) "your turn now," and he got up and I got down and the next thing he were thrown down on top of me. There were a bloody sniper that were up there that I fired on that night. He had to fire a bit quick. The bloody bullet went in here and come out here. Went right through under his cheek, corse the other buggers had all fallen asleep. All along next to me. We couldn't get out cos we were on the bloody end and specially after he done that to my mate. I couldn't wake those buggers, I throwed a bloody stone. I couldn't get out of the trench I couldn't swing me arm up or nothing look and 'twere a bloody hour or two before I could hear anything moving. When eventually they woke up I called out to them, I said, "ere my mate been wounded here," would have bled to death normally, look. Corse I put a bandage round there and then corse weren't too bad then. Went in the cheek and come out there. Didn't do much damage and so one of them got on to the officer. That officer, bloody hopeless what we had at the time. And, "Oh," he said, "I can't do nothing about it for the moment as they can't get out," I said: "He can't stay here like this, bogged down all day like this." so he said: "If you can make it, run for it," so I let he go first, then

I crawled out over the trench, a bit quick. Only a matter of a yard or two and then we were all right down flat. I went back, he were walking wounded, corse I went soon after he got out of the trench. I went back for three days rest as I had been up there longest. Snipers were quite dangerous, and I found out afterwards they on the tanks got 'im that day, first sniper. Then I saw the bloke he shot afterwards. He thanked me and said I were bloody lucky. "That were a bloody sniper," I said, "he fired a bit too bloody quick," I said, "he happened to miss the vital point in your head, that's were he meant to have hit here," pointing to his forehead.

That was the trouble with Bren guns. They always put you on bloody crossroads or somethin'. I were the first one that Jerry bumped into if it they come hand-to-hand fighting. I said to our sergeant, "How's it I am always on the Bren gun?" There was always two of you and one with a rifle, look, you had the magazines.

I come back when the war ended. Went back up to Scotland and Liverpool and then back again to Pirbright. Then six months till I got demobbed. VE Day I had just gorn back to Scotland after me leave. I knew t'were coming to an end. I come home on leave November, early part of November they always had a good sale, and I come home on the Friday. This wood sale was two o'clock down the pub, they always took the money from you twelve o'clock and you pay so much when you buy it and the rest the following year before the sale started. I bought one piece knowing that I would be demobbed in the following months. Got a catalogue, hadn't seen the wood or nothing because I had only just got home, but I knew 'twere a Saturday. I bought one piece and it were the very same piece that I had made my first hurdles in a few years earlier. Not a great lot to pay for it, can't remember now, I bought some privately, as I hadn't bought enough to last me till the following wood sale. I just bought one piece that Saturday and sold hurdles that same day before I had even started making them. Hurdle dealers who knew me. Corse I made a lot of sheep hurdles, especially as the older ones have died out. Last one I made was Shaftesbury Show last August.

NOTES:

a) The General is General Pitt Rivers 1827-1900. He inherited the Rushmore Estate, which at 27,000 acres covered a fair bit of Dorset and Wiltshire. He also started the Pitt Rivers Museum in Oxford and had his own archaeological museum in Farnham. Here he had a "Notice to All Visitors, Professors, Pedlars, Politicians and Poultry keepers. Why have you come here and what do you expect to see? Please ask yourself these questions (as all anthropologists have asked themselves). We ask you to read these labels and form your own opinion on the evidence that you will see…" Very open minded for the 1880s. The pub where the wood auctions were held is of course called The Museum. The museum itself was a converted farmhouse which had been a school for gypsies. The Museum in Farnham was closed in 1966.

b) The action on Hill 270 that Mark refers to is well known and was a key part of the battle behind Salerno. Mark was very lucky indeed to have survived that and the earlier bombing of the Guards barracks during the Battle of Britain in 1940 and of course Monte Cassino.

19 Ern Steel: Sparmaker and hurdlemaker, Farnham Born 1936.

One thing I can't do is sit around doing nothing. I shall carry on as long as I can.

I was born in 1936 in Salisbury. My parents were living at Larmer Tree at the time, Father was caretaker at Larmer Tree. The gardens were open then. I was four when we moved away. Father was a woodman on the Rushmore estate, planting up fir trees, trim them out each year. My father's father as far as I knew he drove a steam engine, but I didn't know him, he came from Woodlands near Cranborne. My Granny did live down in the village of Farnham and she finished up with us. On Mother's side, my Grandfather was a farmer, well he run the Minchington Farm down the bottom here. It belonged to the estate. Someone else had taken on the farm and my Grandfer was running it.

See I was born in 1936, we moved away when I was four so that would be 1940. I think that was when the gardens closed. They haven't been open that long, not now. Corse Father was then living at 71 Farnham, that's just down the bottom, and he was working in the woods for Rushmore estate, he was the head woodman there. Then he decided he was going to go into hurdle making on his own although he was still working in the woods. He was still self-employed and he carried on like that, and he carried on the house which was a tied house, but Father managed to start paying rent on it and when I got to 12 perhaps I started making spars. I cut myself pretty bad when I was 13, spar hook went right into my foot, it was pretty bad but I was lucky it didn't cut the tendons. I was lucky, I only had slippers on at the time. We used to do it in the kitchen. He started making hurdles weekends when he was actually working for Rushmore estate then he decided he was going to do it full time so he packed it in. He was buying coppice at the auctions. I did when I started.

The auctions was always held in the club room down there, attached to the Museum. Always had that every year. I should think there must have been 20-odd hurdlemakers and sparmakers and one or two of them buying stuff for logs, pea sticks and bean rods. They used to do a card, you'd always have a card given to you before the sale. And sections were cut out with the number on it in Roman numerals and you'd go down there, value it to see what it was worth. Different people was after different things if someone was after pea sticks and bean rods they'd look for that sort of thing, but for myself I normally made all six foot hurdles, so I used to make sure I had enough of the bigger wood to make the bigger hurdles.

Father, when he was working on the estate, he used to do it his'self marking it up. Then when he left one of the other woodman done it. It was round about an acre each piece, you had odd sizes, odd-shaped pieces and some of it, there was a lot of trees in amongst it where there was virtually no hazel, so you might get one piece that was declared half an acre. You get some stool ash but we used to have the hazel. You could cut the birch, but anything that was liable to be used for timber had to be left. Couldn't cut that for ash, unless it had been cut before. Stuff that was no use for timber you could cut that. I can't remember the prices compared to prices today, must have been pence, we used to buy it by the lugg, a lugg is five and a half yards square, same as a perch. It was called a perch, a square perch, 160 perch to an acre. The rotation wasn't every seven years, some hazel grows faster than others, that's what they can't get in their heads nowadays. Some places it has to be done every seven years and you find some of the wood is not big enough and some is too old, needs to be cut younger. Corse they got their rules which they read out of a book and that's how it has got to be done. Trouble is the people that are running it today they don't know what sort of wood we want. They wouldn't

Ern Steel with some thatching spars

come down and ask anybody, if you understand what I mean, because they know it all. They could organise it a bit better than what they do, the woods is finished with really now.

I started school down Farnham until I was 11, then I went to Sixpenny Handley till I was 15. I didn't get a break, selling logs, making spars. When I left school I started work with Father making hurdles being paid piece work, I started off having a wage, he used to give me a pound and a shilling a week that was what I was getting corse that was a six-day week. I worked with him for about three years then I decided to go on my own. I was buying wood, making the hurdles then selling them. Dealers at that time, there was quite a demand for hurdles at that time. I never made any sheep hurdles. The ones I made were for people's gardens. You couldn't make them fast enough.

I came out of the woods for a time, there was a spell when these sawn out panels came in and of course they competed with our hurdles. We couldn't make them at the cheap price they were making them lapboard things. They was fairly good at that time, they are obviously too thin, but I finished and I went down to Witchampton paper mill and worked down there for about five years. I was earning more money and you had your free time. We did use to work quite a bit of overtime. We was getting about £12 a week down there, mainly card, not newspaper, card for boxes, thin boxes and Christmas card, birthday card that sort of stuff. Made some beautiful stuff there, made from wood pulp, some of it used to come from Russia, came in lorry loads used to come into Poole, and they used to bring it up from there. About 200 worked there. Lot of them was in shift work. People coming and going all the time lot of people wouldn't stick it the noise was so bad. What I was doing, I was working in the packing department. We used guillotines and forklifts and that sort of thing. I used to pack up samples for customers if they wanted a sample. For a trial run they give you a size and guillotine it out and send it on to them. Then they send in the orders see. About five years I was there, then I decided that enough was enough. But I got fed up with it and so I saw a job advertised assembling car engines that was a reconditioned firm in Wilton.

I went up there and got a job up there. Mainly the old Fords but they was turning them out blooming quick. Five of us assembling engines full time just chucking them together. Put together with air guns bop, bop, bop, that must have been the '60s. Anyway I was up there 20 years see. When I started there were five of us on assembling all the time. Others were doing different jobs. Engines used to come in, scrap engines they used to buy. They was completely stripped down reconditioned, they weren't all Ford engines there was BMC engines and Rootes, Hillmans all sorts of basic models that was about at that time. We used to do I suppose 40 of each model on the trot, used to come through like that in batches, and that was damned good. We were getting damned good money. Scrap yards everywhere. Some of them used to come right from Birmingham on artic lorries. No we didn't do gear boxes. All we was doing was re-conditioning the engines. I was living down the village, exactly 20 miles to Wilton, each way. The thing is the pay, when I was down the paper mill I was earning £12 a week. When I was up there I started on £17 which was a hell of a lot difference. I had to travel, to pay the expenses, but at that time the petrol was that much cheaper, paying at that time about half a crown a gallon. Something like that. But we got on a bonus scheme up there where I was earning double wages. And because I had been there so long, I knew how many screws used to go in every one. Sort them out, put them on your bench then bumph, bumph, bumph with the gun. Totally different to the woods, but I have always been interested in mechanical stuff, how stuff works.

Father was still alive but there was virtually no trade, he

was of an age when he wouldn't have got another job anyway. And Michael Pitt Rivers was running the estate by this stage. Eighteen years ago I left up there, they was getting down so bad up there, there was virtually no trade. I didn't have enough work. And there is one thing I can't do is sit around doing nothing. Well from there I found a garage in Wimborne, Wimborne Motors, they was reconditioning engines and gear boxes and I went in there and got a job I stayed there eight years. But there again they went downhill cos they can't compete. It is cheaper to buy a new engine than re-condition them. I got made redundant there and I thought I don't want to go on the dole, so I decided I was going to come back into this if I could and I did.

That was about 10 years ago I started back. Yeah I been pretty busy all the way through, I make spars for three thatchers, but each of them got two thatchers, so that is six thatchers I make for, and the hurdles. Well I got one lot ready to go out. It is quiet just at the moment, but I have been on very long days, shattered some days. In one sense you'd be better to make them up in the woods, but you haven't got the phone there and if a customer is coming to pick the stuff up he wouldn't be able to get into the woods. If a customer is coming at so and so time, I would have to be here and then he wouldn't turn up. You are still working, not wasting time but where you do waste time is when you are out on the woods cutting it out, tying it up in bundles and carrying it back. But if you were out in the woods all the time, you wouldn't be tying up bundles but you'd be coming back at night. This is the best idea, I got a shed here and round the back I can make hurdles and I can sit in here and make spars.

A thousand spars, I like to make just over a thousand a day. Depends on the wood, if you get some good wood I have made 2,000 in a day. That's a long day, normally I make about 1200, something like that. There again it depends on the wood. I had some wood where I only get two lengths out of it. Very short stuff damaged with the deer, that's a major problem. Well they say there are being culled but there are thousands of them about here. There is no auctions now. You just agree with whoever you are buying it from. There's not much decent wood about. Usually you get a piece of wood where some of it is all right and some of it is no good at all. They are not looked after like they used to be and there is too many deer about. You get a herd of deer come in when the shoots are growing they will strip that in a night and then all that wood coming up nice and straight shoots out its branches, so you got nothing that is any good. The stools are quite old, I have seen one or two hazel bushes where one stick has been the size of my body. They are about. The trouble is where it is left so long, you'd find it was spaced out, the stumps are spaced out. A lot of them have died, been killed off. Well now some places they are cutting the wood to let it grow back for hazel, well it's not going to grow it needs to be closer to together. Well they need to plant in between or layer it down but is it worth it? There's not many people doing it anyway. I don't know how they are going to get on. You see they started making plastic spars but they don't like them. I've heard of one place where a thatcher was asked to go and put a roof back on where a so-called thatcher had gone there and he had thatched his roof out, used all plastic spars and they had a strong wind and it blew the whole lot off. So they had to get someone else there, but he was doing it at reduced price. Another thatcher had to go back and put it on again, so it worked out expensive for him. They got to pay twice then. The way I look at it, I have seen one plastic spar, but with wood, when you put the spar in it bonds with the straw that's what I think. Plastic it separates, it is too smooth. Plastic won't bond with straw. Won't stick to it I suppose the alternative is to put superglue on it. It just doesn't work like that.

Hurdles? I do mainly six foot high by six foot wide. I do all sizes, I have done them eight foot square. To start with I got to go up in the woods, cut the wood tie it up in bundles, bring it back on my truck, bring it here. I cut it with a chainsaw not only is it much quicker but the wood grows better afterward which I was very surprised about. You need it cut down fairly close to the ground, it shoots better that way.

Flints I have had that working alongside the road, bits of tarmac got in amongst the stumps. I cut the hazel whatever is usable. I usually bring it back the length that it is, what I can use. Most of it I suppose is about nine foot long. The ideal size for the sails, I use stuff up to two and half three inches in diameter. I mean you can make four sails out of it if you quarter them, I like to split my wood in the hurdles board fashion, so it is white both sides. I put a strip in each hurdle right down the bottom. It is older wood normally 12 year old, 12, 15 year old. And I find that makes them stiffer you got more control over them and as far as I am concerned they last much longer. A customer if he buys something and it doesn't last very long he's not coming back is he. You just as well do it properly, not only does he order again but he advertises for you. I don't advertise.

Sails? With the ones I make it is nine. I have made them where they use eight or seven but if you put less than nine they are not so stiff. I make hurdles in a lathe. As a rule a birch tree cut in half. Some places they call them a mould, some places they call them a frame, but it is all the same. I think round here they used to call them a laithe, but I think really it was a lath, which if you look in a dictionary is a piece of board. What we used to try and do was get a perch pole which had a slight curve on him and saw him out like that, so you got a bit of a curve on him. Because when you are actually making a hurdle you need about inch and a half curve on. Bear in mind when you make them they are green, when they dry out they will straighten out. If you were to make them straight, when they dry out they will turn the other way round, if you understand what I mean. See you need the small wood in the bottom, about eight in the bottom about the size of your finger. Weave that in just to hold the base in, then I normally put some board in to stiffen it up then carry on with stuff that is split in half. I don't use a spar hook. I use a crook hook, this is a blunt hook never been sharpened, I been using him over 50 years. He has never been sharpened no name on it. I can remember when I bought it as I bought four or five hooks at the same time in an auction and they were chucked in a cardboard box. It was at Tollard Green not very far. I have never seen anybody else use a hook like this but I spotted it and I found that I could get on very well with it and I have used it ever since. Had one or two handles on it in the past. I am not afraid to use this one as I know it is not going to cut me. The secret is to just keep it running along the grain. This hook there, keep him out the way. You need some sharp hooks. One of the hooks I use is a knobby hook, got the point cut off and that's for cutting the ends off hurdles once you made the hurdle and taken him out the frame. And take him away from where you are working then you haven't got the ends under your feet. Some people just chop them up where they make the hurdles and keep tripping over them.

Hazel? Well at the moment I am going about 12 miles but I have been to Somerset. Well how I come to get this near Bruton. I went to look at it and bought it but it was in a difficult place to get and I got stuck with the truck about four miles off the road. It was just this side, a fair size not very far from a railway line, it was dark. The first time I got stuck in I bought a winch with a chain, I brought one of them and chucked him in the truck. Loaded up about dinner time and it started to rain it came on very steady I started to move on hard ground and he went bomph straight down on the belly. Stuck proper he wouldn't move anywhere, on his belly. Any way I put this winch on there and I spent five hours towing him out. Now when I did get him out I drove in a tree, never even marked the truck. It wasn't even a proper track I was dodging in and out of the trees.

Some hazel you look at and you think that's no good at all not worth hauling, but others is normally all right. You can usually tell by looking at it. Ideal hazel would be a dull grey, if it is shiny and grey leave it in the woods, it is brittle. Lot of sheep, lot of hurdlemakers. People always making bread they needed the brushwood for the ovens. Bavvins, we used to do a few, there was a bakery, Frecknell and Wilkins. Pea sticks not worth doing probably done about 150 this year. We used to do thousands of them. Some people do use them a second year, as soon as the peas is over if they take them out and brush the dirt of them and got a shed to keep them in they can use them for the second year.

A six by six hurdle I charge £42 and the customer comes to collect it. I don't want to deliver any anyway, several hours work. You can't put a time on it. A lot of people ask that, but there's no way you can look up and say it takes so and so. I mean for instance I have been in several competitions at the Great Dorset Steam fair. We make a four-foot hurdle there, to see who the best hurdlemaker is. I done it four times and I have won it four times and each time it has taken me 50 minutes. But bear in mind all the work is done before, the wood is sorted out you know. The wood is good stuff and ready for you just split it and put it together. They think you are making a fortune but they don't realise the work that is going into it before. We used to do a lot of clothes props, besoms never sell enough to make it worthwhile that's birch and it got to be cut at the right time. I given away more than I sold, get fed up seeing them about.

I may have to retire, both my knee joints are going now and my knuckles are gone. All the joints have gone. Arthritis, me knees they told me last time I went to hospital for me to carry on working till I can't do any more. They can't do your fingers. I know one hurdlemaker at Sixpenny Handley, he's still making a few but he's 12 month younger than me. I was supposed to have retired three or four year ago and he's coming up to retiring age, and there's one that comes up from Cranborne to the Rushmore estate. He makes a few hurdles. Alan Brown he's a good hurdlemaker, he works with his son down near Wool.

The problem is that they are bringing them in from Poland and they are rubbish. Made with very small wood which will last a 12-month, they are hazel but they have been brought over from Poland and shut in a container. They come over and it kills them. But it is small wood and they are not made properly. I saw a fence supplier advertising them. Never seen anything like it in all my life. A heap of four foots and a heap of six foots, now bear in mind these is new hurdles. They are falling to bits. The thing is if a customer thinks that that is hazel hurdles and he puts them up himself they will probably break up. Is he going to buy anymore? It is not genuine hazel. Corse proper sheep hurdles they used to have an extra sail in them, ten sails and that used to stiffen them up and small hole for carrying them. If someone asks you what the hole is for, you say so it is for the sheep to see when the feed is coming to them. That's what I have always told them. But they don't realise that it is the poor old shepherd had to carry them they use to carry about half a dozen. I shall carry on as long as I can.

20 David Winskill: Forester and woodman, Child Okeford Born 1936.

All my life has been spent planting, thinning or extracting. Bluebells were a problem they were dangerous, if you get a slide on, very slippery… You can easily get killed on steep ground. I miss working in the woods.

I was born in Sturminster Newton in 1936, but my parents were brought up in Cumberland. My Father was working on his farm with his father and he suddenly decided to take a trip down south where he thought he might earn more. He eventually ended up working as a forester. Previously he was doing forestry in winter, in the planting season but he still did various bits on the farm. It was called Bracken estates near Penrith. Quite wild country. Both of my parents came from that region and my grandparents.

Wages were better down South, but only just. As head forester he controlled about 20 men in those days for Balfour Gardiner, the composer. Father was in charge of the woods and was just told to get on with it. Balfour was living at Fontmell Hill House. Organic farming was talked about quite a bit, but not a lot happened. I think it was the Glyn estates and then it became Fontmell Hill Estate. He started in 1926.

My Father picked the forestry up as he went along. He was the sort of fellow who had a lot in his head and decided to keep it like that. He got by. Balfour was an old gentleman with a walking stick, very much an English country gentleman. Other composers came down like Delius and Holst. My Father planted everything in that stretch from the airfield across the hill, in various stages from 1928 onwards. Mostly beech, they went a bit mad on beech. It got planted where it shouldn't have been. Looking nice from a distance, the trouble is that beech was very prone to being blown over. Corsican pine was the answer, three lines of each. Quite amazing things happened. The Duke of Somerset had a Scotsman as his forester and he was called upon to give his advice on this softwood planting and so he comes along. True old Scot. I don't know whether Rolf was there, but he offered his advice he said: "You have to plant the right species. It's Scots pine." So off they dashed and got their Scots pine. After a while it was yellowing and a lot died. They didn't make the same mistake again. They asked Mr Milner: "Pity you've gone and put that it, shove some more Corsican on top of that lot." But the chalk was the problem. After a certain time, 10, 12 years, the root system was going into the chalk and they did keel over. Corsican was more chalk tolerant. You could see that on the Forestry Commission, they had some marvellous nurseries on Savernake. And that was where all the plants came from, and Father's idea was to raise his own forest nursery and he did turn out all that he needed and even used to sell a bit. He collected his own seed. He got various other things going, Douglas fir. Father was fond of the larch. The out of work miners were planting trees, quite willing to work. And when they got cracking they covered a lot of ground. Well I don't suppose anyone would be overjoyed at the time. They were from South Wales and lads from the North. I think it was a working holiday, whether they had a shock when they saw the work I don't know, frightened a few of them off. There are odd tales in the pubs of the occasional fights that broke out. It goes on even now. I think they must have been quite good, in some places very good. Yes they worked under my Father, in the late '30s.

Twenty men covers quite a large area. Open downland, sheep grazing hardly a thorn bush on it. They had to do something during the Depression. Uncle Balfour, once he had brought an area into forestry, he was very reluctant to sell it. He would go round and literally talk to the trees. Urging them on to grow. When Balfour died it carried on

David Winskill

the same under a different name. He died in 1950. He had been through the First World War as an interpreter and spoke quite a few languages, a very clever man. Rolf was his nephew. He told me once he hardly ever saw his uncle till he was 12 or 14 years old. We were brought up on the top of the hill, just over the crossroads down towards Washers Pit on the left where Balfour lived surrounded by trees. We had a flat in the house.

Earliest memories? The best thing I saw was a crawler tractor one day. I was about seven years old when I was taught to drive it. Albie Roberts taught me I have remembered most of it. The crawler was Fordson blue, a conversion they done by County Crawlers. These were originally on lease lend scheme. It was built in Wisconsin. We managed to get hold of it for timber work. Still using horses for extraction in 1952. The year that the Forestry Commission went completely mad and planted up in one season what they would do in about five years. Mixtures of soft and hardwoods. An awful lot of maintenance needed if you are planting on that scale and a lot of what they planted never got to maturity. Just keeled over and died. Then came the weed growth. Sprays were available but no one trusted them very much. 245T was around, but the cost would be pretty great.

I was only three when war broke out so I haven't got any great idea. Looked a bit busier than usual, The Compton Abbas airfield didn't come until about 1950, belonged to the Harding family for years. Canadians had the worst record for training. More killed here than on D Day. Killing their own men. There was a stretch from Washers Pit down to Stubhampton all that valley was alive with stuff, and the trouble was getting hold of the ones which were still live. Somehow we had to sort them out, they put lorry loads of DPs, Dispersed Persons from Europe that happened to be around at the time and they were each dished out with a mine detector and prodded in the right direction. "Right you boys get going." They had to clear the mine fields, they were very well supervised, nobody wandered off and got blown up. An excellent record apparently. If you were planting trees it helped to clear the mines first. Ukrainians and Poles, nearly all Ukrainians. The ones I got to know they had to walk up every day from Motcombe where the school is. They had a lorry to get them as far as they could. Refugees in the late '40s.

I went to school in Fontmell. Primary and then Shaftesbury Grammar and left when I was 17 in 1953. Then eventually I was called up to go into the army. Basic training was in Malvern and then after that it became Southern Command HQ. I was in the Royal Engineers HQ which was in Wilton. We got involved in a top secret operation so you can make of it what you like. I used to carry this big map rolled up on my shoulder, looking very important. I think it was a map of England. Then I had to train typists. All seems a bit odd now. I then went for ESD Engineer Stores Depot Long Marston. It was quite a nice area. Then I ended up with this damned great army procession of kit left after Dunkirk dumped in a field and called it a Stores Depot.

I was 18 months in the Forestry Commission. It just seemed a good idea at the time. Five or six of us worked together. Mostly young lads it was a pretty good life if you were single. Based at Sixpenny Handley that road from Handley to Bower Chalke, quite bleak, inclined to fill up with snow in winter, and that was where the main party worked, up to 25 men at a time. They planted for a private owner. That was quite neat and tidy, trouble was he ran short of money. Ashmore woods now belong to John Eliot Gardiner, now Sir John, the old gamekeeper, Joyce Taylor, was telling me about it. Eighteen months with forestry. Bad winter of '47 was really grim. Never been so cold in my life. It froze everything. The tractor froze and split in half. Some people had pumps and got by and kept themselves alive. We were on mains electric which was quite surprising, three phase for a drier at Ashmore. The snow lay on the ground for about six weeks.

After I left the army I met the head forester along the road and he said, "Are you coming back?" and he said I should come back and see them. Very nice old boy, John Humphreys, very good forester. A lot of wood was planted on Cranborne Chase. Deer were a menace really. They stripped all the bark off everything, My father had a thing about squirrels, couldn't stand the sight of them. Tree rats he called them and just blasted every one he could. These were grey squirrels. The last red squirrel I saw was in Scotland in 1958. They have brought them back.

You could see where the charcoal burners had been. Later on the mobile gangs would go round. I did see an outfit that went round on wheels. He carried on for a long time. Twenty years ago I thought about it. Peter Ward said I should get into it. He knew his timber. He was all right. I went back into the Forestry Commission. I came out of forestry school and then spent 18 months around Reading. I went freelance. This went on to contract felling, a chance to earn some money. Felling scrub oak mainly, nothing of any great value, in the Berkshire area. In the end I got fed up and then joined a gang. They didn't steal anything off me but I wouldn't leave anything lying around. I worked in Hatfield Park, Lord Salisbury's. Tidying up hornbeams. They were chopping them down, to get rid of them all. Coppiced very much like we have hazel down this way, some pollarded. The hornbeam was very hard timber to work and once you have got it cleaned up it is a super timber, like beech but more durable. The head forester got a notion that he would clear it roughly then plant it with Scots pine and that was it. Of course they started dying off just the same. The soil again. Young hornbeam branches were used for skimming the dross off the surface of molten iron.

I came back down here in 1962, the end of the hard winter. Some people did very well out of it. But I had Douglas fir delivered just before that snow, young trees straight from the nursery and we dug them in covering them up with soil, spent days doing that. They survived very well along with some Norway spruce. My father had died in 1958. He was born in 1903 and died when he was 55. So half his working life was spent working for Balfour and Rolf.

I was working for myself when I came back down. Making a living on a huge area, then Chris Oliver came along and he got cracking with it. Getting rid of rhododendron. Gamekeepers used to plant it for a pastime just a bit of cover for pheasants, soon takes over, pheasant shooting showed more profit than trees, but needed watching. I started with crosscut saws and axes in the Forest of Dean. Chainsaws were available but not much good as reliability goes. Prone to all sorts of breakdowns. They were quite heavy, a two man job to carry them around. They done a lot of work in their time, Danarm was the one built in this country. Remington was an American saw, German Stihl. The saws got faster and lighter. The more useful saw was the Husqvarna, Husky 90 and it gradually scaled down to a 70cc and that was when I started getting interested. And from then on it took off. The Danarms were 125cc like a BSA Bantam.

I used to race motorbikes on grass tracks, grass track racing with vintage bikes, used to exchange hands for about 10 shillings. Norton was a good bike, BSA's were OK. Ariel a heavyweight machine. Wish I had a Douglas, or a Velocette. We would race. Best of it was Blandford Camp. Track was a death trap. Blokes used to get killed wrapping themselves round lamp posts. Bikes were too good for the track.

Never worked with horses. I had a tractor, a Fordson. Couldn't get any decent prices for the timber. Seemed at the time that wood burners had come into fashion. They all needed firewood. Some pulp went to Kent or Chepstow mainly cardboard. Always a mystery where it ended up. Birch would go into Mere the brush factory 7ft 6 inch lengths. They worked on the broom head, had the holes drilled in it. Still there now. Still a lot of it growing up in Hampshire. There were hurdlemakers, blocks of hazel sold on, the autumn auction at the Museum pub off the Rushmore estate. Trouble was it was not just the hurdles but a certain amount of the wood had to go up to the House. If it didn't pass the guv'nor said so, they would have a big bonfire. I used to deal with the Forestry Commission. Pitt Rivers was all right if you were working there.

I worked in West Wood. It was planted in 1952, next door to a block my father planted. Thinning for years on end. First, second and third thinning. Quite a respectable wood now. Bluebells were a problem they were dangerous, if you get a slide on, very slippery, couldn't turn the tractor. A load could get away from you. You can easily get killed on steep ground. Wiltshire coppice was nice and flat. Cecil Coombes had an area in there. He could charm his way in anywhere, he'd walk everywhere. All my life has been spent planting, thinning or extracting.

Then I worked down at Wareham, that's a thing on its own. Same could be said for Ringwood. Lived at Shillingstone Lodge in Iwerne Minster for 33 years. I got Parkinson's 18 years ago and went on working for another 10 years, so I only stopped working about eight years ago. It seems to affect people who work outside; fumes from chainsaws or the early sprays. I had white finger badly, which meant your fingers went numb when it was very cold. I used to warm them up over the tractor exhaust. Comes from using early chainsaws, the vibration. I miss working in the woods.

21 Richard Hayward: Sawmill owner, Bulbarrow Milton Abbas Born 1950.

Work outside when you are young… We use every scrap of wood right down to the last bag of sawdust. 50p a bag. Will last a hamster about a year I have been told.

I was actually born in Wimborne and brought up in Pamphill. We moved out to Winterborne Stickland about the early '70s. Father was a bricklayer and plasterer but he did actually go back to the forestry side of it as he started on as a forester during the war. He worked around Wimborne and other areas around Dorset. Grandfather on my Father's side was a joiner, ex-farmer and Grandfather on my Mother's side, he was also an ex-farmer and then he was invalided out of the First World War. He had one leg I believe. Never met the chap. My Father's parents were Colehill and my mother's parents were Sherborne, Alweston and Bishop's Caundle.

I grew up round Wimborne. We were just on the edge of Kingston Lacy. I was born in 1950 and moved away in 1968. Got married and came here. I came to Winterborne Stickland and worked on a farm for quite a while, at Knife Hill Farm. Dairyman, long hours, quite hard work but I enjoyed it. I wouldn't want to go back to it now. A young man's game. Same as a lot of jobs. We had about 130, 150, all Friesians. And I done all that on my own. It was quite a good system with the Milk Marketing Board but since they let that drop, the price has dropped. Nine years. And then I got itchy feet and wanted to come back to forestry.

When I left school I done a three-year agricultural apprenticeship at Shapwick on Purchase's farm then moved away, got married couple of kids. I wanted to go into forestry when I left school but it didn't quite go to plan. I quite liked animals so I went that direction. I got that out of my system probably had about 14 years of that. Father worked for the commission, specially during the wartime, mostly handwork. Chainsaw had only just come in. In the '50s, that is when he came out of it, they were shouting for builders. He had been a trained bricklayer and it was a better way to have gone as he was starting his family. Work outside when you are young. He was good with an axe and crosscut saw. He taught us all that. We have done all that. Only recently there was a couple of chaps who wanted to use a crosscut saw and I had to give them a few hints. They didn't have a clue. They had to push and pull.

Basically I was doing mostly logs and I managed to get hold of this yard about '76. End of the very hot summer. This was an RAF camp, all to do with communications signals which is obviously now at Blandford Camp. We still got the aerials now. All automatic these days, and I believe people were actually based here till '63. All the lot. Early warning systems, police, army, ambulance, mobile phones. We are right bang in the middle of Dorset. We are right in the middle. Not the highest but very close. I think we are the highest residents 270 metres, whatever that is in feet. Quite misty today.

I started with chainsaws. Originally we used Stihl chainsaws, then we went to Husqvarna. Well we tried about everything there was on the market. There is either a Stihl or a Husqvarna. It goes through phases. Stihl saws are the best, then Husqvarna catch up. Everybody's on Husqvarnas then Stihl catch up. At the moment everybody's using Stihls. You only keep them for about one year if you have worked them hard, then keep that as the reserve, or semi-retirement. Bits.

Softwood and hardwood: Lot of hardwood, basically for logs. Stakes and rails. Beech loves chalk and does grow quite well, but very little market for it other than firewood. Now we gone into saw milling it is very seldom used. Still goes for pulpwood for Chepstow cardboard. They do like beech for

Richard Hayward with his sons Geoff and Bob

that. But of course it is not the best price. It is a lot of work, lot of haulage. Lines, three beech or oak. A few plantations with oak in and the Norway spruce. A lot of that close to me here, some of it is just coming into maturity and it would be more useable if it had been looked after a bit better. The softwood is thinned out, leaving a hardwood. That is the intention but there is still quite a lot to do. There are patches now with all the softwood taken out, not an awful lot, still quite a bit with softwood in.

We got two lads that do the felling in the woods. If it is close enough we bring it back ourselves. Because betime it has come out of the wood and unloaded, it is as easy for him to come back with a full load on especially with the modern tractors. They are so quick on the road you can get back unload in the yard in a better place very often. We are running out of space as you can see.

I rented this place till about '93. All we got is the two-acre site at the very top here. A gradual progression to the sawmill side of it and hoping to expand again. May actually go and buy a new saw this time. Instead of secondhand one. It is going to cost a bob or two. We are doing quite good demand for logs, probably shifting 400 tonnes a year in logs alone, certainly 400 tonnes.

We try to have several things going on, through the year you always get a rush on one particular item, but better than putting all your eggs in one basket. Firewood, doing a lot of oak beams, quite a lot of oak going through the saw now and waney edge board. Of course we do the fencing panels, the odd shed or two, ordinary fence posts, hardest work, last job to do these days, we don't do the tannelising. We have a local firm we take it to, the pressure treatment. Got my two sons working here and two other lads. One lad nearly all the time and one that comes in and helps us and one in the woods. We use every scrap of wood right down to the last bag of sawdust.

I wouldn't actually call it recycling. It's not recycling because we are using the whole product right through. The end product is very often used into woodchips and the greener material and the sawdust, the stuff you can't do with at all is mulched. Most of the compost and mulch goes to the local public, there are one or two bigger garden jobs going on through garden contractors. We do some by the bag but an awful lot is done loose. We can deliver it ourselves in bulk. We do an awful lot of woodchip, play areas, pathways, we have actually started doing some for cattle walkways. They have come to the conclusion it lasts that bit longer and lets the water through. Usually where they have got a walkway for the cattle to extra fields rather than walk on the flint. Which I don't blame them, but at the time it must seem quite expensive to do the job, but well worth it when it gets incorporated.

Most of what we cut is within a 20-mile radius. We did think about running a wood kiln here but because we are in a damp atmosphere, we thought it was quite pointless. Get it dry one minute then stack it in one of the sheds undercover. Then it is going to absorb through this damp atmosphere. We do have some lovely days. We have got one saw down there and putting another one on the end, and some finishing saws in the workshops where they make the fence panels and the sheds. A few little workshops for that.

Recycling with the local council a possibility, but we have no room left. Quite a good system a lot of local people who need to get rid of their green hedge trimming and the odd treetops and things like that and which we can make into a recycling mulch. We turn the piles, we got enough machines to do it but we need a little bit more room.

We are processing a lot of timber. Probably between 14 and 1,500 tonnes of wood a year. Quite lucky, no neighbours to complain to me. I live on site and now, since my wife has gone, I am living on my own.

Very steady market, we don't push to do too many sorts of things. It cuts the price down. It is already tight it gives you no leeway at all. No there could be a lot more work, the problem with any business is keeping the cash flow going. We are fairly lucky, we have got some very good customers. We get an awful lot of people pay straight away. Old fashion business that works. I am still dated myself. I don't look to see for any money for at least 30 days if not 60 days. Don't panic at all. It has taken me a long time to get to that system comfortably. Any bills that come in are paid immediately. Since I done that the business has really expanded. Everything is paid for as soon as the bills come in. Then I know that with anything still owing, I know damn well we are not broke.

Most of what we do is privately owned woodlands. I can't remember the last time we went on the commission land. It is nearly all privately owned. Quite surprising really. We have been very lucky here on this Delcombe estate, they have had a good management team, which we have been able to work with well. The little bit we have learnt over the years and the little bit they have learnt, we seem to have been able to tie it together. And we have got quite a good system going here, about 240 acres just beyond the yard. The tracks are a little bit dubious sometimes but after so many years at it, we have got used to it. You know which you use and those you don't use. Or which way you are going, there's some you don't go down when you are loaded and some you can.

We did think about charcoal burning at one point but it is such a dirty job, I thought we had a dirty enough job already and that was taking the biscuit. We really need to be brilliant at that and understand it, we would be in big trouble here with the moisture.

Here it has only been woodland for approximately 250 years. It was all downland before that, sheep grazing. And probably Lord Milton who owned the abbey didn't like to see the hills with no trees on, so he originally he had them planted. And those massive big beech trees that's how old they are now, they are probably 240s, 260s plus. Over 200 years old. Seldom replant, very often clean an area, tidy it right up for someone else to come and replant but we don't very often replant ourselves, very little clear fell, nearly all thinnings. Very sustainable. Sawdust we do quite a few for stables and chicken. When we have too much we sell it quite cheaply, 50p a bag. Will last a hamster about a year I have been told. I have got one or two customers who come once a year for one bag of sawdust. And they are still amazed it is still only 50p. We have thought about going into it properly, then you would need to make sure it has got to be much drier than what we are using.

We don't use the sawdust ourselves, but as a workshop heater it is ideal, an old woodburner the boys got in the shed there. You can press sawdust into briquettes, it can be done but the machine is quite expensive. We got humidity problem another thing that has to be kept dry, we are not flushed with nice new big buildings. We are actually going to try and put another saw in mainly top cut oak beams and big sections of wood partly to reduce the labour but to reduce the physical side. We are all quite capable of doing it but there are points when it gets a little bit over the top and with all the health and safety aspects. We have had to draw our horns in compared with what we used to pick up.

Cordwood? We try to do that the minimum way possible. Basically a fully automatic firewood logging machine. The hardest piece is to lift the cordwood onto the bench and once you have got it onto the bench, the bench brings it forward chop your log off and it drops into the splitter. Automatically pushes its own way out elevator straight into the truck. I think my father would have a heart attack. I think he was all for progress. But like all machines they do have their hiccups. I would say the one we got ourselves we bought secondhand, and I would say we have more than wrote it off in the first year. Most of the firewood is already cut for next winter and we are thinking now for cutting for the winter after that. We try to keep it for a minimum of one year some of the woods are better, oak will last for two years. Beech is beautiful at two years. Not bad at a year, but at two years it is extremely good. But then you get customers that moan that the wood is burning too quick. No softwood firewood. The hardwood is for firewood, occasionally we do sell some out of the area as cordwood but only by the lorry load. All the softwood goes through our systems, woodchips. If it is bent or grotty it goes through the woodchipper.

The future? I can still see it growing quite a lot, I can see us altering the business slightly bringing the two sons into a partnership properly. I am going to have to be designated to the office these days, which is where I spend most of my time now, obviously I am getting a older and finding it a little bit harder to do the physical side. We got quite a few people who are keen to sell to us locally but we just cannot take any more in at the moment, until we can expand the sawing system. If we can expand the sawing system we have got, we can process more wood, the only concern I have a little bit is the waste off the trees, but we have really got to push the woodchip further again. That takes up all the waste and the real rubbish goes into the mulch. Very often for new buildings and a lot of revamped. Dorset wood for Dorset houses. So much easier to work on metric, so much easier.

Metal in trees? We have had a few problems ourselves saw milling. We were cutting a lot of elm trees when the diseased elm was about and the first four foot, no chance. You could do what you liked with it, you didn't dare put it in the load, barbed wire, nails from farming, fence staples. Terrible. I cut one tree, an elm tree and it had one of the steel cages round. I actually hit into that. I had just put a new chain on. I was not amused, it was rather a large tree probably four and a half foot through, it did get cut down in the end. It didn't do the chain much good at all. But they would never accept anything that was cut at ground level, they would want the first three or four foot taken off.

Saw blades? Ours are now running at £120 a time, we have them down at the saw doctors, the Pulham ones have retired. Ours go to Somerset. There are 14 maybe 16 bands now done in a rotation. They take half away, being serviced, they call it serviced. We call it doctoring. Checking, servicing, sharpening, then of course we got the other batch.

The South of England during the Second War was just one vast army camp. This camp didn't get set up until 1941, for Enigma early warning system, before the actual radars came in, all on that idea. We have had trees come in especially softwood, as if they have used it for target practice. And you will have at least 20 bullets in perfect condition and because they are lead, lovely. We are able to saw straight through them. They were putting targets up on trees .303 rounds in there. But they come out, you could get them out and they were just as if they were brand new. But as regards the elm trees and metal, it was absolutely terrible.

22 Rick Smith: Charcoal burner, Halstock
Born 1960.

I didn't like being inside and so that was the thing that drove me more than anything else. The whole place is based on an ethos of sustainable living.

I was born in Romsey in Hampshire in 1960. My Father was a farmer and my Mother looked after us. There were four children and that kept her pretty busy. It was a mixed farm, predominately arable. My Grandfather was a doctor and my Grandmother was a nurse. He grew up in rural Norfolk. My Mother's family were involved in farming in Kenya and they came back in the 1960s. My family came here in the 1980s. And as there were quite a lot of organic growers down here I thought I would move down here as well and try that. I found it an interesting experience. I do enjoy the work, but I realised how hard it was for potentially very little return. One abiding memory I have is spending an entire day cutting cabbage, for minimal amount of money, which was very, very little and it was due to go off to a supermarket and the whole lot was rejected and came back. That was the memory that sticks with me. You are very much at the mercy of other people. I just worked for somebody else, it was just to see what it was like. At that time I felt that this was not really for me, so I did not pursue it but now I have come back to growing on a small scale. The one thing I certainly wouldn't contemplate doing is dealing with supermarkets.

Initially my Father farmed down here but it was only on a very small scale. They bought a farm which had already been reduced, part of it had already gone, there was a small area with it, he ran some sheep. But he was always an entrepreneurial person and he didn't always stick to farming. Even when I was young he had various different projects going on. He bought up one or two houses that were very dilapidated. One of my earliest memories is mixing up concrete. And at one point he even bought a hotel which was quite run down. Needed quite a lot of work doing to it and then selling it on. He enjoyed getting his hands dirty, he's a very hands-on sort of person. This was a poultry farm, battery chicken farm. I never saw it when it was running but I am told there were about 60,000 birds here so a lot of hens. My Father bought it when it closed and converted the buildings into workshops. That was typical of the sort of thing he would do. He was ahead of his time diversifying. He felt he was the archetypal small businessman and he was always looking to encourage other people through his life. So obviously he was looking to make a living for himself but he helped a lot of people along the way. He knew what it took, it took a lot of work.

I came down here when I was about 25. I never really knew what I wanted to do. The only thread was that I liked being outside. I didn't like being inside and so that was the thing that drove me more than anything else. So it was a question of casting around for things to do. When I was really young the only thing I can remember wanting to be was a gamekeeper. So I did quite a lot of different things, which involved farming or horticulture. I wasn't really interested in growing on a large scale or farming. That never, really interested me even though I grew up on a farm. It just wasn't for me. But what I had always enjoyed was working in the woods, with chainsaws, and that sort of thing. Gradually that's the sort of direction my life went in. I worked for somebody else for a while and then I built up my own business and went and studied arboriculture at Kingston Maurward. I have done very little work with softwoods, all the people I have worked with have told me to avoid it like the plague. I like to think we work quite hard anyway but the there you work yourself to the bone for nothing more or less. I managed to give that a wide berth, so it was a lot of coppicing and hardwood thinning.

Rick Smith, charcoal burner

I was doing tree surgery as well. It is dangerous, but the curious thing is, I was quite scared of heights when I was a child. I really didn't like heights, I still don't. If you climb a tree from the ground, you know how you have got there. But you'd never catch me bungy jumping. I'd never do that in a million years.

Climbing a tree you have to be careful. There's no two ways about it, you have to be careful, you never switch off. You have to think all the time what you are doing. Chainsaws up trees is dangerous, but in some ways it is no different to using chainsaw on the ground. You have to think all the time. In fact I would go so far as to say the really dangerous times are actually when you think you are doing something that isn't dangerous at all. And that's when accidents happen in my opinion. I've nearly had one or two accidents not when I have been up a tree but when I have been working on the ground.

Most of the saws I use are Stihls. The reason primarily is that I started using them and you tend to stick with what you know. Also we have a very good local dealership and if I have problems with the saw I can take them there and they will sort them out more or less there and then if they can do it. I don't know of any other places that will do that. So that's predominately what I use and I find them reliable and good. People have other opinions. People doing softwood usually like Husky saws.

Charcoal? I suppose I started dabbling with charcoal and as you can tell I don't stick to one thing. Perhaps I got that from my Dad, it just grew. The horticulture grew first so to speak. Farming was in the blood, just felt like keeping a few hens, so I bought 30 hens for laying just to see how they go. Black Rocks, beautiful looking. I do see things in an aesthetic way. I suppose it is important not just to regard things just as in monetary terms. We have got just under 300. We have also just got 40 table birds just to see how we go with them, just as a sort of experiment really. It is very expensive to get free range birds, not surprisingly. Having kept hens, there is nothing like having your own, having meat you have reared yourself. We have gone full circle now. It is quite ironic really, that's the way things are going. Battery chickens will be phased out so I think we are heading in the right direction and I don't see anything wrong with small scale. As far as I am concerned the more local the better. Why go Dorset-wide if you can do it in 10 miles? The eggs we sell mostly direct to the pubs and hotels. We do sell some at a farm shop up the road and they also buy herbs and salad bags from us as well. They are a good outlet for us. But then again there are all the disadvantages of doing things on a small scale, it isn't that economic. We deliver and so you have to factor that in, so we are thinking all the time how we can make things more efficient and make things work better, which you have to do. And we have got lots of ideas. Unfortunately we don't live on site, so therefore we couldn't have a farm shop. That is the most obvious way of selling direct to the public. That would be the most sensible thing in some ways but that is not a possibility at the moment. So we have to carry on as we are at the moment, but I am quite encouraged by it really.

Once I started doing tree work, I started selling firewood and I was looking at other ways of using wood. I was interested from an environmental point of view. I felt quite strongly about it. Quite often my motivation is not purely a financial thing. So I start with that and I try and make the maths work, so to speak. I started about three years ago on a small scale. Just bought a kiln, didn't invest a great deal, had the wood already. The kiln is circular metal kiln about six foot across by about four foot high, which you fill with wood to produce charcoal. So it didn't cost me a great deal to buy that. The skill is in a controlled burn. The wood is not actually burning. What you are doing is driving everything off, all the moisture and volatiles, everything that is in the wood. So you are reducing it to carbon. Then once you have done that you stop the burn quite quickly and you do that by controlling the air, by shutting off the air and the fire will die. You have eight ports so you have four inlets and four outlets. The air goes in. How it works you have effectively a chimney, you build a gap in the middle of a circular stack of wood in the kiln, with a chimney in the middle. You have your eight ports and you make sure that the air can get through to the middle and be drawn up through the chimney. It goes back out through the chimneys on four of the ports on the outside so the smoke can exit through them. Approximately half way through the burn you change the ports so your air inlets and outlets alternate so that you get an even burn. The smoke is the most obvious indicator, the smoke changes through the burn. Initially it is very thick, white dense smoke, a lot of moisture, mostly steam. And as the burn nears completion the smoke remains white but starts to thin out quite considerably as the tar is being driven off. If you had a lot of oak the smoke might be denser and more acrid. I think in general the smoke, you don't want to inhale it. You have a tonne and a half of wood and the smoke is very, very dense. It takes about a couple of hours to load the kiln with two people doing it, not a job you want to do on your own. I would stand inside and get somebody to pass the wood to me and load it as I want it. That's how I find the most efficient way to do it.

At the moment the wood is all wood that I have cut. But I shall be buying it in as cordwood. Some woods will rot a lot more quickly than others like hazel or birch. If you leave them too long it will rot, but oak you could leave it for a long time. Conversely oak needs a long time to season out. It is always mixed just as it comes. The firing, the rule of thumb is 12-18 hours but I have known it to go on for longer than that. Depends on the condition of your wood. I don't use kindling to start it. If you are starting in spring you get the kiln going, the ground is still quite cold and damp. But as you go through the season, assuming the kiln is in the same place, it is going to take a lot of moisture and the ground underneath is going to be very, very warm. So it becomes easier to light the kiln and as you go through, you get fines at the bottom of the kiln and that helps to get it going. So essentially what I do is, I put maybe a bit of charcoal or what are called brown ends, the incomplete burn that hasn't carbonised properly from the previous burn, put that in the chimney. Then light a piece of newspaper and drop it down there. I find that works perfectly well. Other people I know light rags soaked in diesel and poke it in through one of the ports but I have never done that. The way that I do works perfectly well.

You then have to wait till you know that the burn is going really well, enough that it is not going out. Then you put the lid on and I put it on chocked up, so it is not actually sat down like a saucepan lid. Then once you know the kiln is going well enough, that is it not going to go out, then you put the lid on properly. You drop it right down, you seal it with soil. The lid sits inside and you put soil round the lid and that stops the air getting in or out. The great advantage of a metal kiln over an earth kiln is where you would have to be in attendance all the time. I wouldn't worry about it when I get it going as I want it to, you know that air isn't getting in or out where I don't want it to. I am quite happy to leave it for six hours, it takes 24 hours to cool down. In practice I usually leave it for longer, a day and half. 24 hours is rule of thumb. I have a burn approximately once a week.

In this case you take the charcoal out, riddle out the fines, the very small stuff. You take that out and bag it up and it's ready for sale and then you are ready to load it up and start the process all over again. Three kilo, sometimes five kilo bags. They go to a range of outlets. Farm shops is one outlet, garages sell a lot of charcoal, butcher's shops are good outlets. Very seasonal, not only is it seasonal but it is confined to the weather. It is a precarious way to make a living. I wouldn't put in the bags in the autumn but I would be happy to charcoal it and put it in fertiliser bags. You have got it in stock then and that's how I try and operate. You have to keep it dry. The thing about it is that you really need to have some in stock and you need to start burning before you are going to sell it, otherwise you get caught out. If you haven't got it that's that. If you burn a tonne of wood you end up with approximately a sixth, reduced in weight, as there is so much moisture in wood. As there is everything else.

I build it up every year, certainly doing more than last year. I don't put my eggs all into one basket. We are competing with imported charcoal, that's how I view it entirely. There are big environmental issues associated with it, I try not to compete with British charcoal. The imported might come from South East Asia, or Africa. It could easily be hardwood and a lot of it is unsustainable. Wood is being cut down which should not be cut down. Whereas all of the wood we use is either thinnings or coppice wood, so it is all part of sustainable practice which benefits a huge range of wildlife. A lot of the imported charcoal is taking away habitats of all kinds which may not be replaced and maybe irreplaceable. Imported charcoal, for example, can come from mangroves. In the tsunami one of the reasons why that was much worse in some places than others, was you had these mangrove swamps which are on the coast act as a kind of buffer if you get those big waves. They will absorb the shock of those waves. Now in this instance it was not that they were making charcoal in this case but it was for prawn farming and for tourism, which is a horrible irony. And that is the sort of thing that is going on. I am very keen that people should be very aware of that and that has not been mentioned in the aftermath of the tsunami. You barely heard a mention of it.

Woods for charcoal? I suppose hazel is my favourite wood. Generally any native hardwood barring poplar and willow, which are very soft, no coniferous wood at all, no softwoods. In a burn you might get oak, ash, hazel, hawthorn, blackthorn, field maple, a whole range of different woods. I have got a small bit of coppice that I work. I have just been hauling some wood back today from a place called Kingcombe coppice which is not far from here and that is worked by a variety of people but I am the only person making charcoal. There are lots of other products you can get from coppice and charcoal is only one of them. Ironically charcoal is a good product from what is called overstood coppice, i.e. coppice that hasn't been cut for a number of years and it becomes much too big for making hurdles. Whereas once it has been cut for charcoal, providing you can keep the deer off it, which is another big issue, and if the coppice then re-grows, then it is ideal for hurdlemaking. And so this wood that I have just cut, when it re-grows it will not be much use to me for charcoal. And there will be a hurdlemaker who will make use of that. It is a very good intermediary way of getting coppices back into rotation. There are a few hurdlemakers, not so many in this part of Dorset, more north and east. There are some, certainly but they tend to be more concentrated up there and more coppice in rotation. Thatching spars is another thing you can make.

Hedgelaying? I do a fair bit in the winter, it is seasonal and you hope these things will dovetail. Charcoal is confined to a small time in the summer so come the winter there is no income, so you have to turn to other things. Hedgerow timber can make very good charcoal, this burn now all comes from a hedge that I laid in the spring of this year. I tend to do more of the flying hedge, typical Dorset hedge. We try and use everything we can out of the hedge, and that is one of the beauties of these things. It is interesting to see how it pans out really, now the Common Agricultural Policy has gone full circle. From being production-based subsidies to totally environmental subsidies which to me seems like a complete nonsense. I have always felt that a happy medium is the best way, and the older style of mixed farming, all these environmental things were built into it. It was just part of the system and it seems ironic that there are all these great subsidies for doing it. As I say it will be interesting to see where it goes and how long it lasts for. Certainly there are a lot of opportunities for hedgelaying and for tree surgery. We did quite a lot of pollarding of willows on farms, big willows that needed to be pollarded. Money is tight in farming as it is.

Pruning we do fruit tree pruning, again it is a shame that's another thing that has gone by the by. Fruit tree, top fruit production, it is a shame. The Dorset Coppice Group is an association of people who work in the coppice industry and it is making great strides at the moment. It started out as quite a small concern but it has built from there, due to the hard work of a few people, to the point where the coppice group has got its own woodland at Bonsley Wood near Sturminster Newton. That is again a coppice that is being brought back into rotation. The idea being that it is a demonstration site so that people can see what people are doing with the wood, charcoal burning, hurdlemaking, furniture making. But also wildlife which will be encouraged by this management practice and there is the opportunity for people to see and study the wildlife and ecology of a coppice wood.

The future? I think that I know roughly the direction I want to go in. I want to do more charcoal. Like to devote more time to the work we are doing here and growing producing food from here. That is ultimately what interests me. Tree work is pretty much a young man's game. I was relatively quite old when I came into it. Much as I love it I am not going to be able to do it forever, so I need to be thinking about doing other things. I still want to increase the production of charcoal but it is making the maths work. I don't know exactly where we will go but I want to pull the whole thing together.

Most people who come to this site find it an interesting and beautiful place. I would like to think that there is some aspect of tourism where people could come here and see charcoal being made and all the different aspects of things being grown here. They say some children don't know that milk comes from a cow. I am sure a lot of them haven't seen a cucumber growing or aubergines. We are looking at a load of raised beds where we are growing a range of vegetables and herbs. We can see rosemary, thyme, dill, chives, coriander marjoram, elephant garlic, just a few as an experiment. I duly left them to see what the flowers were like. We grew some garlic for the first time this year which we put in last November and it was a really excellent crop. Really fantastic so I was very, very pleased with that.

We are looking all the time at how we can sell things, like box schemes and farmers' markets. If you are selling at farmers' markets you are not competing with things from other countries. Farmers' markets maybe a key outlet in the future, we are just growing on a small scale. Just the two of us.

The thing is none of these things are very economic, it is a vocation like teaching or nursing or anything like that. It is just how your life dictates to you how you go. You have to work hard and think about it. When you are dealing with supermarkets you are always on a hiding to nothing. Whereas, if you are selling at farmers' markets or on box schemes you are selling directly and cutting out the middleman. You maximise your own profit.

It makes more sense growing on a small scale, and it is surprising what you can grown on a small area. Similarly with the charcoal, if I wanted to make money I would have gone and worked in the city. I certainly wouldn't be doing this. We have fantastic quality of life and it is hard work, it is a beautiful place to be and a lot of people who make a lot more money than I do would give their eye teeth to do what we are doing.

We see Mr Reynard almost every day… We see the foxes

trotting back and forward all the time, we see the cubs. The key is to make sure they can't get in and get at the hens. We did have a couple of unpleasant times a couple of years back, one time where we had just bought 50 brand new pullets, the foxes somehow got in and they had 44 out of the 50. They just kill for fun. Nobody would object if they just took one hen and disappear, but if they get in there, they'll have the lot if they can. That is their nature but at the same time, it is our livelihood and we can't be doing with that. As I say we wouldn't kill every fox there is. Prevention is better than cure. So we just try and make sure the fox can't get in. We do shut them up at night.

We compost everything. It works very well. We use sawdust from a joinery up the road to bed the chickens on, in the house and when we clean that out it all goes on the compost heap. And so it makes excellent compost and where the chickens are running outside, they are on concrete and have access to a field. But a lot of the time they spend inside on this concrete platform and I have put a load of woodchip on and over time that will all rot down. The whole place is based on an ethos of sustainable living.

Anthony Bailey and his two apprentices Karl Edwards and John Whitman

23 Anthony Bailey: Farrier and blacksmith, Stourpaine
Born 1950.

The old farriers only had to look at a horse's hoof and they would go away and make it and wouldn't have to alter the shoe. It has taken me 20 years to get to that stage…

I was born in October 1950 in Weymouth. Parents were farmers at Clover Farm, Portesham, a mile on the Weymouth side of Portesham just before you get to the turn for Rodden. The ground was clay and it used to crack in the summer, but it was good dairy land otherwise. We had a herd of dairy cows which Father milked by machine in a cow stall, not a parlour as it is today. They were getting on for between 30 and 40 which was as much as he could deal with single-handed and they were mostly Friesians with the odd Channel Island to bring up the butter fat. The milk was taken to Bladon Dairies which then turned into Express Dairies. Taken to Milborne St Andrew and processed there. They used to be taken in churns. First of all we had to lift them straight off the ground with the help of the lorry driver. Then there was a decree that lorry drivers weren't supposed to lift churns and so we had a ramp built and you had a two-wheeled trolley and you pushed the churns up onto the ramp. And from there it was on a level with the bed of the lorry.

Father started farming there in the 1930s as a tenant and then he worked up and had the opportunity to buy the farm which is what he did. He worked it all through the war. His father was a farmer at Hooke near Toller, I think they were dairy. Father was a dairyman and learnt cheese making, as far as I understand he made the blue vinny. We had all the equipment to do it, including a big steriliser and lots of shiny buckets and pans for setting the milk out. But he had stopped making cheese by the time I came along. Mother made the butter which was a chore and we boys had to stay and churn this butter. In the spring it would turn very quickly. Say you might only spend half an hour at it, but in the wrong time of the year you would spend three hours just churning this butter. And as boring a job as ever it was. And you weren't allowed to leave and you had to keep it turning, and this was the wooden churn without the electric wheel, you keep hoping it would turn and it wouldn't. It was the most boring job out and we weren't allowed not to do it. If my brother would find an excuse not to do it, I'd end up having to do it or else I would say it was his turn and refuse to do it. But one of us had to do it. It was designed to keep us out of mischief. We now realise that butter in its pure form is now somewhat detrimental to the health, so we use one of these butter products.

Father and blue vinny. He didn't really understand that was what he was making back in the '50s. Blue vinny was known but there wasn't all the fuss about it today, as there was still the odd producer then. But now of course it is talked about as there aren't the original people still making it and hygiene is cancelled out a lot of the processes. Natural blueing, horse harnesses drawn through the milk and all that sort of thing, I believe. I think they would have had something going off to catch the spores, they would have understood that.

We had pigs he was a great pig man. We even tried sheep but what we found was they kept getting out and you had to run a long way to get them back. So we never really got into that, but we tried them as he wanted us boys to experience sheep. I think he made a very good living if you think he was renting it and was able to save enough through his own endeavours to buy it. That is very good. It was only 75 acres. But that kept over 30 cows going and everything was produced on the farm. He did buy the dairy cake in. His father came from Hooke and on my Mother's side they came from Leigh and Hermitage up round Sherborne. I didn't hear that they were cheese makers but they were dairy farmers. But there was a blacksmithing element amongst them.

I couldn't see the point of getting up every morning early to milk these cows and never ever have a break. That's what really got me and of course the butter making was the most tedious job I could be set at that young age and I thought that is not for me. I wanted to put as much distance between myself and butter as possible.

Earliest memories? Butter, shelling peas and broad beans. Father was a very keen gardener and he kept a very good vegetable garden. It was his hobby as it is mine now. We lived very well, we never dreamed of drinking milk, we used to drink cream.

The pigs were sold on usually as finished bacon pigs. We either had a contract with the F.M.C. and they would pick up a batch. They were graded and you would be paid according to the grade. And we were always striving to get the right size pig for that day. Which was a fatter pig than what it is now. We were trying to get a leaner pig then, but parents were of an age when meat wasn't meat unless it had some fat running through it. And they would make a point of eating fat in front of us at the table and we would be there cutting it off. I particularly would nearly throw up having to eat this fat. In the end they realised that I couldn't stomach it which is why I have always remained in pretty good shape. That's what I put it down to. I saw the light before a lot of people. I couldn't stomach that fat.

Early memories? About two or three years old, we never had the telephone or the electric at that time, but although we had a bull, Father wanted to out cross his cattle. He would have to go to the village to phone up the artificial insemination service and that was from the local call box which was a mile away. I can remember one treat. He went and did that and took me up the road for whatever reason to go into the blacksmith's shop which was by the Half Moon Pub, in the middle of Portesham just above the church and below the shop which was at the top of the village. I can remember going in there and seeing the sparks and the stuff sizzling in the water. They may have put on a display, could only been about two or three years old and from that moment on I knew that was what I wanted to do. The noise, the lot, the smell that seemed to me what I needed. They were general smiths. There were two farms in the vicinity that had horses, there may have been three. There was one at Abbotsbury, one, Mr Male, who had shires and continued to have shires 'till recent years. He did his work with tractors but he was known as quite a horseman and ourselves, we did all our work with shire horses but the others had tractors. We had to do it all by horse until they retired in 1966.

We had contractors in as well. I think the big influence was my Mother who was also a farmer's daughter and they had always been in horses and she was a very keen horsewoman at the time and that was one reason. She wasn't mechanically minded as I can remember from her driving a car. She was also frightened that Father would turn the tractor over if he had one. And that was quite a possible thing in them days. They would hitch in the wrong place and up end them. When they hitched on if you didn't know to keep the hitch low you could up end them. And many a person was killed for that reason or they would drive up their silage clamps and turn the tractor over as quick as that. There was no safety frames in those days.

What used to happen was, they'd come to you. I don't remember the horse being taken to the blacksmith. Blacksmiths had in their day a very good eye. Well I think we got the same today, well they would either measure it or come with the shoes and they wouldn't dream of doing it hot, they would do it cold. But there was a problem with our horse, he had what was called "the itch". And that meant he had mites in his feathers and he would stare and stamp, and I can remember he took out one or two floors of the stable, just by stamping all night long. And of course with shoes on he would rattle them loose and then lose a shoe and in the end Father decided he might get away without shoeing him and he did. He worked that horse and never trimmed his feet, never did anything to him and the horse was worked and he never went footsore as far as I could work out. But he would still stamp his legs and still gnaw because of the mite. There just wasn't the systemic medicine then to cure the problem as there is now. They now give them a systemic injection which will kill the mite. We used to try and treat it with methylated spirit which would in fact kill the mite. The thing was the horse would get the smell of the meths and he would do anything than rather have his legs done.

The blacksmiths? Chief man was Jim Taylor and his apprentice was Don Peach. Archie Rice and he was the chief building side of the business, so they could come in, for instance where they had to renew the stable floor where the horse had stamped it out. That was a job they would come and do. There was small building jobs as well as the blacksmithing side. The one horse we had was called Captain he had a bit of hunter in him and he would jump out if he had half a chance. He was quite a good jumper. So we had to be careful with what fencing there was to make sure he couldn't go.

I went to school in Portesham. First for my primary days then parents tried to get me a better education they sent me to Thornlow which was a private school in Weymouth. It certainly worked for my brother but I think it was wasted on me, not because I didn't try, just that it wasn't the sort of education I best benefited from. Later on, I went to Gillingham comprehensive that was much better for me.

We sold up, had a farm sale, sold the property and everything else and moved to a smaller acreage where Father just had one milking cow which he used to milk by hand in the field and a lot of pigs. That was his sort of winding down phase, we were at Huntingford which is between Mere and Gillingham. Well what happened there was, we stayed there three years. Father was getting on a bit, well into retiring age and he decided he didn't want any animals after all cos we had the pigs and the house cow and so we sold up that and we moved to Stourpaine which was just a bungalow with no garden. But there was an allotment and the allotment is in quite a picturesque situation it overlooks the Stour Valley and if you worked hard at it you could grow quite a lot of things on it. It was coming out of the village going towards Blandford on the left. Mother decided that I was going to have a better job than ever they had, which meant not doing manual work. I ended up at Eldridge Pope's as a trainee manager. That didn't really suit me but I stuck it for seven years. That was at Shaftesbury 'cause it wasn't the done thing to go into a job and just leave it. You had to show that you were reliable. The shop in the middle of town where it had cellars. It was the biggest off licence around up there and we had quite a clientele of gentry and people used to come and collect wines from us because the manager was well knowledgeable and that was to be instilled on me as an assistant. I got quite good at it, they would come to me and ask my advice about it. So that was all right, we had quite a trade there. Draft South African sherry. We had loads of them 12½p for the empty plastic five gallon container and that used to go into our little fund.

What happened was, my Auntie who was the mother of the local famous trainer Robert Alner said that her farrier was only a young man. He was looking for somebody to help him out and he said: "I can't pay you but you can have a go." But it meant that I had to hold down a job and spend all my spare time attempting to be a farrier and doing all the things that farriers do at weekends and holidays. I used to spend half the night there trying to make his shoes for the next day's work. He wouldn't pay you. He was giving you the experience presumably so that you could move on and one day earn a living. It was instilled in you that you weren't useful but that he was just helping you out. Anyway he got away with that because I stuck it out. That was about 1974 -75. Then I got good enough to be employed in that business and I got employed to Wing and Staples. I forgot to mention that when I was at school I got top in CSE metalwork for my year. Top theory and pretty good practical marks and that was the only thing I was good at. So that was encouraging. Then the opportunity came to do courses at Hereford College because I was good enough. I wanted to get a recognised certificate for the job. I felt that there was no good carrying on unless I was recognised. I applied for a job at Wing and Staples at Motcombe and Mr Staples saw the opportunity and took me on.

I did almost seven years at Wing and Staples. Hereford courses were one week, two weeks, three weeks. But that had to be done out of my own pocket. They wouldn't sponsor me for that but I did get some help, a grant from the Rural Industries Bureau, so they did in fact turn round and back me on that. Being honest to my parents when I left school, horses weren't quite so popular. I can see why he did it, but he didn't foresee the popularity that occurred in the '70s. Fair comment really.

I had a Great Uncle who in the latter end of the 19th or early part of the 20th century had left the farming side of it, on Mother's side. He was a Coffin, and he trained at Wallace Titt's, the blacksmith's, and he ended up at Holwell in the blacksmith's shop there. In the last 20 years or so I met the last blacksmith at Holwell and he remembered his father buying the business from him back in the '20s or '30s. I knew that he had been a blacksmith but I didn't put a lot of significance on it. It was interesting to know that there in the breeding it must be there. That was a great comfort. I thought there might be a genetic thing there spurring me on. I had a great passion for it ever since I was two or three years old and taken to the forge for the first time.

What happened was with the introduction of the Ferguson tractor. A big thing in this country was Harry Ferguson's system of machinery. It came just at the right time. It really helped us survive when the embargo was on with Germany, and everybody was going towards machinery. Well machinery meant machines and they couldn't possibly turn out the stuff without being tooled up. And really it started being the end of the blacksmith. apart from the horses. The horses were beginning to die out because the tractor was beginning to take over. '47, '48 they were still hunting, but it didn't take off until the end of the 1970s. And all the people, even if they didn't go themselves, they remembered having a pony when they were children and they wanted their children to have a pony. A lot of trade in the '70s and the '80s in all these ponies. But now I think it is starting to go back the other way.

Shoeing a horse? Well obviously I like to do them hot. You could do them cold depending on the circumstances. I think the great turning point was Wing and Staples in 1978. The gas furnace came in, the Calor gas furnace and they were a sort of a homemade thing with fire bricks and a jet sticking into a box. And you could get your horseshoes a dull red and that meant that they was hot enough to burn them on to a horse's hoof. And I remember they were against it at Wing and Staples and other places really because they had always done it cold. It was quite a skill to shoe a horse cold and they didn't really see that the extra time spent doing them hot was going to be any advantage. So I remember going to the Great Yorkshire show and there was a chap up there who had made a lot of these gas fires and I bought one out of my own pocket. And I asked Mr Staples if I could use it and he said, "yeah we have got people who would like a hot fire." He was very good. He paid for the gas and I used to go out shoeing them hot. Now I only did that because I had an exam to pass. It was important that I got above the cold shoeing so I really needed to shoe hot. These were the first of the mobile ones because before that they used a round cold hearth on a short pedestal with a hand blower which they would wind up. That is as if they were keen enough to do it hot which they would wind up at the person's yard. They had them in the back of the van smouldering away and when they got them in the yard they would wind him up and blow up the coals and away they would go.

Blacksmiths had been mobile back in the '20s when vehicles came in. Before that they were the village blacksmith and for whatever reason, if a horse could not come to them, they would go to the horse. They would do it in a cold fashion and take a cross bar of a bicycle and hang their shoes on there, with their tools on the pannier behind and whip round to the farmer and do it maybe in an emergency, like that morning's mowing. You can just imagine it. They did a certain amount of mobile stuff then but they preferred to have them in the forge. Obviously hot metal is pliable like plastic and cold metal means a lot of beating. But they had a very good eye. Obviously the further we go back they had a very good eye for shape. The old farriers only had to look at a horse's hoof and they would go away and make it and wouldn't have to alter the shoe. It has taken me 20 years to get to that stage.

When I first started out, they always had the names of the customers' horses on the wall and that was the way of getting you to keep occupied; he would take the shoes off and you had to replace them. Wing and Staples had a similar thing. Walls with hooks on and names on and you had to replace the shoes and you were kept busy and you were never without a job then. The hind foot is the shape of a coffin, an open ended coffin, and the front foot is a circle with a segment cut out. The thing that the horse can't understand is the smoke rising up. He thinks it is some horrendous spirit and they have to be taught to ignore it and that would take four or five shoeings of being calmed and reassured not to react to the smoke. You get the idea of where to tie the horse in the stable, to get the best effect, how to organise the handler to hold the horse that sort of thing. You really need somebody who is good at holding the horse. You are underneath and there is not a lot you can do. And you do depend on the man holding the horse's head. I wear leather chaps but I started out wearing a leather apron. The apron always ended up on the wrong leg as you can imagine as it would go round the waist, but the chaps are now round the thigh and they don't move and it is a lot better.

The metal you want just under white heat, just under a heat where it would start to deteriorate through melting and that will give you enough heat to make half of a shoe. And then you put it back in and make the other half. Time to make shoes, it depends on the size of the shoe and the weight of the metal. If you had a medium size set of shoes to make you could probably make the whole lot, that's nails, holes and clips, finished off, filed up and made to look smart in about twenty minutes. Stud holes, the lot.

In recent years, especially this last year, it is doubtful whether it is going to carry on in the same form that it has. And I have started to diversify into old fashioned blacksmithing service. So I go out on site welding for people, I go out on site fitting up jobs that they have asked me to do such as gates and gazebos and stuff like that. And they also come here and give me jobs. But I still got an apprentice. We still do horses as well. But I can see a day when it will be cut right down and I will be glad that I have become more versatile.

I am on my seventh apprentice and I expect he could

well be my last one because there isn't probably going to be the money there to give them the work to pay them. They are nearly five years. The apprenticeship is four and a half years official, that is how long they spend at college, and they usually do another six months to round it all up and show no ill feeling between us to finish off. At the beginning it is very intensive training them because we have got all the health and safety aspects to make them think before they operate but once they got them trained by the end of the second year they are really useful.

The blacksmithing is pretty much dead. All the decorative work is being imported from factories in Italy as far as I can work out. And most stuff comes in from there and fabricators adapt and copy through fabrication methods the old blacksmithing ways. From health and safety point of view this is good, so you are in fact going to see the demise of the true blacksmith as it has always been.

Blacksmiths? There are a lot of farriers about, there's no shortage of them. You only have to look in the yellow pages and you probably see four or five and a lot don't advertise, so that's well covered. Actual blacksmiths perhaps only two or three because it is really fabricators doubling up. They just don't need to be able to bend metal hot they can do it all cold. Steel comes from stockholders I put an order in when I need it. It comes in sections and there are a lot of stock holders about who buy it from British Steel.

The tools haven't changed at all. You need pinchers to pull the shoe off, you need a hoofpick-cum-knife to pick the hoof out. You need a tool which is a bit like a chisel with a handle on, called a buffer, to knock the nails up on the hoof so that the nails don't pull straight out. You need hoof trimming tools, so that would be a knife, a pair of cutters that look like pinchers, very sharp and in my case I use the old fashioned toeing knife, which is a piece of bayonet with the point taken off. And you have a mallet which is now nylon and not wooden and will last forever and you hold it flat and parallel to the hoof and take off slivers of hoof to the level you know it has got to be to receive the shoe. You have to be careful of the quick which is why all these young farriers use these marvellous precision made cutters and they are reluctant to use the old fashion toeing knife and blade. But because I wanted to be good, I taught myself and found out how to use that blade, and I have taught all my apprentices how to use it. But when they leave me they go and use the new type cutters, they won't use a blade very rarely now. But at least they know how to do it. I find you can take a foot off level and you don't have to use a rasp if you are good at it.

Takes me an hour to shoe a horse if I am doing it hot. Some of my colleagues can do it in 20 minutes. I have to say there are colleagues out there who can do it in 20 minutes and their method is obviously not quite as thorough, they don't use any heat. And they would probably have to compromise on shape but it seems to do no harm whatsoever to the horse. And it is more a field shoeing that the army used to use. They had to get over it in a battle and a horse had a shoe off they had to get on with it.

The customers would like them to last eight weeks and they do try and get that. It depends, but if you are exercising your horse every day you will be lucky to get three weeks. But if you are riding it quietly during the week so you might be missing a day, you'll get six weeks and if you are really economic you'll get eight weeks. I like to shoe a horse at seven weeks, then we got a nice bit of foot to cut off. We can really make a difference to the job and the hoof is not too long to be detrimental to the action of the joints.

Retirement? It looks as if we will all have to work till we are 70. I have achieved what I set out to do. I have enjoyed myself.

24 Walt Pitman: Shepherd, Compton Abbas Born 1924.

I love horses, I love ploughing with horses. I were only 10 and ploughing with a double furrow plough, not a single one. I liked the way farming was done. If a shepherd had 700 sheep that was his job. Now the shepherd has 1,200 ewes and all these lambs following on.

I was born at West Lulworth in 1924 on a farm on the Lulworth estate. I stayed there till I was about 12. My Father was born in the Dorchester area and they went to work for a man called Mr Diffey at Lulworth and Father was driving three horses as a carter. Carter, that was his job. We used to walk five miles a day, two and half miles each way to school. We lived at a place called Sleight. Coming up over that hill, there's a camp to Durdle Door. Where I was born was two and a half miles off the main road across the fields up a track, the houses are demolished now. My Mother came from Woodsford near Dorchester. I am one of eight and then we moved from there to Gillingham. My Grandfather was carter and we have been in the farming all our life. Father I remember once he went milking cows for my brother-in-law who had a farm near Gillingham. We used to milk 100 cows and we had eight to milk by hand. And two of my sisters used to milk and two brothers, more or less a family affair. And the milk we used to put in those 17-gallon churns. My brother-in-law he had the farm and the thing is they used to come round with a big lorry picking up churns.

Well then when I was 16, my brother left school so I moved out for him to take my job so I went from there to East Knoyle and worked for Crawshawe Bailey and looked after the hunter horses. He used to have three hunters and then he had a farm and so I did tractor driving as well. I left school at 13 years old and started milking a dairy and they found out that I wasn't 14, so they sent me back to school for two months. Then when I left there I went to Witchhampton along with my sister and went to lodge there just to help the farmer. Cutlers, harvesting. He used to send me out ploughing at six o'clock in the morning. In between harvesting, we used to get the ground ploughed with the older tractors. Only the old standard Fordson, pre-war, no hood just the rattley seat. He had two carters over there and we used to haul the corn with horses and wagons and on the farm we used to build the ricks ourselves, or stacks as we call them. I stayed there longer than I intended to. And so then I came to Harding's. Went up for my medical with the army, passed A1. And I had a letter come within a week, and said I wouldn't be needed for National Service could I continue working on the farm. So at the time, I just accepted the fact and went on working. I came here in 1940 and I went to lodge in Hawkcombe Lane, Rixes's down Twyford. When I came to Harding's first I was took on as head tractor driver. I remember it very well. In those days he never had the tackle we have these days, then he said one morning, "would I help milking cows?" so I went relief milking for him at four o'clock in the morning, half past four, and for a bloke called Maloney. Had the dairy from Harding's, then I stayed there milking till he got another man. Then I went on tractor driving for about 12 months, then he said he would like to have foreman on the farm.

Wages when I came to Harding's first, I was getting £1 10/- a week and 9d an hour overtime. And then when our first boy was born I was getting £2 10/- a week. 2/6d and hour overtime. People wouldn't believe it today. I came here in 1940 and got married in 1948.

Harding said to me one day: "I am away a lot I would like to have a foreman on the place." He said in the morning I will take you in front of the men. 'Twas awkward really, we had 22 men at the time, so I met him down there, and he said: "In future you will be taking your orders from Walt, he is taking over the management of the farm." Three men walked off the farm. Well. I was about 18 or 19. He knew that I could do the job, he must have seen the sort of work I could do. Well these three men, two of them five o'clock at night came back and asked if they could get their jobs back. I said, "I never asked you to leave, so I am not taking you back." Straight as that, I said, "no." We had never had any upsets with them but they weren't going to take orders from me. 'Tis an awkward job to do really. In those days you didn't have to give notice like today. I can honestly say that I have never had man turn round and say he wouldn't do a job that I had asked him to do. We had 1,500 acres and three tractor drivers. Then I ran 800 sheep as well as running the farm, 800 ewes for Harding and we lambed outside. We used to put those great green tents, marquees, and the rain came on in March. And then when we got rid of the dairy in Fontmell, I took over the yard. I lambed in the yard down there, the concrete yard and all the loose boxes, well that was different.

Well then, when they did the combining I used to drive the combine myself. Always did. Before we had the combine we used to cut with a seven-foot binder, corn and sheaves. Albion and a Massey Harris we had one year, and the Albion was one of the main binders. Harvesting to my mind in those days, we used to get people out here looking for rats and rabbits and all the rest of it. I used to get people hyling corn, more what I call farming then than today. People used to come out at weekends and come out voluntarily. Used to get rabbits. Well of course the thing is that harvesting then was a big job. Well we had to make stacks and today we just have the combine. We bought our first combine a Massey Harris in '46-'47 I used to cut most of the time and Mr Harding would take over at lunchtimes and that.

Crop yields? We used to get say two ton an acre, that was a lot. One and a half, two ton an acre. Well this year my boy cut four to five tonne an acre wheat which makes a lot of difference from Ashmore into Tollard Royal. The thing is I supposed we carried on doing the same thing every year, we used to have two or three men cutting hedges with hooks, reap hooks. We never had no flail or hedge cutters. Hedges were kept down to height then. I saw a hedge laid the other day, nice to see someone out doing that sort of thing. You don't see that very often now. If you go out through Springhead a chap just laid a hedge there beautiful. Stake and bound. I think what's happened. Some used to tie it down with string but Father used to have a peg. My Father used to lay hedges as well, and he had crook pegs and it looked better. I've laid hedges myself. I've done most jobs on the farm.

We used to fold sheep on turnips and swedes. We used to feed for the ewes and lambs and then there was the shells, and we had a hacker who would hack up all these roots and used to turn the other dry sheep on them behind the ewes. I've done all that sort of work carrying hurdles. My Father used to carry nine on the spike. That was a hell of a lot. Father was short. These were four foot six hurdles. Father was a stocky bloke. I mean the thing is now we used to pay £1 for a six-by-six hurdle and 10/- for an ordinary hurdle. Used to give them a different patch every day. George grows 100 acres of roots for they sheep and he lets them in the field of 20 acres and let them have it in one lot, but he has used electric fence with the kale in one strip at a time. We used to have Suffolk cross Scotch half-bred then, the ones now are the mule ewes with a Texel ram on them. When I went to Gardiner's first I would like to buy sheep.

I were at Harding's about 40 years to the day, I thought to myself, I was about 58 in 1982. Parsons came here and didn't want to take any of the labour on. John Eliot phoned me up through Colin Kay at Melbury. I went up there first, looking out to the cattle. The place had never been farmed very much, just a few sheds, and he had that shepherdess up there, Georgina. But when I went up there at first they didn't have too many sheep. Then he went to import these sheep from Wales, Kerry Hills. You know what foot rot in sheep is like… I was on the phone, it came on the wireless one morning, I didn't hear it but

Walt Pitman with his chickens

Jeanette Harding did, and he said about all this trouble with his sheep, he gave me a good name on the radio.

When I decided eventually to leave he said: "Well I'll have to get someone in to manage the place." George didn't like sheep. Our boy doesn't like sheep he's more of a digger man, he does all the arable work, the ploughing so I used to go back up there and help him thrash and that. Organic wheat reed. I went back up there funnily enough to build ricks. We'd better make some stacks. You know Frank Bradley? Well, Frank he's still alive, he went up there, you got go round and tie him in. I done that for years, my boy was managing the place then, one day I went back up there, we had a thrasher come from Bridport, old Bert's died, we had a bloke from Bridport and he had the baler. No we stopped doing the straw, done it for a couple of years after I left. Widgeon: Always grow Maris Widgeon, tried growing it last year and for why? They grew Widgeon. a very poor yielding wheat, good straw. I don't think they have grown any this year. Stitching up, hyling we used to call it, corn hyling. At the finish we had the job to get the labour.

Peter Hood he used to get one or two helpers from Springhead, they helped us for a year or two, and the price went down as people went for the foreign water reed. Martin used to buy all our straw for the ridge, 'twas nice straw but if you worked out the labour, I can quite appreciate it now, you got to cut the corn, got to go out and binder it, stack it, hope it doesn't rain, cos the last year I did it myself. It rained, all the sheaves grew out. And the wind came and blew a lot of it flat. And the binder won't pick it up. I think that made Mr Gardiner think more about it. It used to be about £400 a ton. Martin used to try and get it as cheap as he could, the price gradually went down and down, and the demand for it went. The amount of men on the farm, Bert's binder, Sixpenny by Horton. Said you can have my binder if you want it and we went and bought the thing. We used it for a couple of years or so, and they went for scrap after I left.

But farming today they haven't got the labour and at certain times of year they need the labour and skilled labour at that. Now there's several jobs on the farm like fencing, that sort of thing and they get contractors in rather than paying farm workers. I ain't very keen on contractors.

Changes in farming? I may be critical but in my time I liked the way farming was done. Better than today because I see tractors laid about in the field, nowhere to put them. I was brought up that everything should be in a shed, like stabling your horse, corse in those days we never had the machinery, but what we did have, we used to look after in the winter. And with the amount of labour I had we could afford to do that. But the cost of labour was nil more or less. I mean the farmers, I think myself if one can look out to 300 cows they can't be looked after 100% I think they go through the milking parlour and I still say, with the amount of sheep, if a shepherd has 700 sheep, that was his job. Now the shepherd has 1,200 ewes and all these lambs following on and what they buy in from Scotland. Then we got two to three hundred beef cattle indoors. Have you seen the new shed up there, all open at the sides? A German invention. He went to Germany and saw it, and what the difference is, they have machine in there, two big square bales and he chucks it 20ft in amongst the cattle, you don't have to go in there. You learn more feeding animals slowly. You can always watch out to them but now we have got to the stage now where there's a few less dairies and too many cows, and say up to a thousand cows. And how can one man or two look after 300 cows. One a worker and the other's a farmer. They start five o'clock in the morning 800 litres a day and a bloomin' great lorry turns up, you are not restricted on the amount you produce cos one time if you went over quota, you had to chuck it down the drain. And that's another thing I don't agree with as they are importing milk.

Foot and Mouth? Never had Foot and Mouth. And that's what finished me with sheep. There was so many restrictions with what you could do and what you couldn't do, and all the rest of it, and I thought, I said to Mary, "I'll lamb them down this year and let that be the end of it," 2001, and so I took all my ewes over to Frome market and they sold quite well. All Suffolk cross ewes. I used to like Dorset Horns one time but they sort of went out round here. They weren't very prolific, that's true, but I think a lot of it today is that we find with the lamb prices, there is so many dairies going out, there's more sheep about than there has been for years. And where they were getting £70 and £80 a lamb, they get about £50 something. But if I made £50 a lamb that was good. I used to go to Frome to make 50 quid.

Sturminster's gone now. Pity that was the worst thing that could ever happen. Now they're building there, and a little slaughterhouse in East Orchard, Dick Moody's and that big place, on the right. We sell all our cattle in Devon, Lloyd Maunder and so do the sheep. A lorry comes and takes them straight off the farm, 100 a week. Much better for the animal, they been on about it for years, export if you were to go to Frome markets and the foreign trade was closed the price would be down like a shot. But these dealers really got the hang of supplying so many lambs, contracts to fill, well the only thing I miss, we used to kill lambs for ourselves. And now we haven't got any, and Mr Gardiner used to give me a lamb every year. But I lost all that. No free lambs now. You don't think he'd miss one do 'ee?

Out of 2,000 but I will say that for him up there, I reckon there's too many animals for one man, but the lambs do exceptionally well. Chalk ground you see, the price of corn has gone down, and they paid farmers to grass down places for the birds, etc. Mr Gardiner caught hold of that thing and one day you get a message, "can you plough that field?" and the next minute you got to cultivate it. And you be told what to do, and I watched a programme on the telly the other morning, we'll pay the farmers if they could let us have 10 or 15 acres, we'll pay good money. But when you look that's another way that farming's altered. The farmer is in between two stones. That 40 acres that big field is under some 40 acres, we would have liked to have bought that field, you ain't allowed to cut that grass, just top it once a year. But it's a different way of farming. Personally I would like to be young again, but I don't think I would like to be farming today. Too much bureaucracy. On the other hand somebody must be doing well, I said when they got rid of all these dairies, the one that got them has got to win somewhere along the line. But the price of milk doesn't go up and the price of land doesn't go down. But if a farm goes empty, there's always houses going in there. I never seen anything like it. One or two farms I knew just build with flocks of houses, That's the way it's going. Gillingham where our Shirley lives, there's no end to it.

Field names: Barns, Blackclose, Squires, Twin Town, Coombe Bottom, Hegthorn. When you have worked on a place as long as I have you see, and I am still interested, Charlie comes in I am always interested in what they are doing. You know I may be critical about it, farming from carting, all horses right through to almost automated farming. I broke-in horses for Harding's when I came here. I broke three mares in and took the cup three years running at Gunville, one mare. And I broke a black mare in with a chain harrow, put three abreast out there. Nobody didn't like horses much out there, but I love horses, I love ploughing with horses, My Father where I was born at Sleight, I stayed there and I was 10 year old, my Father's mother died in Dorchester, and me Uncle and he went to the funeral and he left me – I don't believe it myself – he left me in the field with three horses, and 10 year old! I were only 10 with three, four-year-olds, and ploughing with a double furrow plough, not a single one, and my I remember my uncle saying: "Never let that boy do that," but that were years ago. You wouldn't be allowed to do that today but I was brought up like that. And they would "come round" and "walk on". If you look round this place I am all horses, and we got horses up here. But I do love horses, but out of the eight, out of the three brothers, I was the only one who loved horses. I am interested, I like to see them horse shows. I used to pop down Motcombe down that show field, once a year, that big show for horses, beautiful horses up from Suffolk. I love to see that, that is my way.

Ploughing with a furrow, 'tis easier with a two plough furrow than with a single. But the thing is we used to use two horses with a single plough and three horses with a double plough and the art is. when you strike out keep it straight. I can remember when I was at Fontmell. I was good at ploughing though I say so myself. I was ploughing down at Fontmell. Ryall had the other farm, and Bert Shute, do you want to cast your glance across that hedge, old Bert never seemed to get the hang of it. There's a difference in how you set the plough for the lay over. I used to love ploughing. You got to vary the plough with the ground, there's two wheels on there, one in the furrow and one on top and with horses, one's in the furrow working. There's difference in ground, this ground ploughs beautiful, there's sand in it, loam. Up the top of the hill, that's all stones, you want to keep hold of the handles, I don't remember if you remember that bloke up the top, Siegvart? I used to like him, he ploughed that bit up the top, Siegvart's, we got it grassed down now. I always hoped that the chains wouldn't break because he used to put the rope round his neck, the two horses. But we always kept one in each hand. The reins, I always remember seeing him do that, He never used a tractor. He were a damned nice bloke. We met him several times before he died and he used to have Gore Farm during the war. That first crop of potatoes was phenomenal, I can see him now ploughing and putting in potatoes. He was a hardworking man, very mild, no vice about him. The thing is I remember he used to have a lot of goats.

How long did I work for John Eliot? Nine years, I enjoyed doing what I did up there. When I went up there the first year, I wondered if I would like it. But he was never there very much see, away a lot, for six or seven months, he said to me once, and we were harvesting, and he used to come back, pitching sheaves, hard work, good at loading on top to make a good load. "I am sorry you are leaving," he said. "I used to go away for five or six months and not worry a bit about the place."

Always smoked a pipe, then gave up one day. The bloomin' shop shut, Compton Abbas. Out of baccy for about four days and I thought just as simple as that and never took a cigarette or a cigar off anyone since. I went doing this contract fencing, but I went out doing it Mary used to think I was a fool doing it, but then he used to offer me a pipe of baccy and I never did. Now I never think about it, I used to smoke St Bruno. Mind you some farms they would never allow you to smoke on the farm, my brother-in-law he worked over at Jeffreys at Donhead and if you were found smoking that was that. But a barn load of straw, personally I agree with that.

Lulworth fishing? Well yes they were all called Millers. David and Jim Miller were his sons. Number three the Coastguard cottages. My uncle lives in Wool now. He had the shop in Lulworth and his mother had the shop there before him, 91 now. And we went to his 90th birthday the other day. When I went to school down there we used to have swimming lessons in that cove. The farm is still there but the cottages at Daggers Gate, we used to go across the fields, about two miles say a mile and half, and those cottages are gone, I think we used to have a well, no bloomin' electric, just oil lamps, old toilet, bucket toilet. That was how you were brought up. My Father used to push bike to Dorchester, 12 miles each way and get enough meat for a week, cos there was 10 of us. Eight children and my sister, who just died last week. I remember when she was five year old we used to go two and half miles to school used to drag her to school near enough and father used to be ploughing as if it 'twere yesterday. If you told somebody today you walked five mile a day to school they wouldn't believe you. And I were only saying to my sister the other day, do you remember when we come home and we used to bite dog biscuits, cos Father ueed to have a few sheep besides the horses, and we were eating dog's biscuits on the way home. We weren't starving, these are biscuits. But we were brought up very primitive, no harm at all. I very often say to Mary. Well she used to work in Shaftesbury Post Office and she used to push bike in the mornings at seven o'clock and a policeman used to be coming up from Fontmell on his pushbike and he used to come home with her most days. Dark very dark then and then she'd come home for lunchtime and push bike back again, twice a day. Tell people that and they wouldn't believe you. And what was it £4 a week or £3 a week. Her mother was took ill and she died at 50 her mother did.

I remember the boats and then we used to get the old steamer come in from Weymouth, now where we were at Durdle Door, we use to take our sheep dogs down to Durdle Door on a Sunday morning and put the dogs in the water. Well I were brought up down there, I used to go swimming down there. If you go up through that camp, you're supposed to pay. The farmland went right down to the coast, used to plough right on top of the cliff. Well I think we had about 800 or 1,000 acres, and we used to have three carters there. My uncle was carter and I used to get up at half past four in the morning, and plait their tails up and then they would lay in and feed them with corn and we used to go out seven o'clock in the morning. About two hours then go back and have your breakfast. Feed them five o'clock two or three feeds, clean them down, comb them down, then go back and have your breakfast, harness them up and out of the stable by seven o'clock. We used to put in 15 acres of corn with three horses in a day, up to two o'clock, we used to shut them in. My father had three four-year-olds and they were good. My uncle were in the same stable and his horses were always poor. They used to say that a good carter would always pinch for his horses, give them a bit extra. We used to be allowed two sacks of corn for three horses, 2cwt West of England sacks, two of them per week. We used to do the harness, the furniture, father used to put two in the shafts on a double wagon and then haul furniture from Dorchester. Then the bells on the horses, riddin' day, father moved one firm from West Lulworth. Used to pull a ton, one horse up a hill, a fair weight and he had some good horses. And that is why I come to love horses. They fascinate me, and Mary was the same.

'Tis nice tis a thing you go to races, I like to see the horses. I don't put a lot of money on the horses. I love horses, I like horse racing. I might put a fiver on. 'Tisn't the same as watching it on television. But seeing a good working horse is something else, lot of people wouldn't know how to put the harness on.

But the thing is the day's gone where everything is now in such a hurry. What we used to do is when I worked on a farm, we used to start in the morning seven o'clock. Stop lunch at ten and have a mouthful. Then go to one o'clock and that were dinnertime and now 'tis anytime. Don't matter so long as it is daylight but with horses they need the rest. Pulling those great binders, the pole on them that were hard work. Now we grow oats for Quaker oats, porridge oats and rye for Ryvita.

John Cluett at home in his garage

25 John Cluett: Lorry driver and folk musician
Born 1932, Sturminster Newton

You name it, we bloody did it. I had quite a chequered life. I never stopped anywhere very long. We never had no teenage years.

My Grandfather had a small farm and haulage business at Sturminster and Father worked for him. Father were born in 1901 and he left school at 13 on the outbreak of the First World War, because his two older brothers went in the army and he basically run that farm single-handed all through the First World War. My Aunt Eva, she used to help with the milking. Eva was deformed, she had what they call a curvature of the spine, one shoulder higher than the other. I expect there is some fancy bloody name for it now, she was a strong woman, the finest hand-milker you could find in North Dorset. She milked a cow out clean and wadn't long about it. And they were on that farm, I suppose they milked, I suppose it is nothing today, but they milked about 15. I would think, which when you had to milk them by hand was a lot of work. And they survived off that quite well. They lived quite well, he did the milking, and then would be off with horses and wagons during the day and back for milking in the afternoon. But of course when the farm were on haymaking, ploughing and all that they had to fit it all in somehow. I don't know how they did it but they did. It was down behind the church, what they call Tanyard. Yeah, and interesting to think in later years when I was driving for Harry Brown at Stalbridge, I had to go there with a load of gravel and got down there and this posh woman come out: "Oh you managed to find us then!" "Yes madam… I was born here."

I did not ought to call myself a Dorset man really, because Mother was from Scotland, Mother was born just outside Dundee, on the old Perth Road and she was born in 1898. And her Father worked on the farms as a casual agricultural labourer. But as a very young man, he used to go out on the whaling ships out of Dundee out on to the Arctic up to Greenland, and he was a big man getting on for six foot six, six foot seven and damned near six foot across. And he was the harpoon man and stood in the bow of the rowing boat and actually harpooned the whales. But he got fed up with it, he married twice, his first wife died in childbirth, and when he married the second time my Grandmother, she managed to talk a bit of sense into him and got him to work onshore. He was a bagpipe player and he was quite a character, but I didn't really know him too well cos to go from Sturminster Newton to Scotland before and during the war, you can go to Australia a damned sight easier now, look than what you could get up there. 'Twas a 15,16-hour journey on the train.

However, Mother joined the Women's Royal Air Force or its equivalent in 1916 during the First World War. Anyhow, she never really went back to Scotland, she worked in an officers' mess at Donnibristle in Fife, I believe and then she came to London and when she left the RAF at the end of the war she went to work for one of the officers down near Taunton. And then she left Taunton and came to work for Colonel Bill Adams at Marnhull, and they used to call Bill Adams "Brisket Bill", because when things was hard in the depression in the early part of 1929 when it crashed down, somebody were on that the working people didn't have enough meat to eat, and Bill said, "give them brisket". That is the cheapest bit they can get, so they called him Brisket Bill. So Mother worked for 'ee and Father used to deliver the coal for Blandford and Webb in Sturminster. Used to go to Col. Adam's place at the Grange and he met Mother there and they married and I was the bloody result of it all. I never really knew him. He died very, very young so I was left on me own. I have lived here for 70 years I can claim to be a Dorset man. That's what actually happened. But the funny thing was my grandmother came from Marnhull, she was a Chant, Louisa Chant, Father's mother, sadly I know very little about her. There was quite a few Chants at Marnhull and there was quite a few Chants at Stalbridge and quite a few at Henstridge. It was a local name. She died when I were working on the railways, so it must have been '57, '59. She was 90. But the last 10 years of her life she was totally blind and totally deaf. Fully dependent on my two aunts to look after her, sad really because she had been very active woman look, she never actually milked, but chickens, haymaking... Grandfather was born 1862, that is the same year as the railway was opened to Sturminster Newton. He died in 1942.

Harpooner Grandfather? He eventually moved in to Lochee which is a suburb of Dundee and he had a small market garden. Camperdown was the name of the estate but there was some tie up with the Navy, in the old sailing ship Navy. There was HMS Camperdown. He had several rod allotments, grew fruit, mostly vegetables and he had a four-wheeled totters cart and a pony that were blind in one eye and a dog called Sam. And he used to load this cart in the morning with spuds and cabbage and go all round rows of houses, because they were right next to the jute spinning mills that side. He had a damned good trade. So he carried on for that for years till he died. Grandmother Scott died in 1943 and he died a week later of a broken heart so they said. Mother was the second oldest she had a brother Sam. He was a blacksmith, a shoeing smith in the army in the First World War.

Then there was two aunts. Mother had three sisters Bella, Isobel and Aggie. Bella they always called her, she worked for Dobies the seed people. Aggie worked in the spinning mills, she was as deaf as a bloody post. I went in them mills once, you never heard nothing like it. Bloody belts over the pulleys clack, clack, clack, a hella of a bloody racket, but they did lip-read you see. But if you went out with Aggie a Saturday afternoon down Dundee shopping, she'd see a friend across the road and they'd carry on a conversation across the bloody road, trams, in Dundee then, trams rattling up and down, but she was a great worker. Bella was fiddle player, and she was a marvellous fiddle player, Mother played the fiddle but not as good as Bella. Aggie, the singer, although she was deaf she had the most beautiful singing voice you could wish to hear, and then there was Nell, she was somewhat younger, she married a chap called Bill Campbell he was a postman out by Forgandenny, near Perth. And then there were George, he were a butcher by trade then he went on driving long-distance coaches for Alexander's coaches. George was on the REME during the war, he was one of the few that come out from Dunkirk, stood up to his blooming neck in water for about four days. Poor old George, but it drove him to drink, see he didn't last long after that, after the war. He died very, very young. Basically drunk his'self to death. So that's the Scott family took care of.

Up there, that photograph up there in the middle the three cottages, the one on the right hand side, that's my Great-grandfather. The one on the left is man called John Scott Skinner and Scott Skinner was a very famous fiddle player in Scotland. He wrote and made up lots and lots of tunes and his forté was Strathspey's tunes for dancing, John Scott Skinner with the kilt on and I reckon that photo was taken around 1890. My Grandfather was a Scott but no relation. The harpooner played the bagpipes. No wonder the bloody whales ran away, frightened them away, like the Germans in the First World War, they reckoned they ran away from them. Can't say I blame them. Whale music thought it was a bloody octopus in a kilt. Don't bear thinking about...

Earliest memories of Sturminster? I can remember falling down at my Aunt's place. See that mark on one of them eyebrows, I can remember cutting my eye up there and that's going back a long way. I can remember starting school, I can just sort of remember, that would be the Jubilee of

George V. I can remember going out the recreation ground in Sturminster and getting a Jubilee mug, George V. He didn't last long after that. I can remember that.

I can remember when they had the Foot and Mouth Disease '37-'38 on the Easter Market and a chap from Shroton took two calves in there, and when they discovered it, they shut the gates on the market. And that were it. Everything that were in there, even the dogs, drovers had dogs in they days, everything, drovers dogs and all. They shot the lot, corse the bloody market's knocked down, but if you can remember where the calf pens used to be, then the rest, down the bottom for car park. Well that was a grass field that belonged to the market, and they took on Hammond's the builders. That's what put them on their feet, they got the contract to dig the trench, to burn these animals. And he went up the labour exchange, there were a lot of men out of work and everybody that was out of work, don't matter if they were bank clerks, grocer, baker, candlestick maker. If they could use a shovel, they had to use the bloody shovel. They got them and they dug this bloody great trench and they filled him up with faggots and my Father, Reg Matthews and Garnet Guy, they was haulage contractors from Marnhull. They were pulling faggots and coke from over the gasworks, and they used to be a gas works in Sturminster then, and they pulled all that in, and they burnt all these animals. They set fire to them. Nobody really knew when they were going to set fire to them. My Mother, we lived at Rixon, direct bloody line of that place. Mother had a line of washing out you. Cor bloody hell, you. That smoke come across there, you never seen nothing like it, it was black as black can be. And I can remember that as plain as if it was yesterday. That smell, I can remember that as if 'twere bloody yesterday.

I can remember another thing, And that was in 1939 summer or possibly '38. War started in September didn't he, so must have been June or July 1939 and the Germans at that time, they had Zeppelins, didn't they? The Graf Zeppelin and another one, come over Sturminster and they hung round there all bloody day, just hung round there. I don't know if they were making maps, because old Pitt Rivers up at the Manor he was a Nazi sympathiser. However, apparently, but I can't swear to this, I never see them, people did say that Göring, Hess and Goebells used to come over and stop at Hinton Manor. Now whether this is true or whether it is hearsay or whether people made it up, I can't say. But that was the story that used to go around, and I often wonder if they was up there mapping that day. Because later on in the war, a Heinkel 111 was shot down and crashed at Plumber Bridge. Out on Hazelbury Road, go up The Red Lion, or what was The Red Lion. Turn left, out past the cattle-breeding centre, that was down in the dip, Some call it Salkeld Bridge, some call it Plumber Bridge. He finished up in the stream in the brook. He finished up in there, and people there said, all round Pitt Rivers, all round Sturminster, and that on the pilot's maps, there was a red ring round it. Whether that is true, that is what they reckoned. 'Twere in the summertime, because we rode our bikes out to see it, '43 perhaps, I would think.

There was another bomber going or coming back from Bristol. He come down in the daytime. One had a go at Sherborne, didn't he. Whether it was one of they, there was a fighter base at Henstridge and a fighter base at Yeovil. There was a fighter base out Sigwells up the top of Sherborne. So whether they had he or not I don't know. He didn't get home. Killed them all I think. They were buried in Sturminster cemetery for a long, long time and they'm gone now. Yes there were three or four killed. Poor buggers, though they was against us you don't like to see it not really.

War was a great time for we boys. Yeah we had great fun during the war, as the saying is. We had rationing but rationing didn't mean too much because we had chickens and we used to kill two pigs when you were only supposed to kill one and rabbits I hear Mother say many times, if you don't go out and catch a rabbit you won't have any dinner. So instead of one we'd come back with half a dozen: "What am I going to do with all them rabbits? Take them down to Bertie Duffet," and if they weren't marked, he'd give you a shilling for a rabbit if you had caught him in a net or a snare. And he used then to send them off, he had big wicker hampers, weighed damned near a hundredweight when he sent them off. And he used to pack these rabbits in these big wicker hampers and take them to the station and put them on the train and send them to London. And they chefs in they big London hotels they used to doctor the bloody things up like chicken and turkey. And there were game birds. Bert were getting two bob a rabbit and they were selling the bloody things for about a pound a portion up there look. Especially when the Americans came in, the American officers and that, they had plenty of money. "Dorset Rabbits" in the Dorchester, local food, local grub. We used to catch rabbits and eels, get chubb, dace, pike if you got a bloody great jack pike, cut he in four or five pieces and hand them all around the locality. They'd always taste a bit muddy, but when you be a bit hungry, a bit of mud made no difference did it? We used to use worms and dough. Used to use a dough ball and then catch a chubb, then put the chubb on as live bait for the pike and eels. I used to just chuck in a hook as he was. Just chuck in a line with four or five hooks on and a lead weight. Sling him in overnight and go back in the morning and hope you had something there. Sometimes we did and sometimes we didn't. There weren't many eels in the Stour, no there weren't many eels in the Stour. We used to get a few out the end where Chevrik's Brook run into the Stour. It wasn't a good river for eels. We used to get a few. It was the old story with eels they didn't die till the sun went down. And you used to skin them and Mother used to fry them in the frying pan. You get all these stories of cutting them up and the buggers are still jumping about in the frying pan. I never seed that happen.

Now what else did we do? We helped at harvest. I had to help milk the mornings before school and take the horses up the blacksmith's to get the shoes put on 'em. Ride one and lead t'other. Father was a carter really. I used to help a lot and then we used to get the evacuees come in and we had to shift them. They'd come in as families and they'd put them in temporary accommodation. A lot of girls and boys come down on their own and they billeted out with people. But then later on when the doodlebugs came about a lot of people came down as families see. V2 rockets you didn't know what was happening then in London, and they'd come down with a few sticks of furniture and they'd put them in where Loders butcher's shop is near The Swan. Well that used to be a shop owned by Reg Cressy and he used to deal in sports goods, tennis rackets, cricket bats and football boots and all that business. And on the corner there, I think that corner's gone now, there used to be a flat with three storeys. And then they put them there temporary, and they'd find them accommodation and we used to move them. Furniture with horse and open wagon, used to put the ladders up front and back for haymaking. Put the ladders up front and back, and then put the rope right round the lot and a couple of ropes over, and you had it. My uncle he had a 30cwt Ford lorry, we got modern then, corse he didn't like to use him too much, he couldn't. He didn't have the bloody petrol. See for anything local we used to use horse and wagons. Coal and feed, used to go down Sturminster Mill and get cattle feed. You name it we bloody did it. We used to move farm workers. Yeah that was much the same as moving the evacuees, load it all up. And coming on again, when I worked for Harry Brown I done the same job, on a modern lorry, on a diesel lorry, the same job as regards loading it. We used to do quite a lot of that.

Now going back to the war, on Saturday mornings I had the pony, Toby, and I used to go round the shops with tins of bean cakes or whatever they had. We never had, see, we never had no teenage years. They go to college 'till they'm what 20 then and when they come out of that they still don't know what they want to do do'em? I'll take a year out and all this nonsense… I don't know what the world's coming to really.

We had soldiers, look. The first regiment we had come down to Sturminster Old King's Royal Rifles, London Regiment, which is now part of the Green Jackets, the Rifle Brigade and that would have been Christmas '39. I suppose and they put some Nissan huts up for them over in the vicarage, in the Glebe which used to run right next to Grandfather's place, a wall there. So a few days before Christmas and he had some cider in there and we was in the cider house there, I shouldn't ought to have been there, but I was in the cider house. Father and I, and Uncle George, and Grandfather sat there yapping. So in a minute a head popped over the wall. Corse old man said: "Come on have a drink son." "I can't really." "They won't miss you for five minutes, come on." So two or three of them come over. Look, London chaps can't drink cider. They only smelt the cup about twice and they was out, finished, kaput. So this were all right and we were having a good laugh and the bloody sergeant come round, looking for them. He heard them over there. He come over he stood there, tried to pull them up to attention. Cor didn't he go for they two buggers, he gave them a hell of a dressing down. My uncle see, Uncle George, he had been a sergeant in the First World War in the Fourth Dorsets. "Look come on sergeant don't get like that with them, they'm only boys. Come on sergeant have a bloody drink," and they had to carry the sergeant back! Laugh, I think they all finished up on the bloody fizzer in the end. But then again it was sad most of them were either took prisoner or got killed on the retreat when they came back across France, they was the rearguard. A hell of a lot of them got killed or captured. Lot of them got left behind, they couldn't get off, they was the bloody rearguard, look coming back poor buggers.

Well then the next lot we had come there, now this was a very, very strange quirk of fate, the next lot was Newfoundlanders. Now you know that a lot of people went from Sturminster to Newfoundland in 1850s? Now that was a lot of these soldiers, there was no ties with Sturminster, but you could hear a lot of the Dorset dialect in their speech. Not all of them, but some of them. The dialect words, a Canadian twang, but sometimes you get "thickum" or "theesum" or summat like that. But 'twas there, you could tell it were there. We had one Newfoundland lady, a friend of mine, old schoolfriend of mine, his Grandfather must have went to Newfoundland on the cod fishing from Poole and he married this Newfoundland lady. And come back stopped there a good many years and eventually brought her back with him. And she was a very, very old lady when I knew her and Dennis's mother used to take in laundry and she used to take in washing, and that was another performance. She used to take in laundry on Thursday and Friday was ironing day. And they lived in a very low cottage and she had a kitchen range, and old black-leaded kitchen range and a cast iron box to fit round the range, for the irons. And she had about a dozen or 15 flat irons all cocked up against this box, heating up. And she did move them round and the one closest to the fire, she did pick it up and move the rest of them up, and use 'ee and put him on the back. And you can imagine it, of damp summer's day and washing hanging everywhere, and she had to get the dammed stuff out by Saturday. And you imagine a wet summer's day and that poor old lady she used to sit there right on top of the fire with a long black dress and cardigan and dree or four bloody shawls and man's flat cap and smoke a clay pipe upside down. And then she did cough and hawk, poor old soul but she was damned near 90 when she died, she died during the war. But she was born in the 1850s. Poor old Granny and they laid her out in the front room in the coffin. "Come in and see Granny." "Don't think I will." "She won't hurt."

A lot of folk tunes went out to Newfoundland and America and came back. One that springs to mind that we call Soldier's Joy went to Newfoundland and turned into Old Joe Clark. Well of course it came back again. There's another one which is sort of another version of the Raggle Taggle Gypsies and he went to Newfoundland and came back as Black Jack David. The tune was altered a little bit, the words was altered a little bit. But basically the song where the rich girl marries for love and marries a gypsy and won't come back home and is happy out in the wild, that is the same song. A lot of them went across to America and came back. The Fox went to America and came back. A hell of a lot of them went over.

Dialect words? "Theesum", "theckum", "hoss", " zull" for plough, "plow" for wagon, wheels bonding wheels the same, it was just there you didn't take notice of it. "Nammek" for bread and cheese time, "hyling" up corn, hyling up hay in big rows. Speaking the dialect? No we can use the words but we can't get the intonation. They used to speak different, lower back in their throat "where's bin?" Classic one, the boy meeting his mate. One boy's been to the fair, other one's going to the fair. Conversation went like this:

"Hello Garge." "Hello Bill." "Goin?" "Bin." "Hast?" "Arr." Or the other one when he's rabbiting: "Ere, put your ear down 'ere if you 'ear him in 'ere".

"Sivil" was a scythe. "Whet them sivil," sometimes used to call them a crooked stick, or Eli on the railway, the crooked stick. "She-ap" for sheep. "Bee-ast" for cows, 'osses for horses; funny thing about that my Grandmother from Marnhull she would never say 'osses, she would say "harses," always, she always said "harses". "Tun" was the chimney board, "claviboard", mantelpiece. "Drashhold", threshold, "geat" gate. Joe lived round civil Jimmy in St James. He originated down at Long Crichel. Joe still speak a bit of dialect, he can quote Barnes's poetry like somebody quotes the Bible. When he sees me in The Crown he says, "ah 'tis Bloom, ah here's the road that hauls the load cries worthy Bloom the miller." Joe he's about the only one, corse the children don't speak dialect and Margaret's Wiltshire. But she's getting somewhere handy to it, a "moonraker" she is. And who else is there? There's very few left.

More about the war? We had an aeroplane crash over the junior school what they call the William Barnes school. And we were having a geography lesson and all of a sudden, clatter, bang, wallop. What the hell is going on... And this was a Canadian crew on a Lancaster bomber and he had been over to Germany on one of the daylight raids coming onto the end of the war. Look and he struggled the damn thing back as far as he could and the plane just simply fell to pieces. And he took out, there was a row of elm trees, he fell to pieces on mid-air and there were a line of elm trees, and he took the tops off them. He was going on towards the mill and he took the top out of them trees and a lot of the bits fell off in that field that got houses in now and call Durrant. And the actual body of the plane come to ground, as you go out of Sturminster on the Stalbridge road on the main Sherborne road. Go past the old Red Lion, and can you remember Hammond's had a builder's yard on the right-hand side and at that time it belonged to a man called Harry Turt who had a fleet of lorries? And the body of the plane came down there in that field right behind the office. And one of the engines come down in Stalbridge lane in the halter path and the last time I were down Stalbridge lane and I went down to see Tom Fox's wife about Barnes's poetry or sommat, that dent is still in the ground where that engine came down now. But killed all the crew. People that investigated it said that some of them were already dead and they were all dead bar the pilot and I am not sure he didn't die and lost control of it. She were shot to bloody pieces. That were close. I thought we'd had it for a minute or two. Corse everybody in Sturminster got up in the bloody air as they thought he had come down on the bloody school like, which he hadn't thank God. But that was about the only excitement we really had.

There was two bakers in Sturminster that were Bert Inkpen's on the corner of Recketts Lane which is a bakers shop now but they have moved the bakehouse, is now down in the garden and the bakehouse used to be right on the corner beside the road. And Bert used to like a drop of beer so he had a coal fired oven and he used to fire up, put a batch of bread on, then hit across the lane through the White Hart garden and through the back door.

Bert used to get a drink anywhen, they didn't worry about opening hours, used to help 'eeself and put the tick on the board like, and you could always tell where Bert was because the bloody smoke was flying out of that bake house door, great black smoke, "Bert there's a batch of burnt bread" and he come flying back across and the bottom of that bread was as black as that microphone stand. And he'd still sell it, marvellous bread, marvellous bread that he used to make, 'twas always burnt but people used to queue up to buy old Bert's bread. He had no trouble in selling it. Ready made toast. He used to go round with a Morris 8 van and he used to go round with it. Used to go down to my grandfather's place and grandfather used to turn every loaf over that were in the basket and he would have the one that was blackest. He used to say, I know he's cooked. And then there was another baker straight across the road, Randolph Rogers and they weren't the panache there were with Rogers's as there were with old Bert. But Rogers's used to have their flour and you had to carry it, our father used to take flour to Rogers's and you had to carry it up a ladder, actually up a ladder, two and a quarter hundred weight bag of flour on your back up a ladder. Ordinary thatching ladder used to throw one bag down so the ladder didn't kick then go up, don't know how we got the last bag up I suppose we had to chance it. That's what they used to do. Eight to a ton they used to carry. I bet they were two and a half.

I can remember when the combines first come about look, the baggers, I were working for Harry Brown then and we used to go up to over Turnworth up on the top of Bulbarrow and they had a bagger up there and we used to go up there together, the two of us but if you did get up there on your own they just used to slide them down on the chute on the bagger and leave them where they fell. And if you had to put up ten ton of they buggers on your own and they were catch weight, and they were more than two and a half. I don't know what they were. I used to pick they up and you had to put your arms round them and get them up on your knee up on the bed of the wagon then tip them over, so what you'd do is put up four or five and then get up on the lorry and load them. But you never got caught too many times by it because you always made sure there was two of ee to load the wagons. I have chucked them up on my own off the ground but that is a bloody job. Kill yer.

The mills? He came to Blandford and Webbs, they was the last people to run him, Sammy Elkins was the miller he was still working when I was working on the railway in Sturminster in about '57 , but then I left Sturminster and went to Stalbridge and lost track of what was going on so he must have stopped somewhere about then, Then a chap called Young took him on but only for his own use. He kept a lot of pigs I believe and he ground a bit for hisself on an 'as and when' basis, and then it gradually petered out. Shall we say the mid sixties. I would say about the mid sixties. I would think. And Fiddleford must have gone about the same time. I can remember seeing he working. Roses had that. That was descendents of Job Rose, 'Worthy Bloom the Miller' in Barnes's poem. He must have been related somewhere because he was a Sturminster man. He was born 1815, but he worked up in the gravel pits on Fifehead Common where Vic Smith got his scrap yard, now, and then he left that and went for Mr Reakes who owned the mill and Mr Reakes retired. He took the mill on and they millers always did well, there was a story that one of his relations used to say, cos he was a very big man, used to weigh about thirty odd stone, didn't he, the reckoned he used to ride about in a pony and trap but the pony was what we used to call a half way horse, a cobb wasn't a bloody trotter, wasn't a cart horse like, and they reckoned there was only room for Job Rose and his wallet in that bloody cart. And no room for anybody else, however he eventually took over or bought Fiddleford as well. He had three sons I believe, one son in Sturminster, another son in Fiddleford and he took Woodbridge down here at Hartgrove and run that with his other son, and then when Job died his wife and the son ran that mill, but see then it was handed down. The one that went to Fiddleford, he had a son and then Siddy Rose that I knew, he was a very old man when I knew him, he would have been Job Rose's grandson and Siddy in turn had two sons, he had Howard and Rupert. Rupert was the farmer, Rupert done the farming and Howard ran the mill. Howard never married. Rupert married and had one son, but when Howard died Rupert sold up, so the mill went out of their ownership after what, well over 100 and some odd years.

Sad really but there it is, the miller is still there and the machinery is still there. I can remember Cut Mill working, I can't remember King's Mill working at Marnhull but father would, he used to grow a bit of wheat and oats and they always used to take theirs to King's Mill and get it ground. God knows why, whether they fell out with t'other lot I don't know, but oats they used to grow for the 'osses they used to take it there and get it sorted out. T'was oats for the horses.

Then of course I went to Blandford. I passed I forget what they call it, the eleven plus? Then I left when I was 14 I couldn't get on with it in there. Then I went straight into work. Then I went on for old Georgie Knott farmer down Ham gate who were Grandfather's neighbour. Then I left 'ee and had a few months, a couple of year or more for Hart's the blacksmiths. And then I went on for Richards in the market. I had quite a chequered life. I never stopped anywhere very long. I did get fed up with it. Then I went on for Richards and Senior and Godwin's in the market and then I got called up for National Service. And then I come back out of National Service and went back for Richards for about 12-month, two years.

Horses? I think they used to talk in the region of £45-£50 for a horse. That is the price that comes to mind as being bandied about. Uncle Tommy Knott, he was a great horseman, he knew horses, they was no two ways about it. Tommy Knott married Father's sister, Grandfather's eldest daughter, and any bloody horse dealing was always left to Tom as he could get a better deal than anybody else. I think he knew the gypsies quite well, for he and Clifford Rowland was great horse dealers, Tommy and Cliff Rowland were sort of pals from days back, I think they were in the army in the First World War together in the Dorset Yeomanry. We relied on the gypsies for new bloodstock or local dealers. At Hazelbury there were several horse dealers. There were stallion men but I can't say that I ever saw one, they used to walk the stallion round. They reckon the bloody man used to leave as many offspring behind as the bloody horse. They used to go in the pub, "tell your guv'nor I am here I am around," "lock up your daughters," and all this nonsense.

Well the little grey Fergie put paid to that. When I worked for Richards in the market you see that would have been about that time, I went in the army in '51, I would have been working for Richard's on about that time, and there was a dealer out at Hazelbury and he used to buy all the old horses, look, and we used to load them up in railway cattle wagons and he used to send them off to London for slaughter. And they bloody horses knew where they were going and we had hell's delight to get they in they wagons. Of course they were low and you had to get their heads down to get them in, but I have seen them get that frightened that they kick the side out of a railway cattle wagon, and that was four-inch board, four-inch thick board, and the uprights that hold them up were five or six inches and they were solid oak, all them uprights on the railway wagons, solid oak, must have cost the railway company to build them wagons, or would do now.

And they used to bring their two back feet up and go wham and let go backwards and the whole bloody side could come out, and if they buggers had caught you they would have killed you. No two ways about it, if they had caught you, you would have been a gonner. You wouldn't live to tell the tale. But I was young and supple and I used to load them when I came out of the Army I didn't bloody worry about it. But God, my blood do run cold sometimes, they would have killed you if they had had yer. But it was good money, used to get half a crown each for horses, and two shillings each for bulls, so you wanted ten bulls for a pound but only eight hosses.

I wouldn't be surprised if they did go on for food, there was horsemeat butchers in London and other places yes they used to go on, well on for death and they knew it. They knew where they were going. Fergusons. That's what finished the horses.

Then I left them and went on the railway and worked on the railway for about seven years then I went on lorry driving look. Yeah.

Railways? I was a porter. Started off in Sturminster as a porter and then I worked my way up as signalman at Stalbridge and I stopped there. I liked the railways, it was a good job, the money wasn't as good as some, but it were steady, there was no problem. You knew your money was coming every week. We used to get a bit of overtime. Then this is going to sound bloody funny. On the week that you were on early turn we got £8 15/- but late turn cos you were a bit more overtime you got £10 exactly. Which was good money then. But of course when they started on about closing and Dr Beeching come along swinging the bloody axe about, you see everybody was looking for jobs. I tried several jobs, different boxes, and I tried for gas works junction and got beat on that by one day. The chap was senior to me by one day. I knew the chap quite well and he passed out for signal box on the Thursday and I passed out on the Friday. I couldn't do nothing about it, it was the way of things. And of course I had one child and another one on the way, so I had to do sommat so Hine's down Gillingham were looking for drivers so I went on down there. And that was the start of the lorry-driving career.

Lorries? Oh Christ: Bloody lorries. I learnt to drive on Uncle's two-ton Ford. Petrol engine of course, learnt to drive on 'ee then when I worked for Richards's. We had a most beautiful Sunbeam car. Sacrilege it was, cut the bloody body off and turned it into a tractor and hay sweep on the front. And he had right-hand gate change on him. A beautiful car. If a fella had him now and done him up, I don't know what he would be worth today. Used to drive 'ee sweeping in hay and take the sweep off and take the milk churns up the road, and all sorts with him. Well then of course I drove a bit in the Army as well and done a bit to it in the Army and when I left the railway I went on for Hine Brothers at Gillingham.

And that was on tipper work, sand and gravel work. They ran Fodens, AECs and Dodges. The first one I had was a Dodge with a Leyland engine in and then I went to an AEC Mercury, one of the finest lorries you will ever drive, the AEC Mercury and several Leylands. And then went on for Harry Brown and Harry was a great Dodge man and he had several

Dodges we had up there, and Ford Traders and two or three Austins, BMC Austins. You used to go to Scotland in one of them, I went twice a year I did for seed spuds for Moore's. That were before the bloody motorway used to go all up through, up the left hand side, up the A6 and on up through Preston and on up Shap to Gretna Green and then sort of beetle across. You had to go to Stirling to go across the river Forth and Perth to get across the Tay look, because them firms we used to go to, was down near where my Grandfather Scott used to work, what they called the Carse of Gowrie. That is a very fertile part between Perth and Dundee on the other side of the river and corse you had to go to Perth to cross the river, but there was method in my madness. I had an Aunt Nell and Nell lived at Forgandenny, just outside of Perth on towards Teviot and towards that part of the bloody globe. And now we used to take mining timber from Turner's sawmill at Stalbridge, 10 tonne of pit props up to Shots of East Kilbride, Paisley, all round there, where the coal pits of Scotland were to. So we used to set sail Sunday dinnertime and get, what shall I say, way on above Gloucester before 'ee do stop. Then go on the next day get up Shap and try to get to Gretna the next day. And then the next day from Gretna and unload up over Stirling, Perth and out to me Aunt's place and put a night in there. Next day go down to the farm and load and back to my Aunt's place put a night in there again and try and get back to Gretna then come back down Gloucester and home. That was a week's work just to get some potatoes. Ten ton of seed spuds. Arran Pilot and Arran Banner, Moore's at Stalbridge, a lot of them was broken down and sold by the pound to the local gardeners. Hell of a way. Think nothing of it today, there and back in a day with the motorway.

Then it was sand and gravel, Wareham and West Bay. Used to go to West Bay and pick up pea gravel in bags and they were ever so tiny bags and you thought, "this is easy," and you pick them up and the bugger was a hundredweight. And we used to go up to Sheffield with them and they did line the blast furnaces with them. The blast furnaces had double walls and they had cut out little doors every so often and the blokes that worked there, they had to get inside and pack these bags. The idea was insulation to keep the heat in and after so long they did actually burn and they did shovel them out like a lot of ash. And they had to re-pack them and we used to take them up in bags and that were before the bloody motorway look. They still get them off the beach, they'm allowed so many there is a quota every year. But we used to do that for Browne's in Bridport, (with an "e" as opposed to Harry Brown without an "e"). And Harry used to say, "you got to go down to the posh Browne's." The Bridport and West Bay branch was still there. It didn't do much, maybe one train a day.

Sand and gravel was quite pleasant. Sometimes peat, fertiliser, chalk, lime. Lime for spreading, kibbled chalk and then hydrated lime for mortar. Used to go to Shillingstone Lime Company. They say they opened the pit up after the First World War. The main kiln never went out since it was lit in 1920 till it closed four or five years ago. Continuous flow of lump chalk and breeze coke. It would bubble away then shovel the lime out the bottom. Used to go all over the county taking the lime to lime spreaders.

But I done sand and gravel most of the time. We had some good fun. Harry Brown was the finest man I ever actually worked for. He was a bloody rough diamond and we used to have some terrible rows, and his wife Mrs Brown, she was a lovely lady she was a fraction up the social scale. Years ago, she went to one of these posh schools in Parkstone, very swish and he'd come in some nights cursing and swearing. Tap, tap, tap on the window. "Harry, Harry will come along in and leave him alone. They know perfectly well what they are doing." And he used to mutter and curse and stomp off indoors. Give him about 10 minutes he'd come out right as rain. He never bore any malice, that man, some would have dwelled on that, some would have given you hell for a fortnight, but he'd say: "That aint a bad idea, Carry on and do that." Yeah. He were a marvellous man to work for.

Now I've swapped the gear box for the squeeze box.

Matthew James and his Mother, Ruby James

26 Matthew James: Farmer, scrap dealer and parish councillor, Melbury Abbas and Cann
Born 1956.

There was more freedom, you didn't have the paperwork. You could make a living out of 30 cows. If it had four legs and four teats we used to milk it. As a countryman you are at peace with yourself and at peace with your surroundings.

I was born in Odstock in Wiltshire and brought here at 10 days old. Lived here in the area of Shaftesbury for the past 49 years. I was born in 1956. Father was Wiltshire born and he used to live at Wylye, Tollard, different places round and then his parents settled in Shaftesbury on a farm and he went in the building trade, a bricklayer-cum-stonemason. His parents were farmers. Farming is very much in my blood. Mother's family came from Shaftesbury and Grandmother's side came from Wincanton. They were a mixture of Wiltshire-cum-Dorset-cum-Somerset. We are right on the boundary of three counties. They used to do the fairground, general dealing and all sorts. We dealt in scrap. They done anything. Confectionery. Grandmother used to have the round house, the toll house going into Shaftesbury they pulled it down in 1972 to put the new roundabout up and she used to do garden fetes, Shaftesbury market. Baking the gingerbreads and the sweets for the market sweets. She used to make them and sell them. The roundhouse is similar to the one down at Motcombe turnpike and there was Toll Gate Park that is now Travis Perkins, that was the three tollhouses coming into Shaftesbury. It was fairly well-aged as it went back to the age of the window tax as some of the windows had been blocked up which is some time ago. It was demolished because of the dual carriageway and the roundabout.

Grandfather on Father's side, they were tenant farmers, they worked and they owned farms. They moved farms quite regularly. The tenant farms he was on, were like four or five-year tenancy and the farms were much easier to get hold of in those days. They used to move round to better themselves. A lot of the cases pre-1921 it was the Glyn estate round here and they had their home stock of farms and they just moved their tenants around. As the dissolution of these big estates came about, then the farms were sold off and many of them have stayed in the same families ever since. There was more freedom, you didn't have the paperwork. You could make a living out of 30 cows. When we started farming we started off with goats originally. That was school days almost when we were down at Shalimar. We used to buy goats out of the Western Gazette. We would either re-sell them or they would go through the slaughter chain and end up halal.

I went to school in Shaftesbury. Shaftesbury Secondary Modern school as it was then. We walked there. We were outside the catchment area so it was either walk or cycle. The road was a lot quieter then. Randolph my brother was two and a half years younger than me. The farming started off with a few chickens when we were younger, then we progressed up to goats. Eggs were mainly for ourselves and the cock birds were for ourselves. It was just like a hobby and we sort of progressed up to goats. We only had half an acre. We had a few goats and we used to tether them in our neighbours' gardens. Ride off in the morning with a goat each side. We used to milk them. We did have a bit of bother once. We found out that goats and copper beech do not mix. They eat copper beech quite readily and the milk turns a lovely shade of pink. They gave us extra premium for that. Strawberry-flavoured milk. We used to run these goats on and when I left school I went to work for Percy Perry on Holyrood farm. Grand total of £7.25 a week just under Shaftesbury. Used to be the old sewer farm. Further up was part of the Abbey Fishponds. Later on they converted it all for the sewer farm and they just used to flood the fields and then you had to wait three weeks and then turn the cows on them. Grew a fantastic crop of grass and tomatoes. And I worked down there for two years full-time, left school at 15. First week's wages was £7.25 and I bought a calf for £7 out of it. And didn't have nowhere to keep it at home, so we kept it over at Grandfather's. He had four acres at the time, over at Salisbury road, the scrapyard and we kept it in a lorry body over there. He was still doing scrap there, just one or two calves we just used to rear on in our spare time.

Then I went to Kingston Maurward College for a full-time residential course for a 12-month. An eye-opener. It was fun. Officially I was old enough to drink the day we finished down there. We had to get a bit of practice in beforehand. It was fun we learnt a lot. What was it the principal used to say? "Listen to everything, remember half and forget half." Something like that. Not bad advice. A lot of it, you could pick out the bits that were worth remembering. It was a National Diploma in Agriculture NDA and it was a thorough grounding in everything. Beef, sheep, pigs, poultry, crops, dairy, sheep shearing, chainsaws, spraying, They were teaching agriculture full stop. There was none of your horses or catering or anything like that. There were 32 on the course. It was just on the change round when they had the new hostels built there was four houses with eight rooms so you had a room each. So we had 32 students down there and it worked very well. You done your duties every morning whether it was pigs, dairy, beef or sheep and into breakfast at eight. Lectures started at nine if you could stay awake. You had your lunch and you went out on your practicals in the afternoon. And it was either sheep shearing, castrating, docking lambs. They had their own farm two dairies, their own pig unit, their own flock of sheep, used to keep the pedigree Dorset Horns. And we done outside demonstrations on farms locally, farm walks and when it come to sheep shearing time, you had the choice whether you took the sheep shearing proficiency test or not. I think it was you had to set the handpiece up, shear three, and tie three fleeces up and strip your handpiece down and they gave you 15 minutes to do it in. That was the given time, six of us took it and all passed.

But it was a hands-on agricultural training course, you done everything to the Agricultural Training Board specifications. You took the proficiency tests and you took your craftsmen's certificates. Not all book farming. You had an idea of doing most things and it showed you the correct way of doing it, or rather the way they thought it should be done. A lot of the things like chicken poultry and trussing, because I had done that a good bit earlier from the time I was 11, like on a local farm in the village, they taught us to truss them with needles, and I could do it. But I could just not see the point of it their way. So slow and so boring. I went out to Manor Farm, Melbury Abbas, and learnt off of Roy White. He taught me how to do it for show purposes and when we come to do it at college they taught us how to do it with needles and I could do it but I just could not get any speed at it. Like doing it at Manor Farm we were doing it more or less piecework and we done it the quickest way possible, real farming. And I ended up trussing one the show way of trussing it and the examiner he said: "That is not the way you have been taught," and I said, "no." He said: "Could you show me the way you are doing it? I like the way you are doing it and the presentation," he said, "and the speed." So we went off to one side and I had to show the examiner how I done it and he was most impressed with that and he said you had better do it the way that you have been taught so that I can mark you. So we done it like that and it was a good laugh.

We had three or four cows, couple of sheep at the time. The main of the problem was we didn't have the money. Father died when I was 15 and he left us with a legacy of a mortgage on the bungalow. So we worked if there was something wanted doing and if we could get paid for doing it we done it. So you turned your hand to most things. Randolph went on a three-year day release course. Like from the last year he was at school, he went on day release and when he started working for Nigel Sampson, another local farmer, he went on like that two years' day release. And then he managed to land himself a dairyman's job at 18, at Fortescue's at Wincombe Park up Shaftesbury. So he left Sampson's and went up to Fortescue's and he did that for two years I should expect. He then decided to join me and become self-employed. I have always been self-employed ever since I left college at 18. Main reason I went self-employed, I managed to get enough proficiency tests to get a beef, pigs, dairy, sheep, tractor-driving craftsman's certificates, but you couldn't claim then till you were 21. And I was only 18 when I was finished, and I went to one interview the college had set up and they said that I could have the job but he would only pay me the 18-year-old rate. He wouldn't pay me the craftsman's rate. Just being a bit cocky, I said if you think I am good enough to do the job, then I am good enough to have the full rate. And if you don't pay me the full rate you can XXXX the job. So that was when I went self-employed. Relief milking, turkey plucking, anything. If it was a job you done it.

Turkey plucking? Ever since I was 11. And it started off like this. You go down there at school, mate used to go down there because his brother worked for Colin and at Christmas time you help out by sorting out the giblets, sweeping up. And then you got proficient at that you moved on to plucking wings and when you got proficient at that you moved on to the breast feathers, and then you got proficient at that, you moved on to killing and then onto gutting and trussing and everything else, just a natural progression. In the early days he used to do 400 or 500 turkeys down there. It was more of a social event. We used to have laugh and towards the end we always developed coughs and he was always frightened that we weren't going to finish the turkeys, so the whisky bottle would come out, and then he would be called away and the whisky would disappear. And miraculously the coughs would get better.

He used to have Blandford & Web mill and mix come in and do his own ration. Sometimes the ration wasn't quite right and you'd end up with turkeys in part-moult when you wanted to pluck them, and you had a lot of stubs to pull out and everybody used to complain. And occasionally they had a few livestock with them and you'd go home itching hours afterwards. They would go all over the country. People used to come from miles for them. It was as close to organic as you could really get in those days. Colin never used to use much fertiliser on his corn if any and milled on the farm. A few bought-in ingredients, they were kept in the old-fashion loft style. They were barn-fed they didn't go out free range. Some used to escape so they were free range, barn reared, and done over a long period. They used to have the poults in about first week in June. We used to start plucking around the 14th, 15th of December and that was for the few London ones, because they used to like to have them hung up in the butcher's shop long-legged. The first few, New York dressed, mainly up in London for display and the orders would come back down. And there was geese as well, the waterproof chicken. I could never get into them. I just hate doing geese. At a push I would do them. They take twice as long. I found that the easiest way is to take the main feathers off and take the down off with a blowlamp, and rub them well afterwards. They progressed up and had a plucking machine which made jobs a little bit easier, until it broke down. But if you got 10 or 12 people up there it used to be a bit of a laugh, somebody would pinch somebody else's pliers and feathers knee deep and in your wellies, and in places you would never think physically possible. Get home at night and there was feathers everywhere. The feathers would go up the quarry or burnt. Not much call for them. The feather trade died off years ago.

Scrap? We done everything. The scrap used to go fairly local. Trowbridge, Poole, sometimes Ringwood, sometimes Bournemouth. It just depended on who was wanting what grade at the time. We had all the non-ferrous metals, your coppers, your aluminiums, your leads and they used to go to different yards, because different yards used to specialise in different materials. Certain yards would take dirty aluminium, certain yards would take clean aluminium. Certain yards would take copper, certain yards would pay you better for brass. It has always based on the commodity market. But going back when we had some trouble out in Africa and they couldn't get the copper out of the mines and copper shot from £300 a ton to £1,500 pound a ton overnight, literally. It was almost cheap enough to scrap your old pennies and coppers, worth more as scrap than as money. It went stupid. We used to have a Morris 1,000 pick up and anything up to half a ton of different sorts or a mixture. We had a Bedford TK that would take between four and how every much you could get on it legally. We worked in conjunction with Grandfather, just a carry on from him. We handled batteries, they went depending on who had them, we did actually get up as far as Welwyn Garden City with one load. We were in the recycling business before it was well and truly thought about. So this is old hat, this recycling. We been there, done that.

The farming all happened sort of slowly after leaving college. We met Ann Hodgson, she had that heart trouble and she asked us to look after her sheep when she was working with John Eliot Gardiner. And we done that for a bit, that's how we ended up with a flock of pedigree Dorset Horns. Walking the sheep up Fontmell Hill one day, a lamb kept falling to the wayside. A touch of joint ill and she said take the effing thing on in her normal manner. So we had a goat that was in milk at the time so we put the goat in a pen and the lamb in and the lamb suckled the goat and we progressed up to a rather acceptable ewe. The joint ill disappeared and we bought a bit more odds and sods. We built up a pedigree flock of Dorset Horns at one time and then we started producing the Ile de France blood. Another import via Ann Hodgson, it was an interesting cross. All down to Usky Arthur. Arthur somebody or other from Usk. Ann had seen the Ile de France advertised and she liked them because they were so similar to the Poll Dorset but larger. They lambed out of season and they milked well. And they looked so similar to the Poll Dorset that she bought one and she was selling pedigree Dorset Horn ewe lambs but they were in fact Ile de France cross. Cadzow came from Arthur at Usk. I preferred them polled, they were easier to feed, and if you fed them out in the field and you get the horns in the back of your boots and you were walking along at a merry rate, you suddenly stopped and ended up on your face. And you ended up battered and bruised, easier to shear. It was less trouble on the undercarriage and the trousers. Shearing sheep with horns tends to rip your trousers and everything else. You end up with bruises where it is hard to explain. So it was all right. The wool was always very good on the Poll Dorsets and the Dorset Horns. It is a very fine micron on it. Mainly the reason why they went so far across the world, the merinos. Well the merino is an out-cross.

We built up the sheep, did relief milking, the scrap, a bit of plucking and gutting, logs. If you could see some money in it and you could do it, you had a go at it. We did paper bags, we found that was a niche, we found a market for them, we used to go round and buy paper bags, the same with the fertiliser bags, the cwt ones that had nitram in. There was a very good retail market to re-sell them. Builders used to like them up in London because if they put a skip outside it would fill up instantly without anybody seeing anything. But they could take a 100 plastic bags, renovate the house, have all the rubbish in the plastic bags, have the skip delivered and have the bags carried out and put straight in the skip. So that was a market we found. Well it is finding a commodity for something that is reasonably plentiful and reasonably cheap and finding a market for it.

We slowly built up. Well this field came up for sale seven acres. And it came up at auction and the chap didn't sell it, must be' 76, '77 it came on the market and it didn't sell. The chap that owned it, he had another place on the Salisbury road and we were doing some bale carting for him and just happened to say that if you ever happened to sell that field we would be interested. He said, "no I'll never sell it." About 12-month later we came back home and Mother said that Derek had come in and he'd said that he would sell the field. So we sold everything we had livestock-wise and borrowed a bit of money and bought it as a family, brother, sister and myself. Mother lent us a bit of money to go with it and we could just afford it. We sold everything we had. We were also renting about 10 acres beside off Grandfather, Uncle, Aunt. Different places and we didn't have any stock to put in it, so we saw Johnny Burden at market one day and he said he had 50 ponies he wanted grazing on for the slaughter market and I think he offered us a pound a head to graze them on. So we ended up with 50 ponies grazing for a month at a pound a head which was quite a nice little earner. They stayed in. They were no trouble at all, they were so hungry they ate everything in sight. At the time I had done something for another farmer and there was a dozen ewes with broken mouths and I bought them for £2.50 each and turned them out with the horses so they cleaned up the grass. We were relief milking several farms and one of the farms was Jersey herd and I bought six or seven Jersey bull calves off of them. And when the lorry came to pick up the horses, I said he had better send on a Transit as well, as they had a few ewes up here as well. He did a deal over the phone for the ewes I think they made about £8, £8.50 each which in a fortnight was a good turn round on our money and I said we have got a few calves as well. And the night before the transit come to pick up the horses, we had to rush round and gather up all these odd sheep, calves and a couple of goats as well. We sort of made another lorry load to go on to slaughter at the same time. It is opportunist shall we say. You can't do it with the regulations today. We'd go to market and if you had a cow calve you'd go up to Shaftesbury there and you'd buy a couple of cheap calves to put it on the cow that had calved, so that you didn't waste the milk and keep them on there a fortnight. Then take them to Sturminster and make a better price of them. Calves were always cheaper at Shaftesbury and you could always take them to Sturminster if they had improved.

Then about 1980 we decided to start milking and we purchased a milking bale for a fiver, a bulk tank for £400. The bale came from Margaret's Marsh quite local really. It was a bale, the milking pump, an electric motor and one, two and half horsepower stationary engine for a standby. We brought it back here on a tractor and trailer, set it down on a piece of concrete, bought a small bulk tank from Stalbridge Weston. A chap had given up milk down there. The bale was actually an "in churn" bale where you put the two churns down between the cows and you milked directly into the churns. Four at a time, which wasn't exactly suitable for what we wanted so we went to a farm sale up on the Salisbury Plain and they had a pipeline and I think we gave £180 for the pipeline through this milking parlour. Gutted the bale out put the pipeline in and got it passed and we started milking. We had three cows the first week then we progressed on till we were actually running 70 cows on seven acres at one point. Still in the bungalow. We had 70 cows on seven acres and we used to rent grass keep. If it was close enough to walk the cows to within a mile, we used to walk the cows night and morning back to here to milk and if it wasn't close enough we would zero graze. So we carried on like that for a bit. Then after quite a monumental struggle with North Dorset we managed to get planning permission to build the house.

We didn't have enough money to build the house, to have anybody in, so I think I went to the Bath and West Show and I bought a trowel, a level and a line. And thought to myself it is not an awful lot different to stacking bales. So with a little bit of help, got put right a time or two, we bought the stone at Swanage undressed. Hauled it all back on a Bedford TK dressed it, put it up on the scaffolding and did the scaffolding ourselves. Built the house. We started in '82 and it is now 2005 and we are still not finished. The great move was in 1988 we moved in to the house up here with nothing on the floors apart from bare concrete, no doors on, no ceilings in the kitchen, utility room, larder. Mother loved it. Living on a bloody building site. The stairs were in place but not fixed, no hand rail, no hand rail round the landing no doors on upstairs and a curtain on the bathroom door, the Rayburn was fired up and going, the electric was on, the phone wasn't connected and we had to rough it for a day or two. Because in the meantime we had bought 50 acres on the Salisbury road just in Wiltshire. Right opposite where my Grandfather was and to finance it we were going to sell the house. But Mother decided in her wisdom that the bungalow after being there for 25 years was about time to modernise. So she suggested that we sold the bungalow and moved up to the farmhouse and as it was a new house it was not going to need anything done for a few years. So that was what we done, the bungalow sold a little bit quicker than we thought, so we had to move a little bit quicker than we thought. Everything fell into place in the end, the chap that bought the bungalow was a merchant banker and we had a bridging loan arranged to buy this other land and he very generously said, "there is no point in hanging about. You don't want a bridging loan," he said, "leave things to me to arrange." And the next morning the solicitor phoned up and said we have got a banker's draft for the money just like that. He was a merchant banker in London and he had arranged to have the finances carried through so we got away without having a bridging loan.

So we had 50 acres at Salisbury road and seven acres here and rent about another 50, 60 acres besides. We were full-time farmers, both of us. We went up to 70-85 cows. That was full-time work and what with a succession of BSE it knocked everybody back. '86 that started off, we used to take calves to Sturminster Market. Charolais bull calf 10-day to a fortnight old, £330. We had several calves that topped the market at £330-£340. Then BSE struck and the panic started and Johnny Burden was having calves dumped outside his gate in the morning. He would buy 10 calves in Sturminster Market and he'd go to pick them up and there would be 20 in the pen. People were just disposing of them just to get rid of them. That had an effect and what with everything else.

The Milk Board was still going. We were on about 23, 24 pence and after the dissolution of the milk board it was all very rosy for the first few years. We never had money like it, 30 odd pence a litre. We had a mixture of cows, we had Jerseys, Guernseys, Ayrshires, Friesians and Brown Swiss, Shorthorn crosses and every cross in between. If it had four legs and four teats we used to milk it. Herefords, Angus. It was extremely good quality. We were bordering the 5% butterfat all the time. It balanced out very well, We were selling to Dairy Crest at the time and Highman's were buying milk in at Blackmore Vale Creamery. They would have three loads every day from Dairy Crest five days a week. Then they would take the Channel Islands' milk on weekends which was only one load, and there was two local Channel Island farms so they used to pick up Arundell's and

Jeffery's and then pick up our milk to go with it, as it was high butterfat and that would go into the creamery for the weekend milk. We used to get paid on the butterfat but then it started this price war and nothing didn't go any sense and brother died. It was a blow. That was '86, September '86. Well I carried on as long as I could and it got to the point where foot and mouth came in and the milk price dropped so low and the penalties. You had your haulage taken out, your deductions ended up more than your milk cheque sometimes and it was barely covering the feed costs, so I had a dairy inspection and it passed and then it was a chap from Milklink came out, the farm assurance, and they were talking about spending £30,000-£40,000 on the dairy and I said "well I have got better idea. If you want to milk the cows you go ahead and do it and spend the money. If not, don't send the tanker in after Thursday night." He said: "What do you mean?" I said: "I am giving up. Watch me." So this was on the Tuesday and I gave up on the Thursday. I sold a lot of the cows and then foot and mouth came in and that was another nail in the coffin. So I have just cut back down now to 25-cow beef herd, single suckle them. Less hassle. Just as much hassle with the paperwork, and they don't handle as well as they aren't being handled every day like the dairy cows. I kept the land. I still miss the dairy cows, I miss the milking cows, but I don't miss the hassle that is involved. I can lose less money by not milking cows that I can by milking cows. Even the big herds aren't making money now. So I took the right decision but at the wrong time. I should have taken that decision seven or eight years earlier. But then again it is hindsight. So I have slipped back into my old ways.

As for sheep shearing I have never done a llama yet but I have sheared most things. I've trimmed up the odd dog or two, goats, Angora rabbits. Out on a farm one day and the bloke only had six or seven ewes and he looked a bit in puzzlement, "got a little favour to ask, you wouldn't mind doing us a little favour, me daughter has got a couple of Angora rabbits." He said: "You wouldn't mind having a go at shearing them?" I said, "if they are alive I will try it." And we stretched them out on the shearing sheet, one held onto the ears and the other held onto the legs and we stretched them out a couple of blows up each side they were fairly well shorn then. They survived funnily enough. But we used to go shearing the odd few flocks, never done too much of it. Shearing when you don't know you are doing it, that is when you start doing it well.

Scrap has been in the doldrums since the last six months up till now and everybody is doing it. Now is not the time to go in when everybody else is doing it. So we'll give that a miss for a bit. So I am lorry driving at the moment. Rob Beale doing temporary toilets and security panels stuff like that and I am covering an area from Lambourne, Reading, Basingstoke Winchester, we are now increasingly south. Yesterday I done Bournemouth Wimborne, Winterbourne Abbas, 300 miles yesterday. I get involved in festivals and that is an eye-opener in itself. We don't do Pilton, Glastonbury festival, that is just a nightmare. We know the firm that do it, and we have been asked if we would like the odd day or two's work down there, but that does not appeal. No, we do East Harptree where they have the Great Green Gathering. That's an eye-opener, everything powered by sun, wind and pedal. It's an education. Living rather a sheltered life you do get educated on some of these things. It isn't only topless. When they are putting up tepees absolutely starkers, not a pretty sight. It is unbelievable. You'd never think that people would live like it. They seem to be quite happy. Funnily enough you get less trouble and less damage at an event like that than you do at something like the steam fair, where it is normal people, shall we say. They seem to respect the equipment, they don't damage the loos, but if you get up the steam fair, the toilet paper is always pinched the holders are twisted and bent, the seats get broken. It is unbelievable the damage that gets done.

Double booking occasionally mishaps happen. Yesterday I got back in the yard and there was an awful panic on somebody wanted to know where their loos were. They had a party last night. Started at eight o'clock and at five o'clock they had no loos, and it was a panic and "could you just?" No trouble, put two on the lorry drive like hell for an hour and set them up just in time for the party. Sneak out the back just as the guests were coming in the front. It's different. It's a laugh.

Parish council? Too many years to remember. Must have gone on there when I was about 22. Here was a vacancy. Brother went on at the same time. This was for Cann but it is a joint parish Melbury Abbas and Cann, but we went on for the Cann one. We were down there at the time and some of the old boys in the village had had enough and they wanted to retire. And it was about time they had some young blood on the council and we duly got elected. I don't know how it happened but I ended up with the vice chairman's job. And ended up with the chair at 25. There was some consternation because everybody thought I was too young to do it. I thought to myself, the thing is if you are in the chair that is your job, and you tell everybody else how to do the work, and you just delegate. In fact the chairman's job is one of the easier ones, rather than treasurer or clerk. If it becomes a problem with footpaths, you delegate that to the footpath department. Planning to the planning department. You try and keep order. Only had to shut one meeting down in a hurry but we reconvened the following week after the storm had blown over.

The road? That is the main problem at the moment. It is as everywhere, the traffic has increased and not only is it the size of the traffic. The weights have increased, the damages from each vehicle is less. The higher the weight the more axles they got, less pressure, it is the actual pressure of the volume of traffic that is causing the problems. We are on a B class/C class road here and we are now carrying more than A class roads. It has taken a few years to get through, but Dorset County Council now have decided that we are one of the most dangerous roads in the county for accidents. The C13 the 3081 which extends from the Somerset Border at Hunter's Lodge right the way through to Ringwood. That's the 3081 and the C13 branches off it at Cann Common here and goes on through to Blandford. We are carrying anything up to peak flow, 12,500-13,000 cars a day. Last week we had a lorry from up Grimsby way heading off to Spain with a cargo of monkfish, 13 tonnes packed in ice worth £80,000. He actually got half way up Zig-Zag and got through his gear change routine to get up the steep hill which is one in twenty gradient. Fairly steep and I think he must have let his clutch out a bit sharp, because the fish took off in the lorry slid the length of the bed in a curtain sider. Didn't break open the back doors, the ice and the fish smashed through the back doors, left the catches intact and landed on the road and it was not a particularly warm morning and with the ice in place the whole lot froze in one lump. I think a few of the fish managed to get rescued first. And they were placed in freezers. The council then took seven or eight hours with JCBs and tipping lorries. It was all lost. But that is a normal occurrence.

Watercress beds? Remember them well, that was I suppose right up till 1974-75. All from Ludwell. Fed by five artesian wells down there behind Grove Farm. EEC regulations won't allow it now, they have to be gravel bottom and concrete sides. The investment, when you look at the price of watercress, it makes you wonder. This was all the Lawrence family. It was a big industry, there were five or six men down there cutting watercress. And it wasn't only the watercress, they used to coppice the willow beside the water cress beds in the boggy area. The majority of that used to go on for spar making or thatching, they used to keep the reeds cut back all the side channels mud-free, so there was no flooding. The water used to pass freely and there always seemed to be an awful lot of wildlife, while they were working, There was more wildlife then than now it has reverted to its wild state. So it was better.

Up on the down? I spent quite a few years up on those downs, we know them like the backs of our hands when we were up there with the sheep you were up there virtually every day of the year, if it was snowing you knew which way to go to get out of it. You knew where the sheep would be. Sheep walks, they take the level path, you don't get soil erosion. Once you've lost the topsoil on the down you have chalk and nothing won't grow there any sense and it takes years to replace.

Melbury Hill? We had a rather good bonfire up there. This was going back to the Armada. A timed bonfire. We had permission from the National Trust, we were part of the national chain. I think we had to set it off at 9.17. We managed to acquire a lot of timber from Wonderland Caravans over at Shillingstone. And we built quite an impressive bonfire and they also let us have 25 gallons of cellulose thinners that they had finished using which we thought would make quite a nice pyrotechnic effect. We poured the 20 gallons on top of the fire to let it soak through and we had a piece of metal guttering with sawdust in coming away from the base of the fire which we soaked in cellulose thinners. Bob Blades actually lit the fire as one of the older residents of the village, and as you know, Bob had a wooden leg and we gave him a bean pole with a sock tied on the end as a torch. And the idea was he dropped it in the guttering tray and the fire went up. But the fire went up slightly faster than we thought and Brother and myself we had to have one arm under each side of Bob and get him away from the fire slightly faster than his good leg and wooden leg would carry him, before he actually caught fire. From Okeford Fitzpaine it looked like an atomic bomb going up. Straight up and had a mushroom of flame. Pyromaniac? No we like a good bonfire in the village. We have done enough of them.

There are people who have slaved all their life in London, they have taken second mortgages, they have worked God knows how many hours to buy something we have had to pay nothing for. We have had this view, we have enjoyed the area. People pay a fortune to do it. We have it for next to nothing. What more can you want? Somewhere you enjoy living. Something you enjoy doing. As a countryman you are at peace with yourself and at peace with your surroundings.

Arthur Watson and his famous restaurant at West Bay

27 Arthur Watson: Riverside Café, West Bay
Born 1939.

West Bay is an idiosyncratic place, lots of variation, all sorts of people... The old Channel Pilot used to say avoid West Bay in all weather conditions.

When I first came here it was 1939, the outbreak of the war. I went to live on East Cliff and shortly after that we moved to West Cliff. My father went off to join the Navy. During the First World War in the Army he became an expert in machine gunnery and when they wanted to arm trawlers in the Second World War, they asked him to instruct trawler skippers in the use of machine guns, so he disappeared in 1939.

There didn't seem to be any fishing going on particularly, till old Frank Butt came back after war with a boat called the Redwing and you used to see it going off down the Chesil Beach, every day of the year to catch fish. But the main thing one remembers from those days is the mackerel seining which was always very, very popular. We all had drop nets for prawning and would take them out onto Table Rock, off the pier. After the storms that was the time, when it was all muddy, you never went there when it was clear, you never caught anything. But there were always cleverer people who were more athletic, who could get further out than we could. There were days when you came home with two or three hundred and days when you came home with none at all. West Bay prawns in September, just the best, fantastic.

I remember the watchmen on cliff tops looking out for shoals of mackerel. It was just wonderful to see them rowing out round the shoal to capture them with a seine net. And then haul it up onto the beach and the whitebait would come in first, whitebait jumping into shingle. Of course we were always gawping at this. We were always a nuisance. But we always got ten or 20 to take home. It was just what they did. Burton had a lot of myths, some of them true, some of them untrue, but Burton had a mystique all of its own. It was virtually 1,000 miles from West Bay, they were so separate and distant. And almost dismissive of West Bay. Three parishes meet here. Symondsbury, Bothenhampton and Burton Bradstock. Burton still comes to the very eastern edge of West Bay and owns the golf club.

During the war they had tank traps. Access to the piers and promenade was totally restricted. But people obviously did go fishing for the food side of things. There were areas they let us on to, but a lot of training for cliff climbing took place here. So they had to be careful not to blow each other up. There were tank traps and lots of barbed wire. They worked mostly off the beach. Most young men were at war and it was the old boys who hung about and they didn't go very far. I think they recruited some of the local soldiers to help them. I suppose Lyme Bay was quite dangerous, there were a few E-boats around.

After the war, seine netting continued for quite a while. The last seine netting I saw was about 12 years ago. Reg Perrott, Forsey, Hawkins and Hawkers, they did it a bit. In the end they just gave it up. I think that great episode when the Russian trawlers were in Falmouth and Weymouth, they so damaged the English Channel mackerel stocks that it almost became not worth while. That was a big mistake to allow the Eastern Europeans to hoover the channel almost dry. I think it's beginning to come back a bit now.

Seining they'd soon learn again if there was money in it. Spring right through till September. Whitebait used to go and then the sprats came after, very often, the sprats were unpredictable. Ten years of nothing and then suddenly they would be everywhere, and the boats would come back. The Peace and Plenty, Rex Woolmington, Eric Hamblett, Barry Hawker absolutely laden to the gunwales, almost dangerously so. Full of sprats then they wouldn't know what to do with them, as they are not the most popular eating fish. They were mostly sent off for factories. A bit to Holland where they were processors, there is for everything in Holland.

Conger has always been here, skate has been good, Dover soles. Now the John Dory, red mullet come this far north with a bit of warming of the sea. Never used to see them earlier on. Plaice, bass, great mystery of the sea bass. That's what's been so good, it has not been a centre where you could guarantee to get a lot of anything, it has been a mixed fishing. They never seemed to know what they were going to bring back. You could never order anything except crabs and lobsters.

Minimum size? Most fishermen are absolutely excellent at observing it, except sometimes the weekend potters and divers who will almost have a go at anything. Berried lobsters and old lobsters. The last person who supplied me, he never brought one in, he felt that an old lobster that had got to 25 deserved not to be caught. And the berried ones are the future of the fishing industry so they must be left alone.

Conservation of stocks? Mortgages have to be paid. I think a lot of fishermen would welcome prohibition and closed season. Closed boxes. No scallops, no this, no that, and so there would be complete ban and they would know within the context, that that wasn't an option at that time in the breeding season. It seems we like to blame the foreigner but a lot of it is our own fault. A lot of our fishing quotas are sold to Spaniards, who now own our fishing quotas and export it quite legitimately to their own country and if there wasn't a willing seller there wouldn't be a willing buyer.

Herring? Occasional, very occasional. Of course when I was young the porpoises used to come up from the west. Come through the bay here, after the whitebait and the mackerel, pass on along the piers, one particular day towards the east and then September they would all come back again. It was almost that you could set you calendar by the regularity of it all. It was a real delight seeing the porpoises going up the channel. You knew that spring had started.

The occasional whales were spotted by the Daily Mail. Never pilchard, no sardines, the odd moonfish over the years. blinn, the odd shark from time to time. They do quite well with cod from time to time. I used to go out with Mr Thomas who was wholesale game merchant up in Salwayash, he had a boat in West Bay and we used to catch blinn, he used to know his marks. However much one needs seafish, no one seems to be able to eat blinn or pollack. Squid which is one of the most expensive single items on the menu was thrown away. Just such a shame. 'Till people went to Greece and the Mediterranean they couldn't contemplate eating squid. Squid and shark share more waters than any other species of fish. More common throughout the world, they have survived with different shapes in different areas.

Newfoundland? I've always had this wonderful romantic memory of the great Portuguese sailing ships setting out from Averio and Figuera da Foz and going off to the Grand Banks and chucking off countless dories into the mist and fog. And these poor men just having these long lines spending days in these little dories just fishing up cod from the Grand Banks amongst icebergs and fog and ocean liners. And of course a lot of them just disappeared forever and that accounts for the Portuguese melancholy which enhanced all their music, dance and song, as they have all lost somebody to the sea. Bacalao. Salt cod. The old aristocrats used to love skate and I am told they hung their pheasants up on lines and when they were ripe and tender and the maggots just moving, and the skate the same, hung up skate, when the skin began to peel off on its own that was time to cook it.

Smokery here? Don't think so. Over East Beach there was a chap called Hawkins who used to cook prawns on an outside brazier and you used to go everyday about two o'clock to get a bag full of prawns, and there was the most wonderful smell of salt water and prawns cooking.

Incredible. The salt house. Just a store forever and ever.

Salt smuggling? The great Basque fishermen were going to the Grand Banks long before Columbus was ever thought of. The gold of those days, preserved fish. The greatest trading currency. The fish and the salt. They match one with the other, the priceless commodity of food which was traded throughout Europe.

Seine netting? One man stood on the top of the beach and sometimes one man on top of the cliff and they would see the sea boiling with the mackerel coming to the surface to feed on the whitebait. And they would then get a general direction in which way the shoal was moving and they would then yell down to two men usually, who had an oar each, moored about five yards off the beach and a third man with the net which was piled on the stern. And then as the shoal moved nearer, they would get it past them more or less, and then row as fast as they could and surround it with the rearmost man chucking the net in and the two oarsmen rowing as hard as they could. Then once they had surrounded the shoal, they beached with as much velocity as they could and leap ashore. There were wings to the net rope, wings which they pulled in till the net started hitting the beach and then they'd get the strain onto the net and then the boat would go out and tie the cod end with a sort of loop. Then having got the cod end sealed off they would then commence to haul it up onto the beach. The first thing you would see would be the tiny fish that had escaped like the whitebait and the tiny mackerel who would fling themselves onto the shingle, and then gradually they would pull the net in. Sometimes it was bursting and it was really exciting and sometimes practically nothing, as they would have missed the shoal, which had changed direction. Great skill was needed, hoping it would not change direction.

Lengths of net? They seemed to go out about 50 yards out and 50 yards back Anything more would have been hard to handle. About 200 yards of net. Heavily tarred nets, cork floats, no terylene or propylene. All were tarred and mended, they often snagged on rocks, they all had cork floats. The seine netters still around now some of them. Frank Butt did a bit, Reg Perrott was always there, a chap called Forsey, the Barnes brothers, the Hawkins and the Hawkers, Pat Day who lives over the other side of West Bay, Cliff Samways was making nets, Dessie Gape, Bert Miller…

The restaurant? Like most things, we drifted into it. Mother had this restaurant to help my sister out in the '60s. And then my sister got married to Cliff Samways, and they moved away and my mother was stuck with the restaurant and post office, so I decided to help for a little while in 1962 and never got out ever since. But fish was a very minor item in the early days. People didn't really want it apart from fish and chips, Dover soles occasionally, but mostly people went to the Smithfield Show in their suits to eat Dover sole, they didn't eat them at the seaside. The great houses that had their turbot kettles, didn't eat out, they didn't have any money.

The turning point was 1980. We did lobsters before, but then in the '80s second-homeowners came down. They were a big force in changing things. They didn't want traditional seaside fare they wanted more elaborate things, they wanted fish with a bone in, not a fillet. They wanted scallops and they wanted us to suggest other things they hadn't had before. So really we were partners with our customers, they asked us to do things and we did them and introduced them, so we have grown up as a partnership. Seafoods, all still fresh and local, what's in season when we can get it, deep freeze we hardly use at all. Once it is run out, it has gone, no reserve stocks of anything. We change our menu every day according to what arrives. Not all of it comes from West Bay. Some comes up from Brixham, Sidmouth, Seaton, wherever there is a landing of fish. We must sell about 20 tonnes of fish a year. We are known for fish. We try and keep it simple.

Not too complicated, try and avoid marketing gimmicks. Word of mouth.

West Bay is an idiosyncratic place, lots of variation. All sorts of people, from the most eminent to the most ordinary. Fishermen give the port its flavour and atmosphere. Nothing less interesting than a fibreglass cabin cruiser. Nothing more dangerous than fishing. The old Channel Pilot used to say, "avoid West Bay in all weather conditions." A place for everyone, a wonderful future.

28 Dave Sales and Peter Newton: On board the crabber Gillian S, West Bay
Dave born 1937. Peter born 1955.

Dave: I was the King of St Alban's race for 28 years, and you had to be shrewd to do that. It was a pretty evil place to fish.

Peter: Shut your eyes and pray, if you stay in a straight line you are all right but if you don't, then goodnight Vienna.

Dave: I fished 33 years out of Swanage. They had it a lot harder when we first went to sea, the fishermen, because the gear we were using, all natural fibres. Lobster pots if you didn't make them in winter you didn't have any, you couldn't buy them off the shelf. Today you can go and buy a thousand off the shelf if you want them. We made a first step up from the inkwell ones. The Frenchmen used to come into Newlyn and pick up the shellfish from Harvey's, and you see these hoops, chestnut hoops from round barrels and we used to make a jig, and used to make the entrance out of willow or cobocane and make them out of chestnut hoops and knit a wire mesh bottom in it. Only one entrance, inkwells. One of the biggest problems was that the netting was sisal and we used to dip it in Cuprinol or tar them. Didn't seem to worry them, in actual fact fishing at Swanage and the last place we could get old fashioned tar was at Bridport because of the gas works. It never had the guts taken out of it and 40 gallon of tar would last a bit, the ropes either sisal or manila. Sisal £8 a coil, 120 fathom and Manilla been £12 a coil.

1956. Not that many fishermen around. Fishing inshore, fishing still a cottage industry, the whole of the English Channel, Lulworth, a few in Weymouth and in Swanage, only three or four of us not even a boat potting at Poole and only a few at Christchurch. There wasn't many around then. I am a member of the Sea Fisheries Committee. We had 200 boats on our books in 1956. It did peak at 800. From Lyme Regis to Portsmouth but it was a cottage industry primarily.

The fishermen were in tune with nature and the gear used to wear out and if you were using a seine net, and if you didn't dry it and put it down in a heap it used to rot. So that in itself was a restraint on the fishing. We used to dry them off on posts, trawls and all that sort of thing. Corse with the advent of synthetic fibres it was a new world, they didn't wear out. Lobster pot season was middle of March till October, there wasn't the demand. We used to sell our lobsters to a place at Wall's Ash at Southampton and they used to go on the liners. And in those days they used to keep them alive in big tanks. A pub called The Rising Sun, the pub's still there but that was the main lobster trade. The price I used to get was 3/3d a pound and they're moaning today because they are only getting £4 a pound…

But as technology improved we were able to fish longer periods. Two or three things happened about much the same time. We got kicked out of Iceland, early '70s and about the same time we joined the Common Market. We had no trade for spider crabs till they started to export them to the Continent. It opened up a whole new trade and now Pete deals with the Spaniards, and they bought the brown crab as well and it all created a new market. In actual fact the fleet on the south coast owes its prosperity to the continent. In the '70s you could chuck a shilling out and get a quid. We worked hard for it mind, crabs and shellfish.

Before that we used to go sprat fishing in the winter but of course we had synthetic nets. Then of course various navigational aids came in and we were able to range further afield and the inshore fishing industry expanded out of all proportion. What happened was the liner trade closed down because of the aircraft. Continental demand was greater and prices, I can remember they went up to 6/- then 7/- then 9/- a pound, vans to pick up. Still do on Tuesdays up to Poole. It is a fantastic trade now, in the millions. Poole is the centre of the shellfish trade now from Scotland, Ireland, Outer Hebrides. All goes through Poole. Monday, Tuesday, Wednesday transhipped back to Spain by Thursday, a very highly organised business. Without them we would collapse.

For what we catch, the demand is not in this country. For various reasons the fishing industry undertook a great deal of contraction. We over-fished it, we got too greedy. It is coming back, but very slowly. The EU are slowly turning the screw. We were the small inshore fishermen and got overlooked and the big boys over-fished it. The regulations coming in now are beginning to hit the big boats and making them uneconomic. Small boats like this which have always fished out of harbours like West Bay and Lyme, and have done over the centuries, were squeezed for a number of years. And now it is good news.

Fishing out of West Bay? About half a dozen boats. Jack Woolmington, New Aquarius, Donald Johnson, Seagull, Pete Newton, Gillian S my old boat, Garry Copp, Trace Sea, Jamie Smith, Valiron, John Wordswick, Blue Horizon and John Smith, Christine Anne. This used to be my boat. I have only got a small one now. Sixteen years from West Bay, built in Falmouth, Penryn, Yes she's always been a good boat an inshore crabber, 26ft long. Fish all the year round, with synthetic ropes and gear. The gear's out all year and never comes in. In terms of economics today nobody stops and makes pots. I've had pots delivered to me and they been out at sea the following morning. There was a time when lobsters were very scarce, and in their wisdom MAFF increased the size. Whether it is global warming I don't know, but there's more lobster around and sometimes they can breed, not once, but twice or three times. See when I first caught £1,000 of lobsters in a day. It is true. Haul three tides a day, 120 pots three times a day. We used to haul £300 on the first one, not quite so much on the next and the last one of the day was usually the best one. Done it many time. We have had so many lobsters we never knew what to do with them. There's many moaning today about the price of lobsters but they are catching a lot of lobsters. One hundred and twenty pots is a doddle today. I used to work 300 with this one, I've hauled 150 a day on my own with this one. See we have improved on the hauling gear, hydraulic haulers. Well we had capstans, more dangerous you see. Run off the engine, very crude. Used to pull 10 mile of rope a day. You knew all about it, I had a second hydraulic slave put on the crabber on the South Coast and it was like coming out of the Ark. Don't touch anything now, just touch a lever. So what, if it is making your life easier, at the same time it enabled people to haul up many more pots, and with this quota system there's too many boats, not here, but on a national scale gone crabbing because there's no quota on crabs. And the reflection on that is in the price. I mean the prices we are getting now are half what they were 15 years ago. And it is purely because the market, you can't complain about it. The market is the market... There's limited demand for so much and we have just gone over the brink. You get these super crabbers that land 20 tonnes of crab a week, well the economics are that they can do that for a pound a kilo... they have to, got to get shot of them.

How far afield? I used to go about 10 or 12 miles off the coast. You had to share the ground with scallopers and trawlers. You had to use a common sense, certain ledges, and by and large everybody works well, for the amount of mobile gear out there we get away very well. There are odd instances where pots get caught up and nets get towed away. Donald puts nets out at night and if they are out there at night and a big beam trawler comes in, they can't see them. But even so it is a rare event. I've stood at Abbotsbury Hill at midnight and counted 27 beam trawlers out there once, when the oil business was on. I don't care where they've gone. Bloody

Dave Sales and Peter Newton at West Bay

good riddance to them because it is good for the little man. The whole of the south coast is programmed for the continent, there got to be 20 lorries going to Scotland every weekend. Then drive back down to Spain.

Spain is a tremendous market. Spanish have been fishing in the Western Approaches for donkey's years. Before we came out of Iceland we never had any boats going down there. All those boats got scrapped. we started to build on the prosperity of the Continent and built bigger boats and started to go where the Spanish are. Turning round and saying it is our fish, we weren't out there 300 years ago.

Mackerel? I go out catching a few mackerel. But they have got that very tightly controlled with the Norwegians, and as it is, only large boats that catch these mackerel off Scotland almost industrially. They catch tonnes, they know exactly what's caught and that's the end of it or they have to move from one sector to another and they fish against a scientific quantity, a quota. It could be regulated a lot better. No good fishing a stock out to extinction.

Fishing out of West Bay in winter? Been a bastard. No doubt about it. It's a very difficult harbour. Going to be super when this new harbour is done, isn't a bad thing that it has been like this, it kept the amount of boats out, t'isn't everybody wants to face West Bay in the winter. We've all come in there when you've needed a roll of toilet paper. Timing it right with the waves, got to be on the ball, all had narrow shaves in our time. Been one or two in our family..

My Grandmother's Grandfather was James Hammett, one of the six Tolpuddle Martyrs. They got let down by the clergyman, who perjured himself in court. They had come to some agreement with Frampton the landowner but after this the men were arrested. The clergyman was present at the meeting as a witness but in court he went back on what they had agreed and sided with Frampton. Then my Mother's father, Jacob Gibbons came to Studland as head gardener for Sir Eustace Fiennes. When he was 36 he had peritonitis very badly and Sir Eustace paid for him to have an operation. As a way of recuperating he arranged for him to have a passage as a steward on the Titanic. He was working in the bakery and when she started to sink he was allocated to boat no 11. The sea was dead calm. Most of them didn't believe that she would sink, their boat still had spaces in it when it was launched. He was signed off at 2.30am and his pay stopped there and then. The band kept playing "Nearer my God to Thee". When they got to New York on the Carpathia the crew were kept at a secret location and paid 2/6 a day to keep them from talking to the Press.

Then during the First War Jacob Gibbons went to France to Calais as a cook for Lady Fiennes's hospital and then he joined the Red Cross and served as a stretcher-bearer at Verdun. Would never have a bad thing said about the French after what they went through at Verdun. In the Second War my father he was in Tobruk, the siege of Tobruk and helped direct the artillery barrage when they broke out. The Black Watch just kept on going, they went for two hills called Jack and Jill. Took them with very heavy casualties and pipes playing. Never seen anything like it, just kept going. On my Father's side both he and my Grandfather were professional golf players and made golf clubs, the wooden ones, very skilled.

When I was 14 I started working on farms and then went fishing. That was 1956. Had a good run at it. I fished in my time right the way down from the east of the Isle of Wight off the Nose east of Ventnor, the west side of the Isle of Wight, all down across Christchurch Ledges, Poole Bay, Swanage down Weymouth, down as far as Lyme Regis. Somewhere or another I have fished on it. I was the King of St Alban's race for 28 years, and you had to be shrewd to do that. It was a pretty evil place to fish and a lot of them tried to push me out of it but none of them ever succeeded. You had to stand your ground, but there used to be a tremendous lobster fishing there, you had to know the tides, specially in them days. The one revolution is the spinner, that revolutionised the fishing in the English Channel, what used to happen if we got in at strong tides or spring tide, the tops of the pot used to wind up and what this does, the pots swing, we wouldn't be fishing out in the English Channel without that spinner, just that little bit of technology. Old Geoff Nantes invented it at Weymouth and it revolutionised fishing. You could fish where you had never fished before or you had to be very cautious over the tides. No I fished two winters round Portland, Portland Race had a gut full of that in my time. Well the worst race of all is St Catherine's, off the south of the Isle of Wight. St Alban's if you know your way around you can keep in tight under the shore. But St Catherine's you can't avoid. I came through there one October, November time in a force eight. Took 12 hours getting back to Swanage, But what on earth I was doing up there I don't know but then we were young and stupid, The Start is nowhere near as bad. Portland is probably the worst of it. St Alban's wants some tackling on a spring tide. Never launch a boat on a Friday or paint it green.

Peter: I now own Dave's old Boat Gillian S. I bought it off Martin who bought it off Dave. Spent 30 years fishing, mostly out of the Blackwater on the Thames, trawling and eel trapping. with fyke nets, not as good as it was. Not many people doing it now. Eels declined over the last 20 years. Elvers, very small elver run at Maldon but none really did it. Saw one elver run at Beeleigh Abbey more black eels than glass eel, use them for re-stocking, weirs thick with them.

Trawling, Dover soles, skate in the spring, 28-ft wooden trawler, all glass fibre or steel now. A wooden boat an awful lot of them. Still a fishery, mainly on the soles, herring on the winter. Totally different stock of herring, smaller herring Blackwater and Thames estuary herring. In '77 I bought my boat for herring drifting in March, and in July they put a three year ban on herring drifting, stocks were so low. Ended up doing different things. Once they opened the herring fishery up again, there was loads and loads of herring, but the market, we lost the market and turned them into rollmops or they went abroad for canning.

Drifting? Seasonal start end of September/October in the evenings and go through to April. Night fishery after Christmas used to drift through the day, but in the autumn surface drifting didn't catch much in the day. Nets were old East Anglian twine herring drifts 30 yards long, ten on a drift, four fleets. So shoot 1,200 yards made by Gundry's, East Anglian twine, plastic or cork floats. Scottish nets were too deep really, 24-foot lead line, leads catch the shoot.

Been down here 20 years. Used to come down here on holiday, sick to death of the rat race, pace of life. Easier to live down here, Dave had the boat 16 years. I bought this one in February off Dave. Had an Islands' plastic 23 before. Gone now. Fair Trade living up in Portsmouth now. Go out on my own, lobsters, crab, cuttlefish, just about finished now. Rest of the time it's crabbing and lobsters, fishing when the autumn is here after spider crabs have gone, too many spider crabs on the ground. Mainly Dover soles, plaice, a few skate you go out netting for soles. Samways, Brixham, sold on the market. I have got a couple of private customers, the bulk of it goes to market, you can't market it, too small for customers really. They always want fish 12-14 oz. Just doesn't work like that. On the lorry and sold in one lot.

About 100 pots, 150 I suppose, 170 only once a day, Dave talks about 40 years ago and they did do the double hauling but with parlour pots once the stuff's in there it normally stays, lucky to get one. You don't get heaps now, you get enough. Minimum size from the back of the eye socket to the back of the abdomen 87 millimetres. Any under chucked back. Quite happy to go back straight back to the bottom.

Scallops? Another world diving for scallops. That lot that just passed us, that blond lad is a mate of mine from Essex, moved down 10 years ago, "will I make a few quid diving for scallops?" I said, "I should think so." If I had known how much he made I would have dived for them. Young and fit. I would be daft to do that now. Cod on the tail end. If you went out on the wrecks you'd get cod, pollack and conger.

There's wrecks out there I don't go anywhere near them. Boats come up from Brixham. The Patricia M comes up wreck netting. All the rest are netted from France or Brixham, real good year this year. The season don't seem to end. Spider crabs are a prime example. When I first started down here I would get spider crabs towards the end of May. By the end of Sept they had virtually gone from inshore, now they are there 12 months of the year. They are berried up, hibernated, they are about, they do migrate, the big ones they are certainly more active. Lot more bass than there ever was. Other fish, very occasionally trigger fish on the Chesil Beach. Well there's been trigger fish here for years, I had nine in one pot. That's not a sign of global warming, the North Sea's warming up that's why the cod have moved out of the North Sea and there was never bass in Yorkshire, there's quite a thriving bass fishery up there now. Everything is creeping further north, spider crabs from Eastbourne never went that far up, not the cold winters every year they creep further up there.

With the new pier it will certainly be safer to come and go and there is a limit to what you can fish and this will be a lot better, 100 times better. As Dave said it will take away the fear of coming back. If you go out and there is a big swell, what's this swell going to be like when I come back in six hours time? Am I going to have to go to Lyme Regis? Now with this new entrance you won't have to worry about it, it won't be a problem. Like surfing, sling a basket out the back and just let that slow you down, and there's no boat other than a RIB which will out run it, and dance on a wave. You have no steerage as the water's pushing you and you're knackered then shut your eyes and pray. If you stay in a straight line you are all right but if you don't, then goodnight Vienna.

29 Humphrey Bickford: Fisherman, West Bay
Born 1954.

Mackerel skies and horses' tails make tall ships keep big sails… West Bay no fatalities, they just die of old age.

Born and raised in Seatown. Known West Bay all my life. First boat when I was aged 11, 39 years ago. Seine fisherman? Russell Hodge lobster pots, out every evening looking for mackerel. And it was great fun. Marvellous. Odd 10/- or a quid. Straying not so often now, close inshore and circle them. Following the whitebait, one end on a rope to the beach two people rowing, Russell Hodge himself shooting the net. He also had a lorry, driving all day, morning and evening, sat on the cliff, sit and look at the sea. Plenty of time, May water, planktonic water, the mackerel don't stray then. In June it clears again. From early May till late September then the sprats. Then spratting. There was a fish merchant, Cutty Thorner, Laver brothers contracted to buy fish by the stone, 3/6d a stone, 5/- a stone, a very good price. Two tonnes of mackerel in a good haul 100 yards long, very swift, mackerel.

At Abbotsbury they went venture seining, very long rope maybe 200, 300 yards long then come round in an arc. And then another very long rope back to the shore, the two teams on either end then gradually work their way in closer and closer. The net would stay on the bottom stir up the mud then drive the fish into the path of the seine net. Not quite like trawling. They work systems like this in the North Sea called fly shooting and anchor seining, so it is more along those lines. And rather than catching a shoal of mackerel it was called venture seining because it was just a chance thing. They used to do very well but because they weren't straying or feeding on whitebait, they would last a lot longer because the whitebait weren't putrefying or fermenting in their intestines. That was one of the things.

Fish from Seatown? No such thing as smoked mackerel then, that was a '70s thing, probably it went up to Billingsgate or local fish shops never terribly sure. I have always had little boats. I was about 22 and the seine fishery had stopped. I thought why not continue it. I made a seine net, bought a boat from Rex Woolmington who is a great legend around here, unfortunately he died a couple of years ago. I caught the mackerel but I could not get the market for it in those days. Samways might take it down to Brixham markets for you. Ron Laver might take some, there are a few seine teams left. I don't know about the Abbotsbury team. Chickerel, Langton Herring. Nineteen seventy-six that was the last time I did it myself, big hot summer. The last time I saw it happening was 1982 and that was the photographs I was talking about. There were a lot probably about five or six teams working then, a difficult beach to seine. But the Abbotsbury lot would come down and haul their boats up on the beach and upturn them and camp under their boats. It was true that the women were stripped to the waist topless, nobody minded. A wonderful thing a fishermen's holiday. That was where the mackerel were. Mackerel don't behave like that any more. You don't see mackerel straying right in close to the shore, a huge shoal I saw the biggest I have ever seen, about a month ago at Seatown offshore, the mackerel still prolific. I have a little boat on Seatown, started feathering for mackerel about 10 minutes to catch about 20 fish. Underrated, so prolific, very easy to deal with the bones, were it a scarce fish, it would be valued.

Other fish? If we are talking about seine netting there were West Bay cod, perfectly legal to catch, made of silver and they used to migrate up rivers and come from Iceland, John West's and sea trout and mullet and bass, and a few flat fish. Gillnets, just bought a licence for this boat and work about 20 pots and a few nets, price isn't brilliant, so

Humphrey Bickford at low tide

many lobsters. Had 10 lobsters out of five pots once, that is the best I have ever done in my entire life, legal lobsters, everybody said it was just extraordinary. Lobsters behaving differently, very specific about where I put them. Price £11 a kilo, privately £15-£20 a kilo.

Herring? Last time I shot the seine net I caught quite a lot of herring. No pilchards, conger, not conger fishing. In the Channel Islands they long-line for conger and they have a big fishery. The fish is valuable in France or London or ethnic communities or exported. Bass is a valuable fish, its price has come down because of fish farms in Greece.

I have had various boats. I then went on to fish in the North Sea out of Lowestoft for a couple of years and then eventually got my own boat a 50ft French trawler. Sole, plaice, red mullet, glut price, still falls through. Very basic economics. Supply and demand. Red mullet prime and sought after fish, monkfish, squid. Then eventually I worked on an old Channel Island trawler but it was bigger than mine and then fished down through the English Channel and out into the Western Approaches. Depending on the area, our catch would be megrim, monkfish, John Dory, big hits on that, lemon soles, red mullet, Dover sole, plaice, ling, pollack, cod, haddock. Landed into France, Brixham and Penzance.

Vulnerable species, small rays can't get out of large mesh nets, tenth of the amount of ray on the rough ground, trawl net a sort of conical net held apart in each corner of the cone, two bridles wire ropes which lead out to 100 fathoms. Two doors or otter boards, wrecks well charted, if you snagged into a wreck, would rather you lost the gear. Main damage the sea bed, rocks, according to the scouring exposed or not, go over the foot rope then rip their way down the trawl, fairly basic sort of damage.

Area ledges, in West Bay, inshore just to the left, little lump called the Ram, the Pollack Stone leads into a bit of ground called High Ground, nearly a mile off-shore and about a mile long comes up from 45ft to about 18ft, a lot of fish on there. Lot of bass on that coral, there are corals, Ross coral. Other ledges, Bob Knight's Ground, Swyre Ledges, Abbotsbury Ledges, ledges around the Met buoy six miles from here, three miles off shore. Dead reckoning. Decca which was one of the best things that ever happened to fishing or the worst, developed for D-Day landings. For trawlers, bottom trawling. Midwater trawling for mackerel or bream then you would use your echo sounder to get the depth of the fish.

Russian trawlers in Weymouth and Falmouth, Klondikers in there in the '90s, but the Scots came down with their purse seiners and their pair trawling, it must have made some impact. Stories about the vast amounts, even the boats from Lowestoft would come down here. They were dealt with by Klondikers. Mackerel went up to Scotland for canning. Cornish fish lorries, most of it was being tinned and exported to Africa.

North Sea and the English Channel weather same rough rules of thumb apply. "Mackerel skies and horses tails make tall ships keep big sails." "Wind afore rain your canvas remain." Superstitions. Trawlers out of Lowestoft white-handled knives unlucky, green was an unlucky colour, if you saw a nun or a priest before you came down to the boat. That has died a bit of a death now but that was very unlucky. You didn't call rabbits "rabbits" you called them fluffy tails, you didn't call pigs "pigs" you called them curly tails. And you didn't call rats "rats" you called them long tails so you had fluffy tails, curly tails and long tails, unlucky if you called them anything else.

At present day, harbour changes, knocking down one of the old piers then putting in a new pier with rock armour on the outside, and that leads out beyond the old East Pier and will form an entrance to the south east rather then the south, getting in all different states of the weather. You still have to have knowledge of the place, think twice about coming in with the new provision. Fishing now? Not in a big way. Gave it up eight years ago, now working in construction. Quotas. OK. Where you can target the fish as in North Sea, but in a multi-species fishing in the South West can't target haddock, whiting, cod a by-catch. Jack Woolmington, sole, knackered on a 50 kilo a month sole quota, he might catch in one year what a big Brixham beamer might catch in a week. That sort of difference. They might land 35 grand's worth of sole in a week. Overfished? The fishery is not that local, Brixham beamers inshore. Seine netting indigenous. Seine nets made of cotton, in the '60s then nylon. Seine net cost now £2,000. Mackerel, catch say two tonnes of mackerel, 200 stone of mackerel, £5 a stone that's a grand.

West Bay no fatalities, they just die of old age.

30 Dessie Gape: Seine fisherman, Burton Bradstock 1931-2005.

All right if it were not too rough. A co-operative venture, in they days. When they had to go, you had to go. Sea good to you and bad to you.

Lerrets? That the boats they used to use, I don't know where the old man got theirs from, I think they come from up Chickerell, get four or five blokes in there, double-ended split the wave see. Later on we had a square stern, wasn't so good the bloody waves would catch you. All right if it were not too rough. Nets, fathoms in they days, and then they got the ropes. Bexington we worked off. Father and Grandfather, seine fishermen that was all they had to do up there, in they days. Worked on the land. Night time and Sundays. Never fished Friday night nor Saturday, never sell it. Sundays they were on the ball, nothing on Friday nights, couldn't sell it see. Lookouts on the shore? Not really, tell by the birds, mackerel straying. They didn't mind that sort of thing. Came in, when the whitebait came in. They were the bait, lovely to eat but no good to sell, the bellies pop on them. All right to eat.

Shooting the seine? You have to put the net in a boat and that. You got to see it, to watch it to be done. Sewn in, they pack it in, you had to put it in right for it to come out right, two of them there fold it in. You had to pack it in right like a parachute. Cotton nets, no nylon, cotton stays fresh, had to dry them out every night otherwise they bloody rot. Gor, 'twasn't the cost they put it all together themselves, patched up each year, they do all that. 'Tis cleaner as you go up along. Down quick, circle it round and bring it back in.

If you was half way out and they turned back you had it. I remember about two or three. Contracts, I don't know so much about Burton, water is shallower, old man Bullock, they wasn't so big, they used have little teamers. Venture seining, so much rope, so many fathoms, that was what we done, all depends how many turned up 14 or 16 pulling, sometimes seven or eight in they days that was all they had down there. That was up that part of the world, done in your spare time as and when. When I was up there, only a youngster, thick rope, one inch thick, but the rope was smaller to start with. That was thinner but when you got to the end of the seine, he was thicker altogether. He had to do a lot of work, venture, no whitebait, that was only when they was straying. Good shoot, thousands, not always mind, lot of time we had nothing. Bloody shovelled them by hand, dip net, and you had to carry the buggers, hard work in they days. Most of it went to London in they days, still seine netting at the beginning of the war I remember all that, that is what I am talking about.

I was born in 1931, Father was in the First War. Second, he was a coastguard down on the bloody beach all night. Used to have a little hut down there, just room for two blokes to get in there. They reckon they had to walk the beach at night for an hour each way, supposed to have done. Not many people to check on them.

Seine fishing died off in the '80s. Nineteen seventy-six, feathering then. We did have a little seine, couldn't use it very much, bloody great boulders and that out here, but we used to go up between Clayvend and Swyre, go up there for a few hours on a Sunday morning, five or six of us that was about then '82. Chickerell way, very rare don't think there's any at Abbotsbury. Garlands. Oh Yes. May Day. All the cowslips used to do the garlands up. Walk from Puncknowle down to the sea and chuck it in. Most of the village was there, we villagers used to be pretty united in those days. Although you still got the odd one or two, if you know what I mean.

Any other fish? Pilchards, plaice and all manner at one time. Didn't catch much, shoot the net against the tide and used to pick up all sorts then. Venture seining, net goes right down until you got into a reasonable way. Weights, stones, leads as well, drill a hole and they had to be the right weight, smaller ones up the front and the bigger ones at the back, the po stone and he were heavier take the bunting down, cod end, the bag. Cod never much. Silver, West Bay cod one or two of the queer ones, caught now and again, always put them back. They's all farmed now. Very impressive stuff in those days, glutted some days.

We used to go up Seatown at the back end of the summer, that was when we caught the stray lots down there, that was when you couldn't catch anything venture seining. The Abbotsbury crew used to go up there, I used to go with them. Yeah.

Holiday? I don't know about that. Women every where. Superstitions? Loads of them I can't remember them. Lucky stones, used to have a couple of they on the boat, with a hole in, lucky to find them on the Hive.

How many crews on Chesil? Can't remember. In the war there was only two at Swyre, Churchills and ours. When I was a boy, only about 12 year old, plenty of mackerel around. After the war, '50s, we was busy then, what did we get for a stone? Wasn't a lot of money 3/6d but was a lot if you didn't have any. Boat belonged to somebody like my old man and then the boat's share was taken out, a third for the net and the boat and then the rest was shared out. Shared out proper. All bloody knew what they had to come, to the bloody penny, if you knew what I mean. A cooperative venture, in they days that was all they done.

How would you cook the mackerel? Which ever way you like. I always ate mine fried, the Mrs likes her's grilled. Best way is to fry them. With herring, between Puncknowle and Swyre we used to salt them in, in a bloody great boiler, about three parts as big as this table, and then you took three or four. Nobody ever pinched them, if you were caught you'd have your bloody hands chopped off. You can't get people together, now. Everybody got transport.

Other work apart from seining? Worked down at the fish place for 35 years, Samways, and on a farm before that. In the Army for a couple of years National Service. Lentell he went to Australia, Dorset Horns out there. Only two or three fishermen left, Donald, Dave Sales, Jack Woolmington. Getting off the beach. One rowing up there two pushing off, pulling it in. Oiled boards to run it down on timbers, can't pull it on a beach, grease, dripping, old cart grease, lard's the best thing, I think one or two tried it. Dripping was better on them boards than it was on toast. That was what they used to dip them out with a dip net. Weighed in stones, this was caught night time, cooler, no lights. Never had a light on a pushbike!

Cider shed, they used to have that down the beach, at Symondsbury. Yeah I used to go up at Ash at Abbotsbury quite a lot 1966, '67. Net making never done much, old man used to make them. Buy the net and put them together, used to make up some nets outside nets. Netmaking sheds, cider sheds between Puncknowle and Swyre, the shed up there at the beginning of winter, take the nets apart and put them back together again. The bloody shed was as half as big as this area, and all round the back. All they barrels were in there and all the cider that I can remember was made down at Clayhanger between Puncknowle and Swyre, and they made it, down there somewhere. Cider and mackerel, see they never had no money in they days, drop of cider never mind if it was good or bad, never chucked away. Went on and got hold of it I suppose. Strong stuff in those days, dark black. Mackerel in cider for preserving they did have a bit, but not really. Cider and salt, cod and salt beef, bread and cheese with cider, local cheeses, bloody good cheeses in those days, same every day, bread and cheese every day.

Never did lobsters or crabs, never had the rocks up there, We didn't do much of that, shoals of bass, used to get them in they days but mostly under the cliffs. We used to catch a few up there but not very much.

Tons of things I can remember after a pint or two to jog you to remember. Father, he was a quiet man, give you one in the bloody ear hole though. Getting in and out of the surf rough seas up there mind, whoa on the beach and they gone down out of sight. They could handle them bloody boats. Sometimes they could wait for 20 minutes out there till they got a bit of calm, always a smooth and you can get in, but you got to be patient. Bloody great waves, see the boat go down out of sight, frightening, had to be bloody rough, had to pick their time, all smaller gear, smaller boats and when they had the great lerrets there and when they had to go, you had to go. Like I say, I see them waiting and waiting but you get a smooth then row like hell to get in. I'm talking about years ago.

One or two got bruised knees. Nearly all wore jerseys, guernseys, no buttons not to get catched up in the net, no waterproof gear. As soon as they jersey got wet. Anybody lost out there? My Grandfather was drowned out there. Not very old, in his thirties. Got hung up in a net, fouled leaning over the side, pulling it up, lifting the net up and he went over and they pulled him in, in the net. Couldn't swim or got caught up. Had to know what you was doing. But people can't believe when you tell about it, so different in later years. We never went when it was too rough, but was a necessity in those days. Only bloody money they could get. Wasn't never much said about it really. Sea good to you and bad to you.

Half and half, a pint that ain't too bad, that cider. Taunton was good but then that deteriorated, trouble with the apples. Eighteen-gallon barrels along there, Whiteways, 1950's down the Dove. Taunton – Autumn Gold – Bratton, Mitchell and Toms. White's fish shop out Chard way. Used to deliver all around with the fish. Seeing all the shops, everywhere. Bugger me, locally Chard, Ilminster, but then drive a lorry to London Billingsgate six nights a week. Leave here twelve o'clock. Five hours in those days. No motorways then, four or five hours. Crabs, sprats in the sprat season, catch them down Lyme. I used to collect it and go to Lowestoft when the fish was short down here. Plaice and that used to go up there every Sunday with a transit. Ford Transit, twin wheels on the back. Wooden boxes, lot of wooden boxes in they day. Then they changed over to cardboard in the sprat season. To West Mersea in the sprat season, pickled them in brine and send them to Belgium, then when we was really short of stuff we used to got to Grimsby. This is going back a few years 30 year ago.

Worked for a firm in West Bay, Samways, Cliff Samways, 35 year. Got to distribute the fish pretty quickly. Got to know how to keep them, no bloody ice, this is why they was caught by night. Up in Billingsgate by morning. Used to catch them, had to be up there bloody things wouldn't keep. Used to be ice, dry ice, great blocks of it. Used to go to Poole and Bournemouth to get it. Chip it up but then as the years went on and you got the finer stuff. Grimsby was a long way. Bloody long way 30, 40 mile from Grimsby once you got to Lincoln not so bloody clever, Leicester right wheel and on through Newark. Only got the traffic coming back.

People today just go out feathering. Cider, takes the edge off the heat. Mulled cider in the winter. That's what I got for tea, mackerel. Boys had some Saturday, have them for tea tonight. Bit of potting. They do work, more money in lobsters. Birthdays catch a few and then freeze them down, have a big birthday then use them.

Not the same as it used to be once they big trawlers come down. You get them through here. Mind you on the other hand you haven't got the seines out there you wouldn't know. Don't know do 'ee?

Nearly four o'clock letting them out of school early are they? That's all I know.

Recorded in The Anchor, Burton Bradstock. Sadly, Dessie died in June 2005.

West Bay Sprat at the Hive, Burton Bradstock

Postscript

Having completed nearly three years working on this project I thought it worth making a few extra notes and updates. You will be glad to hear that Jim Webber has started another five-year plan for his garden and has just had his driving licence extended till 2008 which is a good thing. Sadly, Bert Vickery's wife Elsie died in 2003 but after her death he discovered that she had written down her own memories of growing up at East Axnoller Farm. She started work in the milk factory in Beaminster and got into trouble with her father for going into a pub in Mosterton singing carols… Later on she would, with Bert, go round the village carol singing with a decorated tractor and trailer loaded up with their old settle and piano. Their eldest son Roy was born by candlelight in the cold winter of 1947 and delivered by Elsie's mother. Roy was the one left out in the fields in a carrycot. It didn't do him any harm and he went on to work for the Natural History Museum in London as a botanist and is an acknowledged expert of local flora. In 1994 he wrote an excellent book, the Oxford Dictionary of Plantlore, sadly out of print. This goldmine of information covers superstitions, herbal remedies and many folk names of plants. By curious coincidence, Bob Tolley, who is mentioned by several Dorset Men, came to Elmore Farm at about the same time that the Vickerys went to Sadborow, 1945, and they knew him very well. Bit of a scamp by all accounts…

Dick Measures was very lucky not to be killed during the war. He was Home Guard on top of a hill near Powerstock and being a very cold night they took up a crate of beer and lit a bonfire. A German bomber returning from Bristol thought this was too much of a good opportunity to miss and dropped a bomb right into the bonfire. They were all thrown down the hill. One of them died later. Dick Measures still rears the odd duck and chicken in amongst his organic vegetables. Not surprisingly his son Mark has gone into farming and is a very well respected soil scientist and has worked for Elm Farm Research Centre, the Organic Advisory Service, and at Holme Lacey College in Herefordshire. Not long ago I met Stuart Dowle, the shepherd for Dupont's, who recalled the terrible winter when the sheep died in droves. Stuart now works for Quicke's cheese as a salesmen and does the shows. Since the Foot and Mouth outbreak in 2001 feeding swill is now banned. Currently, all raw meat and fish from industrial waste must be burned in the UK. All other animal food waste apparently goes into landfill, which is expensive.

John Symonds, by the way, is in good form. No fixed abode, though he does creep on over the border occasionally. Curiously enough I sheared sheep for both his brothers, Howard at Eype and Robin up at Twyford near Shaftesbury. John is a great raconteur and always has quite a female following… Bob Tolley was his best friend and they often went to ploughing matches and heavy horse do's together. I sheared sheep for Bob for many years and also once or twice for Dick Measures and the Vickerys. Shearing sheep is a very good way to get to know people. It sorts out the sheep from the goats, as they say, but you do work up a thirst every now and then.

Norman Strawbridge is still very active and helps out on the shoots. His son is a bank manager and his grandson a wizkid on computers. Norman used to sharpen my sheep shearing gear, the combs and cutters. When he gave up shearing, it was only because he fell off a timber lorry and dislocated his shoulder and they didn't put it back quite right. He was then 68. I took on his round and sheared them for a number of years. Not many people shear the way Norman did, alternating the hand piece between left and right hands.

Norman Purchase still attends the Powerstock cider

gatherings with great regularity. He gave me a bottle of his own cider and it was light and sparkling of its own accord. Norman also showed me a pamphlet issued by Long Ashton during the war instructing people how to keeve cider, i.e. make it is such a way to keep the natural sweetness in it. Not dissimilar to the methods they use in Jersey and Normandy. This involves careful racking at certain stages. The photograph of Norman was taken at Simon Mehigan's in Netherbury.

A friend called Mark Rogers from Wootton Fitzpaine put me in touch with John Gale and Bernie Joy and I am very glad he did. Skilled local carpenters and joiners like them are a rarity these days. Combine that with a love of tractors, a detailed knowledge of Pymore Mill and the river Brit, you have a winning combination. Bernie still refers to John's childhood gang in Bradpole as 'terrorists'.

Nick Poole has enormous energy and his cider festival evenings are packed out. People come from as far away as Aberdeen. Even as I am writing this he is planning a trip to Tim Chichester's all-night horse and donkey driven cider event in East Devon and another cider making event at his shed in West Milton on Sunday. These events are now important social occasions and a new generation of cider makers has been well and truly grafted onto the old traditions.

Thatching is an essential part of Dorset life and like sheep shearing it often goes in families. Richard and Darren Tuck are no exception. In Symondsbury there is an orchard to this day called Willie Tuck's. All the new build thatch will certainly need thatchers in the future. The Symondsbury Mummers' play that Richard describes is very old and one of the last of the continuous traditional ones left in the UK. I saw it once in the old Tithe Barn in Symondsbury. The character Room is literally the room; he creates the stage as the play would have often been performed in people's large houses.

In the 1980s I lived in the Shaftesbury area, in the same parish as Cann Mill. One year I even sheared the sheep there, for Michael's father, Norman. Small frisky little Portlands but the wool was very fine. That five mills should have run off that one small clear chalk stream, the Stirchel, in a matter of a mile and a half is truly amazing and very efficient. Long may it continue. Flour leads on to bread and although the Houses have sold up, the bakery is still thriving. Last time I saw Norman he was sitting in the sunshine reading a book. Graham he said was always brewing beer and making wine as a kid so he has fallen on his feet in Eldridge Pope. Good village bakeries are like gold dust now.

At the other end of the bread chain is the farmer. Will Best and his wife Pam are very well known in Dorset. Their story charts the ups and downs of organic milk production very well indeed, trailblazers as you might say. Will is very much a hands-on farmer and we were lucky to photograph him as he was silaging. He simply jumped out of his tractor cab and jumped back in again. To see a field of organic grass with all the wild flowers in is quite something. The organic milk and cream is something else of course.

Blue vinny is a great cheese. When I lived around Shaftesbury when the bogus blue vinny was being touted around, a friend of mine who worked on the cheese stalls at Sturminster Market told me then that the reverse dating on the cheese packaging was out-of-date Stilton. But as Mike Davies says it did the job marvellously. For five years people were hunting out this ancient cheese, but nobody could find the farm. Then all of a sudden Mike Davies started making it for real and has never looked back. I bought a truckle the other day to celebrate Trafalgar Night. Very good it was too with ship's biscuits made by the Bakery at Old Town Mill, Lyme Regis.

Clive Sage is another Dorset farmer who has diversified and sells direct to the public. Farmers' markets are here to stay and yet it requires quite a bit of nerve to stand out in all weathers selling meat. In the old days I used to shear sheep with Clive and it is really good to see someone who has the vision and commitment to oversee every link in the shepherding process. His ram has, I hope, many enjoyable years ahead of him.

Good meat is essential for your well-being unless of course you are vegetarian, but then again imagine the landscape without sheep and beef animals. They are after all the most cost effective lawnmowers you can find. Simon and Ron were a very good double act and it is very sad that Ron had such a bad car accident. Someone went into the back of him and when I interviewed him in Yeovil hospital he was in a wheelchair but very cheerful. Hopefully he will fulfil his ambition of moving to Beaminster. As he says, personality and charm counts for an awful lot with the customers.

Honey is of course the ultimate sweetener and I met Peter Cariss by chance in his battered Land Rover in Rupert Best's orchards. I was taking a group of schoolchildren round and letting them loose in the orchard to write poetry and make sketches of the blossom. Peter is an interesting instance of someone with a second career later in life. He took over his son's bees. Normally with farming it is the other way round. His enthusiasm for the bee culture is infectious and I learnt a lot by listening to him. Peter exemplifies the gentlemanly aspect of bee keeping, which he quite rightly thinks is a national trait.

Roy and Mel Warburton have transformed their pub into a real home. More than anything they are keen to preserve a sense of history and a sense of place, a sense of belonging which is what all pubs used to have, a meeting place, a place to relax and tell stories. A place to savour local beer, local cider and local food. Successful publicans often tend to be eccentric and Roy certainly fits that category… The last time I saw Roy he was bricklaying, converting an old barn into rooms, Mel was mowing the grass. A great place to stay if you want some marvellous walks.

Mark Harris I first met in Ashmore in 1982. He was shearing sheep for the Bradfords near the village pond. The sheep had been bedded down over night on nettles which seemed eminently sensible. Mark had driven over from Farnham on his motorbike. He was 70 then. The wartime memories were very fresh and he seemed keen to talk about them. No doubt that and the loss of two brothers in the First War left a deep impression. After the war many people like Mark simply went back to what they knew best, and were healthier for it, working outside.

Ern Steel's father, like Mark's father, worked on the Rushmore estate for the Pitt Rivers, but there came a point in the 1960s when hurdlemaking was no longer economic. What is interesting is that Ern came back into hurdlemaking and spar making later in life and demand is as high as ever. Good hurdlemakers are now very thin on the ground. I found Ern working outside his house as I was on the way to see Mark. Thatchers of course are reliant on men like Ern otherwise they have to make their own spars which takes up valuable time.

I worked with David Winskill in West Wood opposite the Compton Abbas airfield for five years at least. Thinning beech and very satisfying it was, leaving a fine beech wood for all to see. It is a real shame he has got white finger and Parkinson's. For many years David lived in Iwerne Minster. I remember his mother in Fontmell Magna where there was a gossip tree.

As I did logs myself for several years round Blandford and Shaftesbury, I was always aware of the Bulbarrow sawmill and Richard Hayward. I envied him his Nissan huts and storage. Wood burners were all the rage then and environmentally they are so much better than oil, gas or coal. The heat is cleaner and healthier than straight central heating, plus you get the exercise. And then you get the woodchips and sawdust. Lucky hamsters.

The rise of charcoal burning in Dorset is to be commended. It is so obvious. Sustainable local hardwoods, mostly coppice thinnings or trimmings from hedgelaying. For many people abroad cooking on charcoal is second nature in outside cloam ovens. With Rick's chickens and herbs I could see an opening for Afghan chicken and frittatas. Most people don't even think where their charcoal comes from… Use Dorset Woodland and Coppice Charcoal if you can. You know it makes sense…

As far as I could see there was only one job more demanding that sheep shearing and that was as a farrier. Sheep shearing only lasts a few months of the year but farriers are busy all the year round. With the demise of hunting it will be interesting to see if there is still the same level of work in a few years time. I found Anthony Bailey through the Yellow Pages. Curiously enough he lives very close to a wood I once used to work in called France Down on the Stourpaine Bushes road.

Walt Pitman I have known for over 20 years. I used to keep sheep on Fontmell Down. They kept escaping on to John Eliot Gardiner's land, so in the end John Eliot bought the flock. I then went back for several years to work night lambing. Walt did the days and I did nights. It was a marvellous place to work, on the Downs chasing sheep with all them rare orchids and butterflies. Not sure which is more difficult, conducting or shepherding, at least the orchestra shouldn't get foot rot.

John Cluett is a great man for sharpening scythes. His command of Dorset dialect and William Barnes is second to none. He claims to be the only person to have read a William Barnes poem in the Corn Exchange Dorchester at a Thomas Hardy conference. And he does a very good imitation of a 'Ruined Maid.' John helped me in an early production of Blood Earth & Medicine. He has nice gravely voice and a healthy liking for cider.

Matthew James and his brother Randolph I knew well. Their mother Ruby was the uncrowned Queen of Cann Common and a great friend of Ann Hodgson's. Ruby had helped to make Spitfires during the war and would go out collecting scrap in a pony and trap for her father. I used to pluck turkeys and geese with Matthew down at Manor farm, Melbury Abbas. Sadly Matthew no longer has a milking herd but their story is one of hard work. Very often with small farming the harder you work the less money seems to come in. The subsidies were all loaded the wrong way, i.e. the biggest farmers seemed to get most whereas the small farmers who needed it desperately, got least. Ruby monitors the road like a hawk and over the years has spotted not only the Queen but also Asil Nadir when he did his flit from Compton Abbas airfield.

As for fishing, West Bay is still a magnet that draws people from near and far. Arthur's is a fine restaurant and Arthur himself keen to promote the history and ambiance of West Bay. What a wonderful place to have a meal or just a bowl of fish soup. Once with a friend from Burton Bradstock, Simon Eastwood, we caught a nine pound sea bass, a marvellous silver glittering prize in the early morning sun light and took it along to Arthur's, where it was weighed up on the post office's scales and a deal struck over the phone. And all this at 8.30am before the post office officially opened. The fish was still flapping. Couldn't be fresher.

I found Dave Sales and Pete Newton via Tracey who cuts my hair in Bridport. Her boyfriend Garry also fishes down there and she thought they might have a thing or two to say about fishing. How right she was. Dave Sales is very instrumental in representing the smaller fishermen's interests at the highest level through the Southern Sea Fisheries Committee and has had many meetings with politicians. In 1968 he had a Churchill Fellowship to study lobsters in Canada.

When I interviewed Humphrey Bickford, it was over a pint of beer in his lunch break and he was working steel fitting on the new pier which is at a new angle facing almost south. This gives much better protection when boats are coming in with rough weather behind them. Since it has been finished everyone says how much safer it is. They can go out fishing and know that they can get back in again without risking life, limb and boat.

Sadly Dessie Gape died in June 2005. I used to see him in the Dove when the village parliament of fishermen gathered there. And then in recent years he frequented the Anchor. Many people will have known him at West Bay where he worked for Cliff Samways. Dessie would often take his sons, Chris and Ricky, out fishing and they would help seining when they were young boys. The boat in the photograph, the West Bay Sprat, belongs to Chris and is still used for lobster pots and the odd mackerel fishing trip. Dessie was one of the last of the old school fishermen around West Bay who remembered seining with the heavy-duty lerrets.

At the end of the book I have included a photograph of Bob Tolley, partly because several people mentioned him but also because he was one of the original Dorset Men that I had hoped to interview. Sadly, he died in 2001 but George had taken this picture a few years previously. I knew Bob through sheep shearing and we often had a few jars of cider after tidying up his rather raggle taggle flock. Bob was born on a farm in Loders and lived there till he was nine or ten then he moved to Elmore Farm. In 1968 he came out of there and got married to Jill and moved to Winchcombe near Cheltenham, where he farmed and looked after horses. In 1970 Honeycombe Farm came up and they have been in Broadwindsor ever since. Bob was always generous with his time and his stories particularly if a horse was involved. He used horses as much as he could. When he was young he was said to be a bit wild… At his funeral the church in Broadwindsor was filled to bursting point.

James Crowden

Bob Tolley, 1937-2001, with Prince and Buster

Notes on Author & Photographer

Photo by Tessa Gilks

James Crowden was born in Plymouth in 1954 and grew up on the western edge of Dartmoor. He joined the army, read Civil Engineering at Bristol University, then travelled widely in the Middle East, Eastern Turkey, Iran and Afghanistan. In 1976 he spent a year in Ladakh on the northern side of the Himalaya and lived in a high altitude Tibetan Buddhist valley called Zangskar. After studying anthropology at Oxford he worked in the Outer Hebrides, Bristol Docks and North Dorset. It was around Shaftesbury that he kept sheep and worked as a woodman, shepherd and sheep shearer. His first book, *Blood Earth & Medicine* charts the annual cycle of farm work as seen through the eyes of a casual agricultural labourer. He then moved to Somerset and took up cider making in the autumn. Other books followed, *In Time of Flood* and *The Wheal of Hope - South Crofty and Cornish Tin Mining* with George Wright, *Bridgwater - the Parrett's Mouth*, *Working Women of Somerset,* with Pauline Rook, as well as *Cider the Forgotten Miracle.* More recent books include *Waterways* for the National Trust and *Silence at Ramscliffe - Foot and Mouth in North Devon* with Chris Chapman. James now writes full time.

Photo by Edmund Wright

George Wright was born in London in 1950. From 1970-1973 he studied graphic design at Wimbledon School of Art and in 1975 he became a freelance photographer. He has worked internationally for many newspapers, magazines and book publishers. His pictures have appeared in *The Independent Magazine*, The *Observer*, *The Independent on Sunday Review*, *Departures* (USA) and *Instituto Geografico De Agostini* (Milan). He has also worked as a stills photographer for Channel 4. His work has been exhibited at the Metropolitan Museum in New York and the Chicago Botanic Gardens. He also has a number of photographs in the National Portrait Gallery collection. His books include *English Topiary Gardens* (1988), *Ceramic Style* (1994,) *Print Style* (1995), *In Time of Flood* (1996), a collection of photographs of the Somerset Levels and *The Wheal of Hope* (2000) about the demise of South Crofty and Cornish Tin Mining. He has lived in Dorset since 1983 and has undertaken many local commissions and arts projects. A large collection of his work is on permanent display at the Dorset County Hospital.

Acknowledgements

First of all I must thank all the 'Dorset Men' for their patience in letting me record them. I found it a great pleasure as I never quite knew where the stories were leading and many unexpected gems came out. It was a real education and it is quite a thought that this book sums up over 2,000 years of working. In some cases, as with Jim and Jack Webber, they are still at it; hedging, ditching and mowing lawns in Stoke Abbot. It is amazing to think that Jim started work before the First World War. Many of the more senior men started their working careers in agriculture at the age of nine, 10 and 11. They were often driving teams of two or even three horses – an extraordinary skill and responsibility. And how many of today's 18-year-olds do their long-range courting on bicycle?

My thanks also go to the two main funders of this project: The Calouste Gulbenkian Foundation, which gave the initial funding to make the recordings, and the Chalk and Cheese Leader + project, which started off in Dorchester but ended up in Sturminster Newton run by Sarah Watson and Ovi Rominger. I should also like to thank George Wright, who has produced another set of magnificent photographs; Ruby Wright for helping with the editing of the recordings; my father, Guy Crowden, and Carol Trewin for endless proof reading; and Sara Hudston for editing and publishing the book.

Chalk and Cheese is a funding initiative supporting sustainable development in Dorset's rural heartland and is part of the UK LEADER+ programme. It is funded by the EU and UK Government and a range of public and private sector donors match this funding. It is managed by local people for local people, the programme supports projects that deliver community-led and innovative responses to rural issues. Chalk & Cheese, Market Place, Sturminster House, Sturminster Newton, Dorset, DT10 1AS. Telephone: 01258 474276 or 474277. Fax: 01258 473690. www.chalkandcheese.org

In the future you will be able to listen to some of the Dorset Man recordings on Dorset Farm Radio, an internet radio station also funded by Chalk and Cheese. www.farmradio.co.uk